How to Lead a
Quest

How to Lead a
Quest

a handbook for
pioneering executives

Dr Jason Fox

WILEY

First published in 2016 by John Wiley & Sons Australia, Ltd
42 McDougall St, Milton Qld 4064
Office also in Melbourne

Typeset in 11/13 pt Weidemann Std by Aptara, India

© Dr Jason Fox 2016

The moral rights of the author have been asserted

National Library of Australia Cataloguing-in-Publication data:

Creator:	Fox, Jason, 1983- author.
Title:	How to Lead a Quest: a handbook for pioneering executives / Jason Fox.
ISBN:	9780730324713 (pbk.)
	9780730324744 (hbk.)
	9780730324720 (ebook)
Notes:	Includes index.
Subjects:	Creative ability in business.
	Success in business.
	Business enterprises.
	Leadership.
Dewey Number:	650.1

Cover design and illustrations, and internal illustrations by Kim Lam

Author photo by Vuokko Salo

Printed in Singapore by C.O.S. Printers Pte Ltd

10 9 8 7 6 5 4 3 2

Disclaimer
The material in this publication is of the nature of general comment only, and does not represent professional advice. It is not intended to provide specific guidance for particular circumstances and it should not be relied on as the basis for any decision to take action or not take action on any matter which it covers. Readers should obtain professional advice where appropriate, before making any such decision. To the maximum extent permitted by law, the author and publisher disclaim all responsibility and liability to any person, arising directly or indirectly from any person taking or not taking action based on the information in this publication.

Table of Contents

About the Author

Dr Jason Fox is a motivation design specialist who shows forward-thinking leaders around the world how to unlock new progress and build for the future of work.

His clients include *Fortune* 500 companies such as Microsoft, PepsiCo, McDonalds and Beam Suntory, and other multinationals such as Toyota, Sony Playstation, Gartner, Telstra, Macquarie Group, Commonwealth Bank, Red Cross, Suncorp Group, Singtel Optus, Origin Energy, AMP, Xero, Bellroy and the International Institute of Research (along with a bunch of universities and other research institutions).

Some of Jason's best work has seen him partner with senior leadership teams to navigate through unprecedented and wickedly complex enterprise challenges. Such adventures typically span beyond a year, and involve deep strategic immersions and a refreshed approach to leadership development and culture change.

In addition to his work as an adviser, Jason is an in-demand conference speaker (frequently booked over a year in advance) who works particularly well with sceptical audiences who have 'seen it all before'. In 2016 he was awarded 'Keynote Speaker of the Year' by Professional Speakers Australia.

Jason is also the best-selling author of *The Game Changer*—a book that unpacks the science of motivation and game design to drive progress and change at work.

When not liberating the world from default thinking and the curse of efficiency, Jason enjoys partaking in the fine art of coffee snobbery, sun avoidance and beard maintenance.

Learn more at www.drjasonfox.com

PS: About the Illustrator | Dr Kim Lam is the much more delightful counterpart to Dr Jason Fox. Kim loves drawing. Drawing stories, drawing diagnoses, drawing in rock-paper-scissors, but most of all —drawing illustrations. At the quarter-life mark, Kim decided to swap her veterinarian-day-job and moonlighting-illustrator combination. She now operates with a pen, running projects as Dangerlam, and saves little furry lives as a rather specialised side-hobby. She loves the thrill of chasing complex ideas and capturing them in simple and compelling ways through illustration and animation.

You can see more of her work at www.dangerlam.com

Gratitudes

Here are a heap of hat tips, hugs and endearingly misplaced/mistimed high-fives to the many fine folk who made this book possible. Without their support, I couldn't have written this book for you.

Firstly, I'm grateful for all of the authors and thought leaders that have gone before me. Writing a book requires a degree of dedication that borders upon ridiculousness. But by venturing through doubt, uncertainty and paradox, these past adventurers have captured the knowledge we build upon today. They're the pioneers, and I doff my hat to them.

I'm also grateful for the folks at Wiley. Thank you Kristen for seeing the merit in this book right away, and for your trust in me. Thanks also to Ingrid for your support at every stage, and to Chris and Alice for pulling it all together at the end. Without your support, I'm not sure this book could have ever been published —I'd still be writing and exploring.

Big hugs to Charlotte, my supercool editor. I was worried that all of the jolly quirks in my writing would be ironed out into something bland —but quite the opposite happened. Thanks to the thorough, clever and effective editing of Charlotte, this book actually makes a bit of sense and has become even more of a delight to read. Huge thanks also to Jack and Mel for your editing support.

There have been a few mates that have been quite influential in my own thinking. Matt Church, thank you for being the pioneer that forged a path for other thought leaders to follow. You've been a mentor and a mate.

Likewise Peter Cook: thank you for helping me stay true to the path. You've both had a huge influence on my thinking. Sweeping feathered hat tips (in no particular order) to a heap of my thought leading mates: Darren and Alison Hill, Jennifer and Dougal Jackson, Amantha Imber, Sean Fabri, Will Dayble, Dan Gregory, Kieran Flanagan... plus a bunch of people who I will no doubt regret having forgotten to mention here. You each inspire me more than you could know.

I'm lucky to work with some pretty ace clients. Thanks especially to the University of Melbourne's Centre for Workplace Leadership. Peter, Sarah and the gang —you guys are legendary, and your support has contributed much richness to this book. Love you guys.

I need to thank my friends and family —they have all been incredibly patient and kind to me as I write this book. I've been that guy who ghosts on weddings and birthdays, and who brings book writing to dinner. Thanks for still liking me and wanting to hang out.

Thanks to all the folks at Industry Beans, Everyday Cafe, Proud Mary and all of the mighty fine cafes in Melbourne. You provided the magic to fuel my writing. Thanks also to my catpanion 'π' who reminds me to be present (by sitting on my laptop).

I'm so grateful for everyone who purchased my first book *The Game Changer* and made it a best-seller. It gave me the confidence to write the slightly more daring book you hold in your hands right now. I'm also especially grateful those who left a kind review online —this feedback kept me buoyed when the doubt got heavy. Thanks also to all the savvy folk who subscribe to my museletter, and who attend our events. I love you all.

But yes, I've been building up to the two most special people I am most grateful for.

First, to my business manager Bianka. Ah B, you are such a blessing. Not only do you curtail all the entropy that comes with a dynamic business like ours —you keep all of our clients thoroughly nurtured and happy too. I love your proactive empathy, strategy and intuition, and your ability to make good things flourish. Thank you for everything!

And finally, my wonderful darling Kim (aka the 'dangerlam'). You have been the most supportive of all. You've been the light in the dark, and you've kept me aloft throughout —even when things became stupidly busy. I literally couldn't have done this without you. I'm so grateful to share life with you, and to have your illustrations in this book. You are pure wonder, insight and delight!

Oh and thank *you*, dear reader, for being the type of person curious enough to read these acknowledgements. I love people like you. People like you are the best.

Introduction

Almost every leadership, strategy and motivation book on the planet advocates the importance of having a crystal-clear goal or vision for the future.

But, intuitively, we know this is an incredibly flawed position to take.

Sure, this outlook may serve in the short term. And, of course, an enterprise *needs* goals. If you want to galvanise a group of people towards achieving a particular outcome, a clear goal or vision is essential. People like goals — they remove the angst of uncertainty, and give us something to focus our efforts towards. Clear goals can also be reverse-engineered and broken down to create a roadmap, with clear milestones and executable steps. Past experience can be leveraged to improve performance, and systems can be optimised to improve efficiencies. Goals are easy to implement and incentivise, and a raft of precedents prove their efficacy.

But what happens if you don't know what the future has in store for your enterprise? What if you don't have a clear goal? What if you only have a vague hunch, or a fuzzy sense that something needs to change? What then? Do you simply wait for clarity? Or do you manufacture a goal and a forced sense of certainty?

Or worse: *What happens if you wake up after a long 'winning streak' only to discover that your enterprise is no longer relevant?*

This is the major challenge many enterprise leaders face, and the fundamental flaw with leadership focused on clear goals and operational wins.

Naturally, this is quite a predicament. We cannot afford to simply *wait* for clarity. But at the same time, we cannot set forth a single, clear vision for the future while knowing that the future is infinitely complex and uncertain. What to do?

LEAD A QUEST

This book presents a different approach to enterprise strategy and leadership. I wouldn't go as far as to say it is an 'alternative' approach; rather, it is something much more complementary: *pioneering* leadership.

Rather than simply work within existing parameters of operational excellence (incrementally optimising your business model to meet customer needs), pioneering leadership sees you embarking upon quests. Such quests allow us to systematically explore complex and uncertain futures. We don't set goals in the hopes that a particular future will manifest—rather, we explore multiple possible futures, and prepare proactive stratagems to capitalise on each.

The result of this continuous and dynamic approach is that enterprise strategy and leadership is enriched with viable, alternative options to pursue. Such options allow enterprise leaders to mitigate risk, obtain strategic advantage and ensure meaningful progress as the world changes.

If this sounds too good to be true, don't worry—it quickly won't.

Pioneering leadership is challenging to initiate and maintain—especially when compared to the established approach that favours fast results with a bias toward prudence and predictability. But! If we can crack through our default thinking, pioneering leadership offers enterprise leaders the chance to obtain the most important thing of all—*enduring relevance.*

USING THIS BOOK

The biggest paradox about writing a somewhat practical book about the dynamic and non-linear nature of leading a quest is that a book is static and linear. Because we don't have the benefit of exploring this concept together over a dynamic conversation with coffee and expansive gesticulation (at least, not right now), the inescapably static and linear nature of a book requires that I arrange relevant concepts into a seemingly logical sequence.

And so, I have attempted to do this. The result is okay—but it's not perfect. In fact, you may find yourself jumping back and forth between chapters.[1] To assist you with this dance, here's a nifty overview of the parts that make up this book:

Part I: Default Thinking and the Kraken of Doom frames the *why* behind this book. Yes, I used that classic approach of framing the problem

---

1 | Think of this book as a *Choose Your Own Adventure*, rather than simply a 'follow the instructions' book.

and context first. Call it constructive discontent. In part I, we explore default thinking, the Curse of Efficiency and the Delusion of Progress. We also review the default growth arc of an enterprise, and discover how great businesses can one day wake up to discover they are no longer relevant.

If you want to get into the meat of the book, you could skip part I—but I don't advise it. You see, I have this terrible tendency to weave metaphors through my stories (rather than use bland corporate speak). A key metaphor in this story—the Inevitable Kraken of Doom—is introduced in part I, and you don't want to miss this beast.

Part II: A Quest Beckons unpacks the *what*—Quest-Augmented Strategy. This is a framework for meaningful progress and enduring relevance, and is the main proposition of this book: providing a means to augment enterprise strategy with pioneering leadership. The model presented in chapter 5 summarises this framework, so, hot tip: if you find yourself getting lost, return to chapter 5.

Part III: Cultivating Options includes the first of our more focused *how* chapters. This may be the most challenging and paradoxical part of the book. Here, we explore infinitely complex and uncertain future contexts. Your existing business rationale is then contrasted against these possible futures, to identify any incoherencies.[2] Such incoherencies may harbour alternative options—new pathways that may be of strategic merit to your enterprise. We harvest these.

Part IV: Crafting Experiments then switches our focus from pioneering thinking to pioneering *doing*. Here we explore how you can support experiments that enhance learning and yield strategic insight. It's through this focus that our alternative strategic options are validated.

Part V: Augmenting Strategy sees us switch back into more familiar operational territory. Here, we focus on how you can augment existing enterprise strategy with the viable alternative options generated through pioneering work. This is how we secure enduring relevance.

Part VI: Making Progress is what happens when we don't succumb to The Delusion of Progress—that is, our tendency to get caught up in the busy work. This section offers some practical insight for enterprise leaders looking to make meaningful progress 'the new normal'.

2| Don't rush this chapter.

Part VII: Pioneering Culture is a whole heap of fun. Having progressed through each quadrant of Quest-Augmented Strategy, we then cast our focus on new rituals you can integrate—personally and with your team—to lead meaningful progress. Through this, you begin to integrate pioneering leadership into workplace culture.

And then it all wraps up with a short **conclusion**. You may find that you are left with more questions than answers. If so, marvellous. This is my gift to you.

Righto, shall we? Let's get into it.

———————————

Default Thinking and the Kraken of Doom

Default [noun]: an option that is selected automatically
in the absence of viable alternatives.

A hoy the default! It's always there, and it's such a time-saver. So handy. Thanks to the default, we get stuff done and we make things happen.

But sometimes—because it's always there—we stop seeing the default. We stop questioning the very thing that influences every decision we make. And, thus, we assume our assumptions are valid, sound, correct and appropriate for the current and emerging context we operate in.

Our default thinking (and the biases it harbours) becomes like air to a bird, or water to a fish. We are so unceasingly immersed in it that we don't even comprehend it to be there. And so the things that we do become the perpetual echoes of things we did before, and the reflection of the norms we're immersed in.

Change, progress and growth only truly happen when we challenge our thinking, and explore alternative options.

But, of course, the default is not all bad! It's actually really rather handy, most of the time. So before we proceed with our fancy future-focused, proactive, default-eschewing, strategic-progress-making magic, in chapter 1 we're going to pay a brief homage to default thinking and the wonderful things it brings. Things like systems, templates and other

Established Ways of Doing Things. Such constructs save us from having to reinvent things or think too hard over every little task we do, which in turn liberates us from duplicated effort and wasted time—efficient, eh?

Naturally these constructs work fine for formulaic work with predictable outcomes (improving efficiencies within existing systems), but this unquestioning approach does not beget brilliant strategy or pioneering growth. In fact, this kind of thinking only leads to one thing: the Inevitable Kraken of Doom—a not-so-mythical beast that feeds upon irrelevance (introduced in chapter 3).

Despite outward appearances, this book is *not* about how to quest towards irrelevance. How ridiculous! It's quite the opposite. This is about ensuring that you, your enterprise business model and your modus operandi stay relevant and useful, and that your work continues to grow and prosper—now and into the future.

And so, before we embark upon any sort of quest, let's explore the current premise that we're operating from. What is informing and influencing your thinking right now? Where do your defaults come from?

———————————

1. The Anatomy of Default Thinking

The 'default' is defined as an option that is selected automatically unless a viable alternative is specified.[1] It's influenced by the sum of our experiences, and is usually the option that requires the least effort (or least angst/uncertainty/discomfort) for the most short-term gain.

'But from whence does the default come?' I hear you ask. Well, linguistically, 'default' stems from the Old French word 'defaut', which in turn stems from 'defaillir' or 'to fail' (from 'fallere'—a Latin word meaning 'disappoint' and 'deceive').

Failure, disappointment or deception, eh? Fun. This connotation of default typically applies to not meeting a loan repayment—but there's an important message for leadership in this, too. Rely solely on default thinking, and you're going to encounter disappointment.

But, enough of that! Don't tempt me with further discussions of linguistics and semantics—I hold a doctorate in philosophy, which makes me quite inclined to engage in confusing and somewhat-irrelevant tangential pursuits of linguistic and philosophical whimsy. *sets cognac aside*

Now, in practical terms, the default comes from our ability to recognise, match and leverage *patterns*.

1| Ah, so…how do you generate viable, alternative options to consider? A splendid question! And also the main thesis of this book.

This is what Daniel Kahneman—Nobel Prize winner and author of *Thinking, Fast and Slow*—might describe as 'system 1 thinking'.[2] This type of thinking is fast, automatic, frequent, emotional, stereotypic and subconscious. The opposite to default thinking would be what Kahneman might describe as 'system 2 thinking'. This type of thinking happens consciously and is, by contrast, slow, effortful, infrequent, logical and calculating.

A lot of my work involves helping leadership teams engage in more 'slow thinking'. It's critically important, and it's how we lead and progress worthy quests. But, in my experience, the framing of a dichotomy of 'fast versus slow' does slow thinking a disservice. Thanks to the Curse of Efficiency (see chapter 2), selling the importance of slow thinking in a world that wants fast results is ... tricky.

And so, I've replaced 'slow' with 'thorough'. Thus, our options are to think fast, and leverage our default thinking, or we can think more thoroughly—challenging our default assumptions by exploring diverse perspectives and generating alternative options. But the detail on that comes later.

First, let's return to the anatomy of our fast, default thinking.

PATTERNS

From the moment we are born, we start to recognise patterns—those discrete, discernible and repeatable experiences. Every such experience we observe is encoded to inform our model of how the world works.

Indeed, the linguistic roots of the word 'pattern' come from the Old French word 'patron'—the idea being that this patron serves as a model or example to be copied. I love linguistics.

The more frequently we experience or observe particular phenomena, the stronger this encoding becomes. It's why we train for sport, and practise mathematics, music and language. Without this incredible ability to recognise patterns, we would never learn anything. We wouldn't

---

2| Of course, he would describe it in much greater depth and with more elegance than I have here. If you're unfamiliar with his work, I highly recommend you explore it.

even know how to communicate. In fact, our ability to recognise and codify patterns to form our own model of the world could arguably be a cornerstone of our existence. #profound

And all this pattern recognition is automatic: by just observing and experiencing the world around you, you are codifying new patterns or reinforcing existing ones.

From a very young age, for example, we're picking up objects and then dropping them. We observe a repeatable pattern, learn it, and are eventually given a label for it—'gravity'. Likewise, we learn about our preferences through our experiences. I commonly order my default coffee preference at a cafe, without even thinking about it. Sure, some fancy new single origin may be on the menu, but I'd need to be aware and mindful to look for it first.

Many of us experience the phenomena of pattern recognition and default thinking when driving (or riding) home from work. If you've had a particularly tiring or busy day, or if you have a lot on your mind, the well-encoded pattern of your usual route could have you arriving home without you even truly realising it. Another example is musicians learning new music by studying patterns of input. It's clunky to start with, but with enough repetition (practice), the pattern becomes embedded, and the music can be played without having to actively think about it. Much like riding a bike.

Think about a software developer writing code for a program. If they have diverse experience, chances are, when confronted with new challenges, they can quickly call upon a rich database of potential solutions. On the other hand, a less experienced coder would need to invest more time to experiment with and explore the efficacy of new patterns, in order to find a solution.

Our memory is a database for such patterns. It stores patterns contextually, and is optimised for speed. This speed allows us to take the cognitive shortcuts that enable us to draw conclusions quickly. And the more experience we've had—the more patterns we have observed—the more cognitive shortcuts we have at hand.

But this speed comes at a cost—accuracy. Despite what we may think, our memory is often an inaccurate source of information, influenced as it is by myriad factors—such as our emotional (psychophysiological) state, time elapsed since we recognised the pattern and our current context.[3] This means that many of the patterns we call upon to inform our default thinking may be inaccurate in any given context or moment—or even no longer valid or relevant in this new context. Thus, without challenging our own default thinking, we may be proceeding with flawed assumptions.

Default thinking is not the result of consideration or any form of reasoned, intuitive or active thought. It takes effort to draw awareness to the potential inaccuracies or inherent biases within our thinking. Such effort is confronting, and slows down the cognitive process and decision-making, running counter to the efficiency and productivity we need for most of our work.[4]

Of course, it would simply be infeasible to engage in slow, deep and thorough thinking for every facet of business—we'd get nothing done. It'd be silly to go back to the drawing board when attempting any new task.

And so systems are created to help us to manage increasingly complex patterns of work.

SYSTEMS

Most organisations today simply would not function without clever systems. Systems keep entropy at bay.[5]

---

3 | Not to mention a swag of cognitive biases (see chapter 14).

4 | You may have already suspected this, but I'm setting up 'default thinking' to take a fall. Don't get me wrong—it is utterly brilliant for 80 per cent of our work.* If you're looking to replicate existing work more efficiently, to simply tick boxes, be productive, get shit done and progress formulaic processes with predictable outcomes, your ability to recognise patterns, take cognitive shortcuts, leverage past experience and run with default thinking is an absolute asset. But—and it's a big but—if you're looking to venture beyond the default, to truly innovate and pioneer into uncharted territory, you need to 'ware the perils of our default thinking, lest we meet the Inevitable Kraken of Doom.

* Where did I get this figure from? Not research. It just seems 'about right'—I essentially defaulted to the Praeto principle, which states that (for most events) roughly 80 per cent of the effects come from 20 per cent of the causes. And why did I do this? Because it serves as a good reference point. And that's what default thinking can be, if we can heighten ourselves to see it: a reference point for decision-making. But not the only reference point.

5 | Or, at least, they attempt to—but entropy relates to increasing disorder (the higher the entropy, the greater the disorder) and disorder will always win, in the end.

Whenever we've got multiple, interconnected patterns happening, we have the opportunity to create systems to increase our efficiency and avoid wasted effort.

I use, and love, a heap of systems—one being the software I'm writing this book with, and the operating system that nests it. These complex systems were developed by very intelligent teams. Short of an ecosystem or the human body, few systems are quite as complex.

But not all systems are of such a high order.

Take the typical sales sequence, for example. I've chosen 'sales' because it is a fairly universal function within any business or organisation—even if your organisation or business unit doesn't sell products or services for money, value is still generated and a currency of exchange is still at play.

The typical sequence looks like this:

1. First, a business needs to generate leads ('leads' being code for 'potential opportunities'). Assuming you are doing something of value, generating leads could look like advertising, marketing, public relations or networking. In my world, leads are generated as a consequence of doing great work with clients (which generates referrals), sharing fresh research and insights (via my 'making clever happen' museletter), speaking at conferences, running our own events, and publishing research and books like this. Each of these activities is also a collection of patterns—but they form part of this bigger sales sequence.

2. Once leads are generated, they need to be qualified. If your organisation trades entirely online, your situation may be that the customer is self-qualifying, and your focus is on enhancing conversion. But if your organisation is service-based, or you engage in business-to-business sales, you likely need to qualify your leads. This means sorting out the valuable opportunities from the dead ends. In my world, we scare the tyre kickers away with our fee guide.

3. Next comes the nurturing. Some sales cycles are incredibly short, and as such, minimal client nurturing

is required. A sales rep might know the typical questions that prospects have about a product, and be able to easily call upon the right answers for these questions. Other sales cycles are incredibly long, and require a lot of client nurturing. An example might be a large organisation adopting a new piece of software for tens of thousands of their employees — it's a big decision. Eventually, with enough nurturing prompts and the right frequency of positive interactions, clients are ready to consider investing in the work.

4. Then comes the pretty proposal. Once prospective clients are primed and ready to buy, some sort of proposal or agreement is required. This may be something automatically generated, like a software license agreement, with pricing structures that scale in proportion to the number of users. Or it could be manually generated. I used to spend a heap of time on these (mainly on design and layout), but over time we had developed enough confidence and experience to be able to recognise patterns and present proposals that frame our methodology and value (without getting bogged down in detail).

5. Then comes doing the work. And providing the value (although of course, you'd want to be providing value before any proposal is submitted). This nests a whole heap of systems and patterns too. Patterns, patterns everywhere! But sometimes we have good systems to corral them into something manageable.

And that's kind of how we make sales happen. Each step nests its own level of complexity but, not to worry — we have a system to manage this complexity. If you're a small business, your system might look like a spreadsheet that lists the current status of particular opportunities. If you're a bit more advanced, you might be using customer relationship management and/or sales pipeline software as your sales system. Thanks to these systems, we can track where various opportunities are at, and can ensure we are investing the right effort in the right folks at the right time.

But this is an incredibly simple example of a very small and agile thought-leadership practice. As things scale up, things get much more complex.

Multinational corporations live on the other side of this spectrum, and need to embrace a broader mix of systems in order to coordinate efforts on a global scale. These may include systems for performance reviews and compliance, inductions and on-boarding, communications, professional development, succession, distribution, legal considerations and disputes, and so on.

And these systems work too — 80 per cent of the time. Until the world changes and they become irrelevant.[6] In these cases, fortune favours those who are able to adapt to new systems. But this only happens if we have viable alternative options beyond the default.

Hey, here's another element of default thinking — and something found within many systems — *templates.*[7]

TEMPLATES

'I'm glad you love Jason's doodle'. This statement came from a virtual assistant I once employed, in response to a senior HR director's email.

The response created a mighty awkward situation, but let me explain the details.

The HR director had just written to express their gratitude for a closing keynote I had recently delivered at their annual conference. In this keynote, I shared some of my visual notes from the event — 'doodles', one might call them. The plural is important.

Around the same time, I had developed some systems to guide my virtual assistant through the complexity of my business. Virtual assistants were all the rage back then, and my business hadn't matured to the wonderful point it is at now where I have a closer and more experienced local team (in real life, not just virtually).

But yes, I'd read Tim Ferriss's fabulous book — *The 4-Hour Work Week* — and I was set to live the dream. I thought that, once I had a virtual assistant, everything would get easier. It didn't. It required me to establish some really good systems, and unpack my default thinking into a whole heap of default templates to live within these systems. These

---

6| Or, in some cases, organisations and their leaders grip onto systems that no longer serve the business model — which is akin to gripping the railings of a sinking ship.

7| Let's just pause and reflect on how bad that segue was.

templates included simple things like email responses—including what to do if someone important emailed while I was out of the office or overseas:

Acknowledge their email [as in, say something nice about something they've mentioned] and then explain that I'm out of the office until [specify day and date]. Offer to be of assistance if there is anything they need urgently.

And so back to my doodles. After my presentation, the client mentioned via email something to the effect of, 'the audience loved Jason's doodles'. But alas! My template did not capture the nuances of such things as the distinction between one's doodle and the doodles one sends through after graphically recording an event.[8]

Anyhoo, I thought this was a good template for a fairly repeatable task. Templates are the physical bits that make up a system and, when they work, they save us a heap of time by minimising any unnecessary duplication of effort.

For example, beyond some basic html, I don't know how to code. I wish I did, but I don't just yet. But, thankfully, website templates exist—which means I don't need to bear the cognitive burden of learning to code. I can use a template and save a heap of time and mental angst.

In an organisational context, performance reviews are a fairly common phenomenon. The common intent behind performance reviews is to periodically assess an individual's productivity and efficacy in relation to a set of pre-established criteria and organisational objectives (defaults). Additionally, the process may be an opportunity to review the employee's aspirations, goals, strengths, weaknesses, learning opportunities and behaviours.

But what tends to happen is that everyone is busy, and these performance reviews become simple box-ticking activities that do little to improve things. Whole industries are designed to provide box-ticking solutions for performance reviews. In these industries, instead of having meaningful conversations, managers can simply generate a specific, measurable, achievable, relevant and time-bound goal, and employees can then proceed to show incremental progress towards that goal. Again, this is fine for formulaic work with predictable outcomes—but it's horrendously limiting for any organisation or leader looking to do something new.

8| I'm sure I could add some pun using the word 'graphic', but I'll resist.

And so, the cracks in default thinking begin to show.

Templates and systems serve our default thinking. They're the instructions and guideposts we turn to when we're uncertain about what to do. And, because we are so primed to recognise patterns and minimise cognitive strain (that is, the burden of thought required to process what to do), defaulting to the assumptions, systems, templates and structures we have already established is an incredibly alluring proposition.

Reverting to the default saves you time, thereby enhancing your productivity and efficiency. But it costs you accuracy, empathy, relevance and meaningful progress.

NORMS

'Erm, that's just not the done thing around here.'

Norms are cultural products (including values, customs and rituals) that represent our understanding of what others do, and what others think that we should do. Norms occur in many contexts, not only at the team level, the organisation level and the industry level, but also across countries, age demographics, cities, suburbs, and so on. For example, I'm writing this book at a cafe in Fitzroy, an inner-city suburb in Melbourne that, according to a 2015 article published in London's *Telegraph*, ranks in the top three of the most hipster neighbourhoods in the world. As such, good coffee, ironic tattoos, beards, skateboards, pop-up stores, ripped skinny jeans, thick-rimmed glasses, craft beer (and so on) all contribute to the norms of this area. I get no comments on my flaming red beard or coffee snobbery in Fitzroy—but very much do when I travel abroad.

Norms influence our defaults. When at a loss as to what to do, our brain will scan for a default. If we identify a pattern we haven't experienced yet, one of the reference points that will influence our decision on how to behave is the established norms. *'What would others do? What would they think I should do?'* The answer to these types of questions is usually something that's predictable and safe.[9]

9| Remember—default thinking favours the minimisation of angst in return for the greatest short-term gain.

As a leader, understanding the values that influence your behaviour, the values that drive your colleagues' behaviours, and the company values[10] that influence the collective behaviour of your organisation is really important.

Norms are powerful. They are frequently repeated and reinforced by the people who surround you. Deviance from the established norms is often frowned upon, and viewed with mistrust. If one strays too far from the established norms, one may be cast as a pariah or deviant.[11] This is unfortunate, because most norms are established in precedence (the past), and are self-validating and reinforcing.

PRECEDENTS

Because our default thinking relies so heavily on pattern-matching, it can be hard for folks to explore or accept new ideas that lack an established precedent. Leading folks through unprecedented territory, towards a future not yet realised, can be even harder.

Part of leading such a quest is the process of *creating precedents*. This is where we gather evidence to serve as a reference point for decisions (covered in more detail in chapter 4).

Naturally, the psychology of what informs our thinking is much more complex than the brief tour I've provided. We haven't even ventured into the territory of the identity you form within given social constructs, and how you manage cognitive dissonance in reference to that.

Suffice to say, our default thinking is a comforting, complex thing that favours efficiency and the status quo. Whenever we believe the world makes sense, it's due to our profound ability to ignore our own ignorance.

---

10 | I'm not talking here about understanding the standard mix of integrity, innovation, collaboration, safety, diversity, community, and other 'default' values. Unless, of course, you've actually done the work of translating what these values mean in terms of keystone behaviours.

11 | Which is why the hero's journey is so challenging, and why it's incredibly important that leaders invest in culture change to ensure the folk they work with are part of the journey too — it's a lonely journey, otherwise. Pioneering strategy requires pioneering leadership, but it also requires a cultural norm that supports it — even if it's a bimodal culture to begin with (see chapter 16).

And so ends our lukewarm homage to Default Thinking.[12]

It's good, fast and often useful. It forms the basis of our 'system 1' (fast) thinking. And a heap of leadership, strategy and motivation books out there support a collection of comfortingly familiar thinking around this.

Keep in mind default thinking is primarily formed through pattern matching—the more experience we get, the more patterns we recognise. This, in turn, gives us more codified patterns to call upon, and access to more cognitive shortcuts.[13] For formulaic work with predictable outcomes, this is quite a boon—it's what allows us to enhance our mastery of musical instruments, or to accurately predict the outcome of things.

Clever systems exist for more complex phenomena, and handy templates exist for more repeatable phenomena. Both of these constructs serve to guide us through complexity and reduce cognitive burden—instead of having to think too hard, we have a system or template to guide us.

With all of this clever, time-saving stuff, one would think that we would have *more* time to work on the important stuff—like strategy, progress, and the threats and opportunities that lie on the horizon.

In fact, in an ideal world, we'd invest roughly 80 per cent of our time doing the core work that needs to be done—the default, productive, operational 'business as usual' work that Ought To Be Got Done, and that only requires fast thinking.

But then everyone would also ensure that a good 20 per cent of their time was engaged in more thoughtful work, and deeper, more thorough thinking. We'd reflect upon our assumptions and the decisions we make. We'd feed our hunches (see chapter 4) and nurture the exploration of new possibilities and options.

This might happen, if we weren't *cursed with efficiency.*

12| My intention with this opening chapter was actually to be all jolly-like, pointing out the many merits of default thinking. But I fear my disdain for unquestioned thought might have crept in. Oh well! Stay tuned...

13| Assuming we've had diverse experience. If this isn't the case and we've only had more experience doing the same thing, our default thinking may just be that much more ingrained and harder to challenge or budge—hence the need for diversity in leadership. This also highlights the effect that fresh eyes can have—without having a database of patterns to call upon, less experienced folks can often ask good questions, or see things others cannot. At least, until the point at which they become 'normalised'.

2. The Curse of Efficiency

R ighto: chapter 2. First, though, let me tell you something about one of the biggest challenges of writing a book—getting the *sequence* right. I want to unpack so much goodness with you, but before we get there, we need to appreciate the context that goodness serves. The concepts of this book are best shared in a certain order, so that the value of ideas may be fully appreciated.

You might have already noticed, but what we are doing here in part I is essentially 'framing the problem'. This is an incredibly useful thing to do if you're looking to prime people to be more receptive to an idea. And the idea of this book is a big one—leaders need to systematically go *against* the grain of default thinking, efficiency and busyness (heresy!), and pioneer uphill, through doubt, angst and uncertainty (madness!) in order to future-proof relevance and obtain strategic advantage. This is too important a notion to not have the problem framed correctly first.

Now you're probably somewhat savvy with The Curse of Efficiency already. And you probably recognise that relentless busyness crowds out our time for good strategic development and meaningful progress. But we can't jump to the answer just yet. After all, leading quests means pursuing better questions—not easy answers. And as you'll discover in part III, staying *within* the angst of the challenge, resisting the urge to jump to quick fixes and conclusive solutions, is a discipline we need to foster—individually and collectively as leaders. Otherwise, we are only perpetuating the existing paradigm of convenient but shallow default thinking.

This is something I see happen in organisations all too often—someone has a brilliant idea, and begins to promote said idea to their colleagues, only to be met with stiff resistance or general indifference. Bah! What ignorant dinosaurs! Why can't they just appreciate how brilliant this idea could be?

Well, a few things are getting in the way—including the fact that ideas are cheap and often poorly framed[1]—but the main thing is that new ideas pose a real threat to people's time. Especially when everyone is so busy being *efficient*.

THE PROGRESS DELUSION

If I had a dollar for every time someone said they were busy, I'd probably have... a few hundred dollars.[2] Being busy has become the new badge of honour. Part of this perception is because we have allowed such a work culture to percolate, but a big part of this is because busyness is just so darn rewarding.

In my previous book, *The Game Changer*, I raved about the illuminating research into workplace motivation delivered by Professor Teresa Amabile and Professor Steven Kramer. This research all started with the question 'What makes employees enthusiastic about work?'—an important question for anyone in management or leadership.

And so, more than 600 managers (from dozens of companies, and at different levels) were asked to rank five workplace factors commonly considered significant in influencing motivation: recognition for good work, incentives and rewards, interpersonal support, clear goals and targets, and a clear sense of progress.

These are all good answers, of course (indeed, the selection of these factors was the result of several meta-analyses). But 'recognition for good work' emerged as the factor considered most powerful at positively influencing motivation.

1| It's much better to focus on cultivating strategic options (the focus of part III) and worthy hypotheses (part IV).

2| The introvert in me tries to avoid talking to many people—so that seems like a big number to me.

It's definitely a great factor, but this result came only from the managers. So Amabile and Kramer also explored this concept with employees, following a bunch of people from different companies over several years, and analysing over 12 000 journal entries to see what correlated to the highest level of motivation at work. It turns out, the number one thing that was most important to the employees was actually what the managers ranked *dead last*—a clear sense of progress.

That's right—the more we sense that our effort is contributing to progress, the more likely we are to stay motivated to invest effort. This Progress Principle was recognised as the #1 breakthrough idea by the *Harvard Business Review* in 2010—and it makes a whole lot of sense.

When it comes to leading for the future of work, providing visibility of progress is our most important opportunity.

This applies to nearly all types of work—from formulaic routine work right through to risky pioneering work. Essentially, the more we reduce the latency between effort and meaningful feedback, the more effort we get.

And so, creating visibility of progress, and using a combination of structures and rituals to recognise and celebrate small daily wins is an incredibly important calibration for leadership in the future of work.

This requirement is far less about fixating upon specific, distant targets, and much more about making work that is inherently motivating. Pay people well, and design and lead work that provides people with a rich sense of progress. This, in turn, contributes to work cultures that are much more future-proof—nimble, adaptive and responsive to change.

Think about it like this. Imagine, earlier in your career, you were given an important piece of research to do. Your boss explains that some colleagues are visiting from overseas and she needs this research completed by Monday morning. You are already very busy but, like many of us, you're terrible at saying no—so you say yes, and you go about doing this research (staying back late and even working on the weekend). The research is hard work but it's kind of exciting and interesting too. On Sunday night, you email off the research report.

Monday comes and no word arrives from your boss. You begin to think that perhaps she did not receive the email, but you check and, yes, the email was definitely sent. You figure she must be busy with her guests. Tuesday arrives and still no word. All you want to know is that she received the report okay—it's like an open loop in your mind, a cognitive dissonance that must be closed. You send an email to check.

Finally, on Wednesday morning you receive an email back from your boss, which simply says: *'Thanks— turns out I didn't need it.'*

Bah! I mean, it's nice that she acknowledged it—but you're not even sure that she read your research. And, thus, somewhat deflated you resolve that, should a similar request be made in the future, you're probably going to default to a conservative level of effort.

Which makes perfect sense—we all have a finite amount of time, energy and attention available to us each day. It's only reasonable that we invest our effort into the things that provide the richest sense of progress.

This is why progress visibility is also our biggest threat.

The things that provide the richest sense of progress are usually our defaults—those routine things we've done before, that require minimal cognitive effort to achieve. These things are easy to do, have established precedents, and often provide a rich and immediate sense of progress.

Now imagine this scenario: you are a senior leader within a large organisation. You've just been to a conference where a few of the speakers shared insights that have got you seriously thinking about the mid-term viability of your organisation's business model. You have a hunch that disruption is just around the corner for your organisation—and, unfortunately, this won't be something your organisation is proactively leading. This hunch is only further confirmed through the things you read and the conversations you have with peers in other industries.

You don't know what to do—you've never encountered this before, and you have no rulebook, gold standard or step-by-step formula to follow. You attempt to share this hunch with your colleagues—it's important, after all—but, alas, they're busy. You put it on the agenda at your next meeting, too, but when the time comes there seems to be more pressing concerns. Everyone is avoiding the angst of uncertainty by defaulting to their defaults.

And so it's just you in a sea of doubt and the angst of uncertainty. How do you make progress in this context? Where do you even begin? Particularly when you don't have the answers, or any solution to offer yet.

Well, if you're like most of us, you'll soon find yourself checking email and identifying small things to micromanage. Why? Because these things provide a rich and immediate sense of progress! Say you start your day with sixty emails in your inbox. By mid-afternoon, you've whittled your inbox down to fourteen. Ah! Progress! It feels like you're winning, and other people in the organisation know that you're putting in effort. Good work! No-one can fault you.

Soon everyone starts to do this. Before you know it, 'reply all' is the norm.

This type of work is so very gratifying when compared to your time amid the angst of uncertainty. It really looks and feels as though you're making progress. And you are! You can look back on your 'to-do' list at the end of the day, and feel content that you're contributing to some sort of progress.

It's just ... not *meaningful* progress.

Hence, the progress delusion.

This state is where we find ourselves saying yes to so many little things that the bigger, more important things suffer.

It is insidious, pervasive and all too common. It afflicts all of us — myself included. And it requires a level of deliberation to lean against the flow of busyness, and say yes to the things that matter.

But choosing to say yes to meaningful progress requires three things:

1. knowing what meaningful progress actually looks like

2. saying no to the work that doesn't add value or contribute to progress

3. creating structures, rituals and support for the meaningful work that matters.

Our activity will frequently default to the things that provide the richest sense of progress. The challenge for any pioneering leader is to shine a light on the path, and create visibility of meaningful progress as you venture through the fog of uncertainty.

Ah, but if only we had a strategy for that ...

TOO BUSY FOR STRATEGY

A good part of my work involves facilitating strategic immersions and leadership development. This work is frequently profound. With the right sequence of pre-framing, pattern-disruption, assumption-busting, and thorough thinking with diverse input within a progressive context — magic happens.

Especially when compared to the default approach to strategic development. Here's the pattern I've observed.

First of all, you need to find an appropriate date for the immersion. This is usually one of the hardest things to do, because everyone is busy, and often leaders are operating in different states or countries. Pulling them all together even for a single day is a challenge.

And with this challenge comes an opportunity cost. The leader organising the strategic immersion needs to factor in the logistical expenses (venue hire, flights, accommodation, catering and so on) as well as the time cost of having senior leaders step out of their normal roles for a day. As such, there's a real imperative to make sure that they get 'real value' out of the day.

Unfortunately, this 'real value' is often expressed in terms of preconceived outcomes. And so a tight agenda is worked up, to 'make best use of the time'.

The leaders arrive at their default venue, with a default room layout, default venue-branded notebooks and pens, and default individually wrapped mints.[3] After a bit of chitchat, they take their seats and then proceed to move through the agenda, which usually begins with a bit of a reflection on the progress made since the last time this group met.

Of course, the agenda quickly goes out the window. One of the more extroverted executives on the team feels compelled to go on a rant and push for something important to them (and them only). Some of the executives seem to be multitasking being present and answering emails on their devices. And some are periodically ducking out of the room to take phone calls.[4]

3| You know the ones I mean.

4| *Look at how busy and important I am, everyone!* (More like, look at my inability to delegate and manage my time.)

A few times, the team encounters the precursor to real strategic development — an important question with no clear answer or possible quick fix. Debate ensues about the best path to take. Conversation gets tense and, due to the poor setup and lack of professional facilitation, things start to get a little bit heated and personal. Little political subgroups emerge — but, ah! Look at the time! The agenda serves as a convenient structure to rally back to, allowing folks to skim past the discomfort of uncertainty. Quick decisions are made to favour the default, which minimises the immediate angst while generating short-term wins.

And so, by the end of the day, the team finds themselves staring at a bunch of goals, eerily similar to last year's list of goals. Things like increasing product sales, expanding into new regions, becoming more competitive in existing markets, enhancing operational efficiency in key areas, and updating outdated service platforms.

Boxes get ticked and people call it a day. They head to the bar fatigued, connect over a drink, and return to business as usual.

This is not strategic. Nor is it a demonstration of leadership.

We've seen this pattern enough times to know it doesn't work.

Thanks to the Curse of Efficiency, our time for thorough thinking is often crowded out by fast thinking. This means: more efficiency (maybe), but less progress. And when the Curse of Efficiency gets in the way of good strategy and leadership like this, only one thing can happen — *a rainbow of growth and despair...*

3. A Rainbow of Growth and Despair

For every business there exists a wonderful rainbow of growth and opportunity. At the end of this rainbow, however, lies not a pot of gold, but decline, despair and demise—in the form of the Inevitable Kraken of Doom. *cue thunder and lightning*

In his 2015 outgoing speech as the CEO of Cisco (a multinational technology company), John Chambers delivered a dire warning to the 25 000 attendees—'40 per cent of businesses in this room, unfortunately, will not exist in a meaningful way in 10 years.' He went further, adding that 70 per cent of companies will attempt to go digital, but only 30 per cent will be successful.

Now, a heap of 'doom and gloom' warnings go out to businesses—and particularly to leaders within large organisations. But this one is worth paying attention to. Before retiring, Chambers had to lead one of the most painful transitions in the company's history (including moving from 62 business units to 18 focused divisions that worked together). Chambers stressed, 'We had to tie together our silos, we had to change our culture ... we had to change, or we would have been left behind.'

And you can find plenty of examples of companies that have been left behind. In 2011, IBM turned 100—a remarkable achievement. To celebrate their relative resilience and highlight just how much had changed in that period of time, IBM ran ads in *The New York Times*, *Washington Post* and *The Wall Street Journal*. 'Of the top 25 companies on the *Fortune* 500 in 1961, only six remain today,' the ads explained.

How do organisations find themselves in this predicament? Why is it that a few organisations are able to maintain resilience and relevance over time, while many others sink into inevitable decline?

How is it that large organisations die?

Leaders do not set about to make their companies irrelevant and extinct. Rather, they find themselves meeting the Inevitable Kraken of Doom as a result of a series of *reasonable decisions*—the type of decisions that are so reasonable, and backed so convincingly by precedent and convention, that you just can't argue with them.

Let's explore what these reasonable decisions look like through the various phases of company growth.

THE DEFAULT GROWTH ARC

All successful enterprises have an arc of life—from startup, to growth, maturity and decline.

I rather like to think of this lifespan as an arcing rainbow of growth and despair. It's all somewhat wonderful to begin with—but follow this one path too long, and you'll find yourself sliding into not a pot of gold but the gaping maw of the Inevitable Kraken of Doom (as per figure 3.1).

Figure 3.1: The default enterprise growth arc

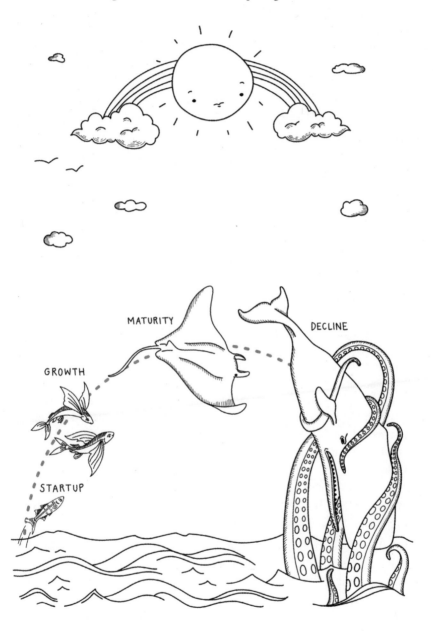

I'm not sure where you are currently placed in this growth arc. Perhaps you have the benefit of being a leader within an enterprise undergoing rapid growth, or maybe you've taken the reins of a senior leadership role for a company that's already feeling the tendrils of the Inevitable Kraken of Doom. Or maybe you're an intrapreneur within an enterprise that's currently experiencing the stagnation that comes with maturity—and you're looking for creative new pathways to reactivate growth.

If your enterprise is in the stages of maturity and decline, looking backwards, you might see a series of reasonable decisions that have led you to this point. Part II explores how to move on from the point you're at, but for now let's have a look at some of the typical challenges any organisation faces at each stage in this path.

The magical startup phase

In the magical startup phase, the focus is on *new thinking*.

Or, at least, it ought to be.

If everything is going well, you'll be very connected with your teammates and your customers, and minimal to no hierarchy or friction is standing in the way of meaningful progress. Feedback loops are tight, and learning is fast. You adapt to change quickly, and thrive on new insights. You pursue hunches via experimentation, sharing learning and insights, and asking progressively better questions. Diversity is leveraged, and feedback is sought constantly. The work is inherently motivating. Discretionary effort is the norm—people do what's needed, when it's needed. No-one is counting the hours of work they're doing—you're looking for a more meaningful sense of progress. During this phase, you have a sense of purpose, you're developing mastery, you have autonomy in the way you pursue progress, and you have the community of your team (and the rituals that keep your team together—like daily stand-up meetings, and beers and pizza on Fridays).

But the situation is not always magical. Startups can be structureless and unfocused, blindly subscribing to default 'proven' methodologies without critical thinking, stumbling from one minimum viable product to the next and hurling prototypes at users until something sticks. Everything is lean, everyone's agile, we're all pivoting and using all the right buzzwords—but we're not learning, or making any meaningful progress. In this scenario, experiments are not informed by any vision or reasoned thought. The 'new thinking' that is the most valuable element of this phase is instead replaced by a desperate need to build something viable to sell to customers. As a result, the focus shifts to improving existing products for existing customers. Such thinking might bring about incremental improvements, but it certainly won't lead to any breakthrough development.

A QUICK NOTE ON STARTUPS

Ah, the startup part of the arc is where the magic happens — where things go from 'zero to one', as technology entrepreneur and investor Peter Thiel describes it (in his book of the same name). And as the co-founder of PayPal and first investor in Facebook, he might know a thing or two. Indeed, in a world enamoured with startup buzzwords, Thiel's contrarian views are quite refreshing.

'The paradox of teaching entrepreneurship,' Thiel states, 'is that such a formula necessarily cannot exist'. I bring Thiel's perspectives into this chapter very deliberately — a lot of systems and templates out there, from 'proven experts', teach innovation and startup methodologies. But in reality, this process is paradoxical. Thiel argues that because every innovation is unique, it's actually impossible for anyone to claim authority and prescribe how to be innovative. He further suggests that if you are simply copying previous innovators and entrepreneurs (read: defaulting to precedents) — you're not learning anything. It's easier to copy a model than to do something new.

(By the way, I hope you are enjoying the irony here as we bump up against these paradoxes. Do you realise how challenging it is to write a how-to book when the very advice you give is paradoxical? We're going to be doing this dance throughout the book. And so, for any concepts I share with you — grip onto them tightly with an open palm.)

This 'magical startup phase' is a very important phase, because it's where we begin to explore *new* pathways, rather than simply enhance the efficiency of existing pathways. But this doesn't mean you need to abandon your position in a large, established organisation to embark upon a quest and make something new. Savvy leaders in organisations are realising that it's possible to create startups *within* their existing enterprise.

(continued)

A QUICK NOTE ON STARTUPS *(cont'd)*

In 2015 I delivered a keynote to senior CIOs at a large event for global information technology research and advisory firm Gartner. Part of the joy in events like this is getting to hear what forward-thinking insights come from a company like Gartner, and this year the message was clear—large organisations need to rethink how they do digital.

Peter Sondergaard, the global head of research for Gartner, argued that leaders need to design, resource and deploy for a world that's digital first (before any traditional forms of business). And in this new model, every business unit should be treated as though it were a digital startup. 'Now is your opportunity to create that team,' Sondergaard exclaimed. 'Partner with the digital startups inside your organisation and prove that you can move fast too.'

We'll get onto this approach in part VI. But the message for now is that it doesn't matter whether your organisation is large or small, or where you sit on the rainbow of growth and despair—the startup phase is pivotal. It harbours important elements of a quest.

I'm a bit sceptical of the zeal many folk have toward lean startup methodologies. The importance of experimentation and agility is paramount—and this is something a startup can do well. But this should not eclipse the need for good, thorough thinking.[1] And that's the risk any good system or template provides—it's too easy to simply follow the formula, rather than thinking for yourself.

But, let's assume all has gone swimmingly, and you've found and made something brilliant—something worthy enough to draw notice in the market. If you're attracting customers and sales are happening, your focus shifts to the crazy growth phase.

1| Indeed, the three elements of empirical science are observation, evidence and reason. And this is guided by imagination, curiosity, doubt and wonder. Experiments give you things to observe, and some evidence to work with, but *reason* is what brings it all together.

The crazy growth phase

Once an enterprise gets over the initial challenges of building a viable new product or service (something that delivers value where none existed before) and attracting paying customers, they are then ready to enter the crazy growth phase.

Now, the reasonable default and reasonable thing to do here is to scale fast — to capitalise on the opportunity before competitors can catch up. When this works, organisations can see rapid increases in their revenue and market share. This is where they begin to reap the rewards of all the hard, angsty work in the magical startup period.

It's a glorious phase, this. You have a growing customer base, surplus revenue, validation and a level of future stability — the opportunities are abundant. It is here that leaders have the greatest opportunity to use the momentum, interest, optimism and confidence generated to venture further into uncharted territory — to keep pioneering, and stay fresh and relevant.

But alas — this is not the default thing to do. In an article published in *First Round Capital*, Mark Leslie (the former CEO of VERITAS Software) points out, 'When things are going well, most leaders are reluctant to take significant, unnecessary risks in favour of market dominance.' Instead, they do the reasonable thing. They focus on what works — building incremental improvements to the product or service, adding new features, and refining things further.

Even if you're coasting along with default thinking, it's not all beer and skittles in this phase. New challenges emerge.

In the magical startup phase, small teams managed a diverse range of responsibilities. But now, in the crazy growth period, it's no longer viable for people to be spread so thin across so many things. And so people begin to work to their strengths. In an attempt to manage increased demand and workflow, the more formulaic tasks are automated or outsourced. Roles are created and a company structure begins to form. More people are hired — a process that needs to develop as the company grows. With more people and more roles comes more complexity, and more risk of duplicated and wasted effort. And so, new systems, templates, policies and structures are created and evolved to curtail the entropy inherent within rising complexity.[2]

2| Meanwhile, the Inevitable Kraken of Doom cackles, seeing the Curse of Efficiency begin to take effect.

It's possible to go from a small team to hundreds of staff within the space of a year. This can all feel fast and frantic, and work culture, vision, meaning and purpose can take a hit if leaders are not mindful through the growth period.

I've worked with a few founders who have navigated the crazy growth period of their company. The common challenge they express is that the culture is just not what it used to be—it used to be dynamic, creative and collaborative, and the team felt a real connection with each other. But now the members of that startup team feel as though they are surrounded by acquaintances they barely know. Things used to be spirited—now they are polite and correct. The initiative and discretionary effort that once fuelled things has now been replaced by slavish adherence to role descriptions. Where once people were motivated by a sense of purpose, now they're motivated by pay and promotion.

The plateau of maturity

Throughout the crazy growth period, the organisation has scaled to the point where revenue starts to flatten, and margins begin to stabilise (to a lower but still decent level) as competitors enter the space.

At this point, you likely have a well-established organisation, with robust systems, policies and procedures. The company also probably has a good base of customers, distribution channels and some brand equity.

In the best-case scenario, you have a level of operational excellence that allows for epic efficiency and impact. With your national or global positioning, you can truly change the shape and nature of industries. You can leverage massive investments in research and development to create groundbreaking products and services in your field. You attract brilliant talent. You can invest in quests and the development of further options, which in turn further enhances business strategy and growth. And, your organisation can be driven by something higher than profit—*purpose* (and the opportunity to do great good).

But, at their worst, mature organisations have a bank of well-established policies and procedures that significantly hobble their ability to innovate or prosper. By following the default path, making reasonable decisions and doing the default thing, you can end up with an organisation full of bureaucracy, friction and politics. You likely find an embedded fixation upon near-term KPIs and shareholder returns. There is no sense of greater purpose—people fixate upon ever-shrinking margins, and seek greater efficiencies.

Here are some of the common challenges I see within large organisations cursed with efficiency and default thinking:

◊ **A distinct lack of ownership exists.** Because people have clearly defined roles and hierarchies, it's easy to simply keep doing the default things in their role description. As a result, peripheral things like quests and discretionary effort just don't happen.

◊ **Vision is blinkered and myopic.** If leadership is operationally driven, established metrics and conventional measures of success will be a strong focus. This serves to narrow people's focus to a small range of tasks, hobbling curiosity and exploration. Further, some senior leaders may only have a few years remaining until their retirement. If this is the case, they may be more inclined to maintain the status quo, rather than take bold risks that might rock the boat.

◊ **Failure carries a stigma.** In mature cultures gripped by the Curse of Efficiency, failure is bad. Very bad. The learning derived from experimentation and exploration does not outweigh the perception of wasted effort — a thing to be frowned upon. This is a results-focused organisation! To demonstrate this, those who successfully adhere to established metrics are rewarded and celebrated. The message is clear: we want you to innovate (of course!) — but don't you dare innovate.[3]

◊ **Friction seems to exist for every action.** The company has a system, policy or procedure to follow for everything. You can't even send a tweet without multiple layers of approval. Everyone is civil and politically correct — but no authentic communication is happening. People aren't being human and real — instead, they don the professional masks and proceed as automatons.

---

3 | Hat tips to Scott Belsky, author of *Making Ideas Happen*, for this line.

◊ **Everyone is busy.** No surprises here, but when things are truly dysfunctional, broadcasting that the work is being done can be a better career advancement strategy than actually doing the work.

Trying to adopt a new strategic direction in this phase is much harder than in the growth phase (where everything is primed). But it's still possible—fresh thinking, a renewed approach to leadership and strategy, and a game-changing approach to workplace culture can turn things around (see chapter 5 for more on this).

For if we don't, we meet... *cue moaning dirge and darkness* ...

The Inevitable Kraken of Doom

Ah! The inevitable demise! This is where companies find themselves entering decline. At this stage, all efforts are a little bit too little, too late. The Kraken is here, and it *feeds* upon the sweet nectar of your irrelevance. If only you were more nimble and adaptive! If only you had explored new pathways to stay relevant!

Decline happens when an enterprise no longer generates value. This usually happens as a result of:

◊ **Default thinking and arrogance.** As we've explored, it's difficult to see default thinking (and the ongoing influence it has on the decisions we make). Deliberation is required to break out of default thinking and explore alternative options. But, even when viable alternative options are laid out, leaders can still succumb to arrogance—to view previous successes as indicative of future success.[4] They stop asking questions, believing they already have the best answers.

4| Not to mention a heap of cognitive biases (see chapter 14).

◊ **Bureaucracy, politics and the Curse of Efficiency.**
Sometimes innovation and progress are halted because of
large egos and/or political manoeuvring. Or decisions are
made just to keep shareholders happy. When efficiency
or personal preferences are given higher priority than
meaningful progress, things begin to decline.

◊ **Disruption.** This usually happens when large
organisations don't have a sense of emerging threats or
opportunities; when they are not attuned to emerging
technologies and intersecting trends. And when they
are not fostering quests to generate new pathways for
strategic growth. As a result, they don't lead proactively,
but instead are blindsided by disruption, and forced
into a reactive scramble to maintain market leadership.
Facebook's 'Little Red Book'—a manifesto of the
stories and perspectives that continue to shape the
company—has a great line: 'If we don't create the thing
that kills Facebook, someone else will.'

Enterprises engaged in this final phase are usually characterised by
desperation. They are highly likely to adopt widely audacious goals, and
risk perception goes way out of whack. They either rally to old thinking,
or desperately put their hope in cheap tech or 'magic wand' solutions.

If an organisation finds itself in this situation, it has either failed to
anticipate or manage an external threat—like disruption from a new
technology, a change in regulations, an environmental disaster—or
it simply has failed to keep up to date with customer needs, let alone
stay ahead of them. This usually happens when there is a combination
of the Curse of Efficiency and dogmatic adherence to default ways of
doing things.

Operationally efficient? Yes. Reasonable? Yes!

But adventurous and pioneering? No. And at this point, perhaps the best hope is that the organisation is bought out by a savvier enterprise, which might use what's left of the customer base and distribution channels to better effect. This essentially resets the cycle, and we go back to the new/ fresh thinking of the startup phase.

There will be casualties, yes. And most won't survive.

Much better to embark upon quests earlier, before things get desperate.

✳ ✳ ✳

This whole 'default growth arc' (aka the rainbow of growth and despair) kind of reminds me of the default life plan, which looks like this:

Get born, go to school, go to university, get a job, save up for a wedding, get married, switch jobs, save up for a house, get a mortgage, have a kid, switch jobs, work hard, get a promotion, take a holiday, have a second kid, work harder, see kids through university, get another promotion, have a midlife crisis, recover, work hard, retire, go on a holiday, settle down, look after grandkids, die.

Of course, that's just the default template.

There is a better way...

Summary

Part I

◊ Our default is the option we select automatically in the absence of viable alternatives. Defaults are informed by our ability to recognise and match patterns. Established systems and templates leverage efficiencies identified within complex patterns. Default thinking is, therefore, fast—but not necessarily accurate or conducive to new progress. Our default thinking harbours preferences, assumptions and biases—many of which we are blind to. It is further influenced by the status quo, conventional norms and past precedents.

◊ A sense of progress has been identified as one of the most powerful motivators at work. The more people perceive that their effort is contributing to progress, the more likely they are to continue to invest effort into that activity. This principle is an important calibration for organisational leaders—it is much less about distant goals and targets, and much more about recognising and celebrating small wins along the way. A deliberate approach utilising the progress principle can make work more inherently motivating.

◊   Unfortunately, when left unchecked, it is easy to become deluded by progress. This is where efficiency and productivity are valued more than effectiveness and progress. When organisations are cursed with efficiency, it becomes much easier to tackle the 'busywork'—emails, meetings and other visible routine or operational tasks that provide a rich and immediate sense of progress. To escape the Delusions of Progress, you need to know what meaningful progress looks like.

◊   Strategic development can identify new pathways for progress, if leaders can suspend the need for fast or immediate solutions and instead engage in a deeper and more thorough level of exploration. If this does not happen, they are likely to default to their defaults, resulting in reasonable, risk-averse strategy very similar to previous iterations.

◊   Such a risk-averse approach is typical of the arc of life for an enterprise. The arc begins at the startup phase (which can and should also occur within large organisations). From there, assuming reasonable decisions are made, an enterprise will grow, mature and then lose relevance and decline into the tentacles of the Inevitable Kraken of Doom—unless an alternative pathway is embraced.

◊   Making viable alternative options available to inform strategic decision-making is therefore an imperative—and the main focus of this book.

———————————

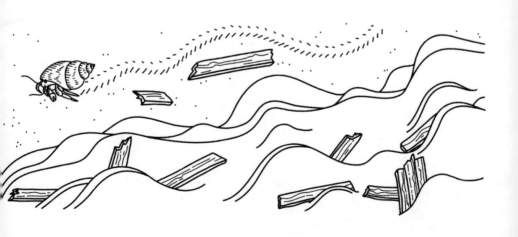

Part II

A Quest Beckons

Quest [noun]: a search for an alternative option
that meets cognitive criteria.

As soon as we step outside the relentless busywork—resisting the Curse of Efficiency and the Delusion of Progress—we can begin to realise and appreciate that our current (default) business model and modus operandi may not be relevant in future contexts.

When you first stop and think about it, this realisation is quite scary. It's an uncomfortable notion to consider—and so many don't. They instead look back to past successes to find validation within their experience, and comfort within existing paradigms of work.

But, for those who can move beyond the initial fear of an uncertain future, the second phase is likely to feel daunting. The sheer scale of the infinite complexity inherent within our uncertain future is intimidating, to say the least. As a consequence, leaders crave a direct and familiar approach to tackle this complexity. They attempt to *reduce* uncertainty.

What this tends to look like is an 'ideas funnel', with ideas being fed into one side and innovation coming out the other. This can seem like a simple contraption that makes logical sense, and it's certainly a tool that gives everyone a sense that something is being done. Indeed, in its worst incarnation, some enterprises even come up with 'give us your best idea' competitions. #facepalm

Such a simplistic approach comes at a cost. By seeking to reduce uncertainty—instead of questing within it—we end up reducing the very things that allow us to pioneer and unlock game-changing strategic innovation: creativity, serendipity, imagination, diversity, experimentation and learning. Reducing uncertainty forces us to rely on simple opportunistic and incremental improvements to the current business model. This approach does not lead to the generation of new or unprecedented progress and growth. Also, such approaches are usually the result of governance systems in which senior decision-makers are the arbitrators of innovation,[1] rather than the champions who enable collective and ongoing strategic innovation.

The third feeling when confronted with the complexity of an uncertain future is *frustration*.[2] If you're a leader of a large organisation, this is very understandable. As we saw in chapter 3, organisations can mature to the point where they become behemoths (in terms of size and/or bureaucracy and arrogance). The pace of change becomes glacial, and everyone is focused on the wrong things. No-one is working together, and no-one is thinking about the future.

And so the big fear for CEOs of large organisations today is that they are simply going to preside over the slow decline and decay of a once-great enterprise. Their legacy, they fear, will simply be a footnote on a Wikipedia page that describes their leadership impact as the stewardship of the enterprise into irrelevance.[3]

So — let's not be that leader.

The only escape is to think differently, and lean into the uncomfortable complexity and paradox inherent within the infinite possibilities of an uncertain future.

The chapters in this part present such an approach. Where part I brought you the *why* behind leading a quest, part II hones in on the *what*—namely, Quest-Augmented Strategy.

This framework guides an enterprise through the contextual activities and pioneering leadership required to explore, identify, validate and pursue new value, and secure enduring relevance.

---

1 | And, by being the ultimate judges of what strategic initiatives proceed, they bring their own cognitive biases and default thinking into the process — making it much more likely that we see more of the same (see chapter 14).

2 | This, when compared to fear and intimidation, is at least a *useful* feeling to have.

3 | And the clammy embrace of the Inevitable Kraken of Doom.

4. An Alternative Option

I n *The Game Changer*, I share an alternative philosophy for work—that is, to recognise that work is a game. A game that can be tweaked and changed, in order to unlock inherent motivation and greater progress.

This perspective was inspired by philosopher James Carse's brilliant book *Finite and Infinite Games: A vision of life as play and possibility*. In this work, Carse argues that life consists of at least two kinds of games: one finite, the other infinite. Finite games have a start and an end point, and are played for the purpose of winning. Infinite games, on the other hand, are played for the purpose of continuing the play. In a business context, you can think of this in terms of maintaining value and relevance.

Many conventional leadership books treat business as though it were a finite game, in which the sole focus is winning. For example, in the popular book *Playing to Win: How strategy really works*, AG Lafley and Roger Martin argue that 'the heart of strategy is the answer to two fundamental questions: where will you play, and how will you win there?'

Such a philosophy has a certain old-school charm to it. It's comfortingly simple and familiar, and a raft of historical evidence supports it.[1] And it might work for 80 per cent of the work—it surely works for defined playing fields, in which the rules are set and the metrics for winning are clear.

1| And it includes sporting analogies, too—keep your eye on the ball, and so on. Because, err…sport! Right?

But I'm not sure how such an approach translates in today's world—let alone the future we are moving into. Technology is catalysing change faster than ever before, which means no fixed playing fields exist. Lafley and Martin argue that 'winning is what matters—and it is the ultimate criterion of a successful strategy' ... but I'd suggest that such an approach is dangerous.

Not everything needs to be viewed through the lens of competition.[2] And, in today's game, we never really 'win'. By the time you master one playing field, the game has changed. Victory is never declared—because the business landscape is always shifting. To say you have 'won' implies that the game has finished—that things have been brought to a conclusion—but all finite games sit within the context of an infinite game. There's *always* the opportunity to create more value.

Taking a more infinite perspective is more valuable—one focusing on progress, rather than success. As Carse explains, 'Finite players play *within* boundaries, infinite players play *with* boundaries.'

In order to lead pioneering progress, you must explore opportunities that live outside the boundaries of existing, conventional playing fields. For busy leaders, this means carving out time for *thorough* thinking—the disciplined exploration of alternative options, both individually and within a diverse teams. Sophisticated, thorough thinking that takes us beyond the safe and warm embrace of default thinking and quick, shallow wins.

This kind of thinking requires leaders to explore the intersection of science and art, and heed the call to adventure.

2| Why do we obsess about competition? Peter Thiel (author of *Zero to One*) argues that competition is a relic of history—something economists copied from 19th century physicists. From this perspective, businesses aren't seen as the creators of unique value, but rather as interchangeable atoms. Thiel further argues that all failed companies are the same—they failed to escape competition.

A CALL TO ADVENTURE

According to the computational knowledge engine WolframAlpha, the word *adventure* means 'to take a risk in the hope of a favourable outcome'. This type of risk-taking also happens to be a significant element in Joseph Campbell's 'hero's journey'. Campbell's *The Hero of a Thousand Faces*, published in 1949, identified what he calls the 'monomyth'—a broad concept in narratology that highlights a common structure to many enduring heroic mythologies.

Campbell identified seventeen stages in the structure of the hero's journey. This structure has since been summarised by some clever folks into as few as eight steps. But now, for the sake of brevity, I'm going to summarise it even further:

1. A hero exists in the ordinary, default world surrounded by ordinary, default people doing ordinary, default things. (A similar world to the one we explored in chapter 1.)

2. There is a 'call to adventure'—an opportunity to obtain a great boon for the ordinary world—but the hero refuses the call. Besides: it's perilous, and they're already quite busy[3] (refer to chapters 2 and 3).

3. A catalyst or mentor arrives, challenging the hero to take up the call to adventure. Maybe the hero has just attended a conference, or read an insightful book. Or maybe, this catalyst is the accumulation of several mentors and catalysing experiences—enough for the hero to declare, 'Enough! Something must be done. We must find a better way!'[4] (See chapters 4 to 6 for more.)

---

3 | At this point—should the hero and everyone around them continue to refuse the call to adventure, the story continues as per the default rainbow of growth and despair, and the Kraken of Doom enjoys another meal.

4 | There's an introverted equivalent, in which the hero frowns and simply begins rescheduling their calendar, carving time out for a worthy quest

4. And so the hero embarks upon a quest, leaving the world
   of default thinking to pursue new and as-yet-unrealised
   opportunities. Inner demons (self-sabotage, assumptions
   and biases) are confronted, and dragons (friction) are
   slain. The journey is fraught with failure—it's really
   challenging. But the hero demonstrates a level of adaptive
   tenacity, and eventually gains powerful new knowledge
   and magical insight. (You don't want to skim this part of
   the story—check out chapters 7 to 12.)

5. The hero returns to the ordinary, default world, in which
   their newly obtained special insight and magic is a great
   boon that can be used to make a difference—namely, to
   inform and progress pioneering strategy and growth. (This
   is where the real magic happens—see chapters 13 to 21.)

And thus, we have the hero's journey (as it applies in this book).

Of course, I have done a crude job of summarising Campbell's fine work.
If it interests you, I suggest you look it up—his ideas are incredibly
intriguing, and you'll see the template playing out in many popular stories
and films. One thing to note: the hero's journey is typically depicted as a
male thing—which is, of course, ridiculous. Anyone can be a hero and
embark upon a quest, regardless of gender.

In the context of business (and this book), the hero's journey is a
challenging one, involving lots of work (which may not work out), and
it can be a lonely journey. The rest of the book helps you with this
journey, but the thing to note at this point is this— *most refuse the
call to adventure.* Oh sure, we *talk* about how important it is to think
differently, and to embrace fresh ideas. And not a corporate event goes by
without some senior executive pointing out that innovation is of critical
importance.

But what's often lacking is threefold:

◊ **A progressive strategy** that goes beyond the default, and builds for future opportunities.

◊ **An enterprise culture that values learning** and thrives on change.

◊ **Leadership that values new thinking,** can handle ambiguity and aspires to make a difference.

All three of these components work together to influence progress—but it's the leadership component that makes the most immediate and direct difference. And it's the leadership component that'll see us circumvent the Inevitable Kraken of Doom.

CIRCUMVENTING THE KRAKEN

Q: How does one escape the Inevitable Kraken of Doom?

A: By finding new rainbows and growth arcs to pursue.

Yes, we *can* outfox the Kraken.[5]

But to do so requires the exploration of opportunities that lie tangential to the default growth arc.

Recall the rainbow of growth and despair from chapter 3. The typical growth arc is littered with default thinking and ruled by the Curse of Efficiency.

But! If some leaders heed the call to adventure, and lean into the challenge of pioneering through doubt and uncertainty, it's possible to unlock new, tangential growth arcs (see figure 4.1, overleaf).

---

5 | I can imagine some serious folks frowning as they read this, so let me just remind those readers—the Inevitable Kraken of Doom is a metaphor for business decline. It's what happens when a business loses relevance. I use this metaphor deliberately, because the alternative is to use buzzwords or lifeless corporate-speak. And who wants more of that? And besides, pattern-disruption is good for learning.

Figure 4.1: Circumventing the Kraken

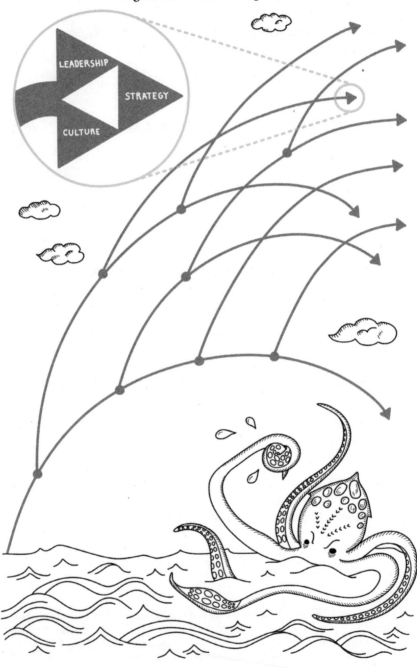

In this scenario, an enterprise stays relevant by exploring new rainbows to maintain growth and avoid despair. This 'growth' may not necessarily take the form of company size or market share, but, rather, relate to relevance, value and significance.

Note the arrowhead in figure 4.1 — it consists of strategy, leadership and culture. These three elements influence the direction in which an enterprise moves: towards enduring relevance or towards decline.

THE IMPORTANCE OF PIONEERING

We've all heard stories of the companies that have had their 'Kodak moment' and veered into decline and the Inevitable Kraken of Doom. What usually characterises such decline is the inability (or a lack of willingness) to pursue alternative options.

Take Nokia, for example. Few realise that this company was founded in 1865 in Finland as a wood-pulp mill. For well over 100 years, this company has been led by opportunity — pursuing tangents and adapting with the times. From wood pulp Nokia shifted to rubber manufacturing. This was in line with a rise in car production (and, therefore, an increasing need for rubber to make tyres), but it also saw Nokia begin to produce cables for electricity and telecommunication. This pioneering model of strategy and leadership continued until Nokia was at the peak of the mobile phone market, selling over 1 billion mobile phones by 2005. By this stage, many considered Nokia to be 'untouchable'.

But then, two years later, the iPhone was released. By this stage, an operationally driven, risk-averse culture had been established within Nokia. By this stage, the company was a behemoth that pumped out *millions* of phones. Any error or bad call could cost the company billions of dollars, and threaten the success it was enjoying. To prevent this, the enterprise culture (and the leadership that informed it) was structured around many layers of approvals and meetings. There was no sense of urgency. In fact, Nokia refused to enter the touch-screen market. The whole system was built to prevent mistakes and preserve the efficiency of the existing business model.

(continued)

THE IMPORTANCE OF PIONEERING *(cont'd)*

And so, for the first period in Nokia's enduring history of pioneering, opportunity-driven leadership, the enterprise stopped exploring. By the time it did react it was too slow, too little and too late. In 2014 Nokia was acquired by Microsoft.

This example is typical of many large organisations in which pioneering leadership occurs far too late in the equation. Or those in which pioneering leadership never germinates—due to a leadership culture cursed with efficiency.

In the next chapter, we'll unpack the crux of this book—a model for *Quest-Augmented Strategy*. This approach ensures that strategy is fed by more than just default thinking, and that leaders have a viable set of alternative options to inform their decisions. Later chapters further illuminate how startups can be created *within* large enterprises—to identify, explore and pursue new rainbows of growth.

But, of course, even when these alternative options are identified, they'll still carry inherent risk. And they'll still be shrouded in a level of uncertainty.[6]

Pioneering leadership is what we need. That, and a willingness to embrace paradox.

PIONEERING THROUGH PARADOX

The word 'pioneer' means a heap of wonderful things, including:

◊   to open up a new area, or prepare a way

◊   to take the lead or initiative in

◊   to participate in the development of something new.

6| Our efforts in part IV attempt to mitigate this, somewhat.

Pioneering leadership means leaning into the challenge of progressing through new and uncharted territory. This form of leadership enables the exploration, development, learning and progress through uncertainty and doubt.

I use the terms 'pioneering leadership', 'frontier leadership' and 'opportunity-driven leadership' fairly interchangeably. I'm not trying to create new buzzwords here—rather, I'm seeking to refresh the appreciation for the significant role of pioneering leadership. It is one of the biggest missing components in large organisations today.[7]

It's thanks to *pioneering* leadership that businesses stay relevant and grow. However, for organisations enjoying the fruits of success in the growth phase, or shrinking margins in the decline, it's *easy* to default to operationally driven leadership and maximise efficiencies where possible.

Operationally driven leaders may believe they are protecting a company's ability to grow. But their bias towards efficiency and predictability, combined with a low tolerance for uncertainty and risk, means that they'll very likely choose *not* to capitalise on anything but the default. And so, dutifully they'll persist along the default growth arc—ignoring tangential rainbows along the way—right into the disturbingly moist embrace of the Kraken.[8]

Embracing pioneering leadership means embracing several paradoxical notions. These may seem to be absurd and seemingly contradictory propositions—but, as you'll find through this book, they harbour practical and progressive wisdom.

To gain certainty, we must embrace fuzziness. Where the operationally driven leader manufactures an artificial sense of certainty—often in the form of clear targets and goals—the pioneering leader feels no such need. As such a leader, you're comfortable making progress while only having a fuzzy sense of the potential destination. You don't wait for clarity or perfect plans before acting. Rather, you progress into uncertainty with adaptability and risk-mastery, learning along the way.

7| Startups generally begin with pioneering leadership by default. However, they can quickly succumb to the defaults of 'proven strategies' and formulas if they're not mindful.

8| This is not to say that operationally driven leadership doesn't play an important role—it does. We need to be able to implement and execute great strategy. We'll explore the importance of this role in part VI.

To build conviction, we must embrace doubt. German philosopher Johann Wolfgang von Goethe once said that 'doubt grows with knowledge'. And Aristotle is said to have once quipped, 'the more you know, the more you know you don't know'. Whereas some might claim to have all of the right answers, pioneering leaders instead value asking the right questions (which, in turn, makes them less ignorant of their own ignorance).

To make progress, we must avoid success. It's tempting to declare victory, and to feel as though we have 'made it'. But pioneering leaders know this is an infinite game we're playing—one with no finish line. You always have more opportunities to learn, grow and develop to stay relevant. Sure—you'll have small wins along the way. But constructive discontent is a constant companion.

Now, you might be nodding along to this, because you're the one reading this book. But what about the other folk you work with?

Don't worry, we'll get to them.

NEW SUPERPOWERS AND THE BENEFIT OF THE DOUBT

The old leadership superpowers favour certainty, decisiveness, self-belief and unwavering conviction. They celebrate an ability to stay firm in the face of change, and pursue goals with tenacity and rigour. Such superpowers are still valid today—particularly for formulaic work with predictable outcomes. They allow us to implement and execute on strategy. These are largely *convergent* superpowers. They narrow our options so that we can focus on the work that needs to get done. They are ideal in the wake of strategic development.

But they don't serve us at the frontier. To effectively lead progress through uncertainty, pioneering leaders need to call upon a new family of superpowers—*divergent* superpowers that open new pathways and avenues to explore.

I like to think of the superpowers as a family. Just as there are the four riders of the apocalypse (death, war, conquest and famine), there are four much nicer superpowers for a pioneering leader. Those powers are imagination, curiosity, doubt and wonder.

It's getting tricky to trust quotes from famous dead people these days[9], but I'm reasonably confident that Einstein once said that imagination was 'more important than knowledge'. But in this family of superpowers, 'wonder' is probably the champion. Wonder exists in the undivided mind, within the overlaps of both art and science. When we wonder, we feel curious and experience the desire to know something.

But, let's not forget 'doubt'. Doubt is like the black sheep of the family—often regarded with less esteem than imagination, curiosity and wonder. And yet doubt is one of our most stalwart companions to any quest.

The three hidden benefits of doubt

One of the best books I encountered in 2014 was Oliver Burkeman's *The Antidote: Happiness for people who can't stand positive thinking*. In this book, Burkeman challenges many of the conventional 'positive thinking' approaches to happiness, instead advocating what he calls 'the negative path' to happiness.

Burkeman argues that, through positive thinking (and related approaches), we seek the safety of certainty. We seek to know of a time in the future in which we'll never need to fear negative emotions again—we'd be ceaselessly happy. But in chasing all that, Burkeman says, 'we close down the very faculties that permit the happiness we crave.'

Instead of trying to actively pursue happiness (while trying to avoid negative emotions), Burkeman suggests we go the other way: look toward negative experiences, and embrace the learning inherent within them.

9| Indeed, as Abraham Lincoln once said: 'The problem with internet quotes is that you can't always depend on their accuracy.'

A similar approach can be applied to the concepts of clarity and conviction. If you want these things, you could set forth a crystal clear goal. You can make it rock solid, and temper it with unwavering persistence and conviction.

Or, you could take a counterintuitive approach, and turn toward the hidden benefits of doubt.

Let's look at a few of these.

Doubt makes ideas stronger
Doubt is fundamental to all discovery, learning and growth. It's an inherent element of the scientific method, and the precursor to all great questions and breakthroughs. Doubt births wisdom. It's what we unpack when we do slow thinking, and it's deeply linked to quality ideas.

We'll explore this further in part III.

Doubt makes leaders better
Have you ever felt that, sooner or later, your colleagues and everyone around you will realise that you're not as smart as people think you are? That you are not really qualified for the position you hold? And that one day you'll be found out. People will point at you and shout *impostor!*—exposing you for the fraud that you are.

I get that feeling all the time. It's called the impostor syndrome, and it emerges when we constantly compare ourselves to our talented peers. Or, more specifically, when we compare our own doubt-ridden internal perceptions with the confident facade that others project.

We feel that a big discrepancy exists between the two—but for all we know, they could be full of self-doubt too. In fact, if they're any good, they probably are.

This sense of 'impostorism' could be seen as a natural symptom of gaining experience. 'Move up the ranks and, if your field's even vaguely meritocratic, you'll encounter more talented people to compare yourself negatively against', writes Burkeman. Some research suggests that the syndrome actually gets worse as you get better.

So, the good news: if you're full of self-doubt, you're probably doing great![10]

Besides, it's much better to feel like an impostor than to suffer from the Dunning-Kruger effect—a scenario whereby people harbour inaccurate illusions of superiority. Unburdened by self-doubt, these people don't realise how inept they are. The fools.

Now, plenty of standard advice is available for managing the impostor syndrome (stop comparing yourself, accept that you're successful, focus on providing value, yawn). Most of this advice is about reassuring yourself.

But you could take a different tack, and *embrace* the doubt.

In my world, I know that sooner or later someone will challenge me on my work. And that's great—I will be prepared for that battle. Or maybe I won't.

Either way, we'll learn something. And in the meantime, I use my awareness of the impostor syndrome to stay ahead of the game. I publish books like this, work with increasingly influential leaders and share world-class research in keynotes. I never settle, and never fall into the delusion that I've 'made it'.

You might like to take this approach, too. Accept that the doubt is there, and use it to do more and be better. This is exactly the quality we want in leaders—the ability to question ourselves, to think deeper and accept that no-one and no thing is perfect, but we can learn.

Much better that than a leader unburdened by doubt.

Doubt makes life more wonderful

We often think about things in binary mode—in terms of what's right and what's wrong. This places us in a near-constant state of judgement—of ourselves, and of others. To be right, someone must be wrong.

Marshall Rosenberg, wielder of daggy puppets and pioneer in non-violent communication, argues that this type of thinking is the very thing that brings us closer to violence. Binary right/wrong thinking

---

10| Maybe.

certainly doesn't enable self-compassion, nor compassion or empathy for others.

'Instead of playing the game of 'Making Life Wonderful', we often play the game called "Who's Right",' Marshall Rosenberg says. 'Do you know that game? It's a game where everybody loses.'

We can play a different game—a game with no clear right and wrong, where nothing is conclusive. A game that always has room for wonder, and win–win scenarios are wonderful.

We see this in science all the time. Theories that were thought to be right and 'true' are dismantled in light of new evidence. Everything is always open to further questioning.

'Let go of certainty,' says author and journalist Tony Schwartz. 'The opposite isn't uncertainty. It's openness, curiosity and a willingness to embrace paradox, rather than choose up sides.'

Want more wonder in your life? Relinquish the need to be right, and instead embrace doubt and the opportunity to learn.

This approach is not always wonderful. In fact, carrying doubt is often uncomfortable. But, all growth occurs just outside of our comfort zone. To willingly step into this space requires courage and vulnerability—the type of qualities pioneering leaders ought to seek to demonstrate.

Beware conclusions

'We can't do this' is an unhelpful and potentially premature conclusion. *'I'm not sure we can do this'* is a bit better. Because there's only one way to find out—try. And then if that doesn't work, you could fall back to the conclusion that you, in fact, cannot do said thing. Or maybe you can keep the doubt alive—maybe it was an issue with your methodology, or some other factor?

The best kind of doubt ends in a question mark
'Can we do this?' Ah. I don't know. Let's find out.

A parting note…
We can easily become lost in the world of divergent thinking. Imagination, curiosity, doubt and wonder are all wonderful—but they need to translate into meaningful progress. This is where operational leadership serves to support pioneering leadership.

In the next chapter, we'll unpack a model for Quest-Augmented Strategy that balances both divergent and convergent thinking, to make meaningful progress happen.

AHOY THE INTRAPRENEUR!

'News team, assemble!' says Ron Burgundy, after blowing into a shell horn in *Anchorman*. If only such a horn existed for the intrapreneurs within organisations.[11]

The term *intrapreneur* is a relatively new one—I had to teach it to my word processor—but it's a concept business leaders are beginning to see the value of.

As distinct from an entrepreneur (who seeks to build their own business around the creation of new value), an intrapreneur is someone who seeks to create new value within a larger organisation. This isn't an employee simply looking to do better in their existing role, aspiring to climb the corporate ladder[12]—this is someone wanting to create something new that doesn't exist yet.

Intrapreneurs are frequently my favourite clients. These pioneering leaders may not carry a senior leadership title within an organisation, but with the right superpowers and savvy, they can make extraordinary things happen.

Gaining these results often means fighting uphill battles, against the grain of conventional thinking. It also means persevering through doubt and uncertainty. Without the support of the organisation, it can be a very lonely and tiring journey. At any point, these emerging pioneers can either succumb to default thinking, or leave the organisation.[13]

11| In the movie, it turned out that Ron's news team were in the same room. I daresay the case might be a similar one with fellow intrapreneurs.

12| Although, just as growth can be the consequence of sound innovation, advancement can be the consequence for an intrapreneur. Those who think beyond their role description—who invest discretionary effort towards the betterment of an enterprise—are usually the ones who advance faster and further. The key is this: the intrapreneur's motive is primarily not self-serving. It's about creating new value.

13| It's never been easier to start a startup on your own (or with a team of like-minded folks) and pursue meaningful work with autonomy.

But some companies *nurture* their intrapreneurs, and provide them a safe space to create. Companies like Google, Facebook, Deloitte and Accenture have formal programs to support employees in creating and pursuing their own projects within the organisation.[14] Given that many startups fail, intrapreneurship can become a very viable alternative to entrepreneurship.[15]

Fostering intrapreneurship is a critical element of pioneering leadership. The way it's fostered doesn't have to be rigid and formal, but it does need to be authentic and real.

By providing support for the exploration of meaningful projects, and by empowering people to improve the business (with autonomy), leaders enhance the diversity of thinking and the likelihood of meaningful growth. An enterprise that values intrapreneurs will usually have an effective internal communications platform[16] and rituals to share learning and celebrate achievements.[17]

When confronted with new challenges, the leaders of traditional organisations call together the VPs and directors of business units to brainstorm a solution. But then, it's always the same people trying to find a solution—and they're all influenced by the same constraints of default thinking. A pioneering enterprise that supports intrapreneurship, on the other hand, has a whole raft of diverse thinking to draw upon, from people passionate about contributing to the company. They're able to tap into the full potential of their organisation.

14| 'Bah!' says the default-thinker, cursed with efficiency and precedents. 'That's easy for them—those companies are different to ours. We can't do something like that!' they proclaim, cynically, without testing the hypothesis or collecting any evidence (beyond assumptions and bias) to support it.

15| I should also note that this is not simply something for the younger folk. Many senior employees harbour a wealth of experience and a desire to leave a meaningful legacy. Allowing them to pursue pioneering projects within an organisation can be just as valid.

16| No, I'm not referring to the intranet. 'It's on the intranet' is often code for 'you'll never find it' in large organisations.

17| These can take the form of hackathons, mini-conferences, fail-cons, and dedicated breakout streams at national events. See chapter 21 for more.

If you play the role of a senior leader within your organisation, know this: you have the ability to pioneer, and build for the future of work.[18] An immediate priority for you is to foster an environment that supports intrapreneurship. In part III and part VII, I'll give you some insight as to *how* you can do this.

If you consider yourself an intrapreneur—or an intrapreneur in waiting—the time is now. Don't wait for the senior leaders to make this happen. Finish this book, and get to making clever happen.[19]

18| Even if you consider yourself more of an operationally driven leader, it is still possible for you to support pioneering leadership in your organisation. With the right balance, things harmonise, and the result is a robust, progressive organisation fit for the future of work.

19| The Quest-Augmented Strategy model we're about to unpack is equally applicable to you. Even if you must start with small projects, I'll show you how you can pursue meaningful hunches, experiment with worthy questions, and build a momentum of evidence to influence progress and change—no matter what position you currently hold.

5. Quest-Augmented Strategy

A nd so here we are—the contextual framework that nests the concepts within this book. Let's just quickly recap.

A quest is the search for an alternative that meets cognitive criteria. We find alternative options by *pioneering*—opening new pathways, and exploring new areas. And, we ensure that they are *viable* options by conducting experiments.

This ultimately yields insight that augments and enriches strategy—challenging default thinking by presenting viable alternative options. This enhances leadership and decision making, which in turn ensures more meaningful progress for an enterprise.

A FRAMEWORK FOR MEANINGFUL PROGRESS

Mathematician George Box once said, 'All models are wrong, but some are useful.' This notion is therefore the ultimate caveat for any model. With this quote, one can make a model for anything—logical fallacies be damned!

The main model for this book—'Quest-Augmented Strategy: A framework for meaningful progress'—is no exception. What I'm about to build with you is *not* the perfect solution to all the enterprise woes we highlighted in part I. But, I daresay it might be useful.

Here it is (see figure 5.1, overleaf).

Figure 5.1: Quest-Augmented Strategy

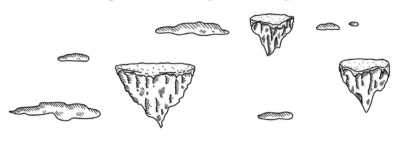

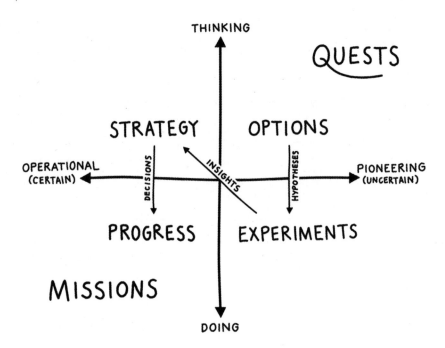

A lot is going on here. Let's unpack the thinking behind it.

Pioneering, or operational?

The primary balance of this model exists within one key distinction — are we playing with boundaries, or within them?

Pioneering work is wrapped in uncertainty and requires a very different style of leadership. In this space, we can't work towards a specific goal, because we don't know exactly what the goal looks like.[1] Pioneering work is work without established precedent. It's uncharted and largely unknown — there are no easy measures for success, and no maps, pegs or guideposts to follow. It's highly ambiguous, and your only reliable companion is doubt. You're wielding the machete, and you're carving out your own path.

In contrast, operational work has well-established precedent to follow. It's much more predictable than pioneering work, carries a higher level of certainty, and is easy to benchmark and measure. It's what all gold standards are built upon, and it's how we make things happen.

In previous chapters, I may have been a tad disparaging towards default thinking, so let's be clear: we *need* it. We need good defaults and cognitive shortcuts in order to get work done. In fact, we need operational excellence for about 80 per cent of the work we do. Without it, there'd be chaos. And besides — our defaults determine our workplace culture.

The trouble is, if you're looking to build pioneering leadership, one of the first challenges is carving out time *within* the context of operational work.[2]

Thinking, or doing?

The secondary balance of this model relates to the emphasis of our efforts — are we focused on good thinking, or good doing?

Naturally, both activities occur at all times — it's hard to separate the two. But for high-stakes work that involves navigating through risk, you need a slower (non-rushed) and more thorough level of thinking to occur.

---

1 | If we *were* to manufacture a specific goal to strive towards, we'd rob ourselves of the ability to explore tangential opportunities.

2 | This is something we explore in part III.

Why? Because enterprise strategy can have far-reaching implications. It could involve expensive acquisitions, or investment in new research or technology. It could also necessitate restructuring, mergers — potentially affecting the lives of thousands (if not more). It's here that we challenge our assumptions and default thinking. And it's here that we move beyond arrogance and ignorance, to challenge, innovate and potentially cannibalise our own business in order to unlock new value, stay relevant and grow.

But what happens if we overemphasise thinking, at the expense of doing? Nothing. Nothing happens. It's an easy temptation to invest too much time in thinking and strategising. Meanwhile, the world moves on. At some point (well, at all points), we need to act.

In fact, the feedback loops for thinking/learning and doing ought to be tight. It's one of the key principles of the lean startup methodology (as popularised by Eric Ries). You need to be doing things if you are to generate value, validate ideas and make a difference.

But what happens if we overemphasise doing, at the expense of thinking? You know the answer — we get more of the same. It's incremental at best. The Curse of Efficiency and the Delusion of Progress ensure that we just get better at doing more of the same things. It's the *thinking* — the questioning, the learning and the challenging of assumptions and convention — that sees us make meaningful progress.

Righto, now that we've familiarised ourselves with the axes,[3] let's have a look at each of the main components.

Quests

In keeping with our philosophy that businesses and enterprises play an *infinite* game, victory is never declared in our quest. We never dust our hands and claim to have 'won'. Instead, we *constantly* pursue relevance and meaning, and the creation of new and enduring value.

This is, at the highest level, what a quest is — the constant pursuit of betterment. In a business context, it's the recognition that our current business model and modus operandi may be rendered incoherent in the future, but that by exploring future contexts and possibilities, we may use this insight to manage strategic risk and obtain strategic advantage.

---

3 | *Axes* is the plural of axis. I had to look that up.

When we quest, we move beyond the boundaries of our default thinking, to bring about something new.

Such a philosophy is naturally quite beautiful—but it also needs to translate into more discernible value to an enterprise.

This is why we identify *options*.

Options

Our default is the option we choose automatically, in the absence of viable alternative options. The focus of the 'Options' quadrant in Quest-Augmented Strategy is to explore and identify future options, and new pathways and opportunities for growth.

It represents the thinking work required for pioneering leadership.

An 'option' can be defined as a possible activity that we may choose to integrate into operational strategy, should an opportune moment present itself in the future.

When engaged in the thinking required for pioneering work, we willingly venture deep within paradox, complexity and uncertainty, and it's here that we start to identify emerging trends—we have our finger on the pulse, tapping into (and pre-empting) the Zeitgeist of our times. By developing an acuity for technological triggers and emerging needs, we can start to explore the future intersection of trends. From this perspective, we ask: how will our current business model work in this potential scenario? What strategic risk does this potential future present to our current business model, and how might we proactively mitigate that risk? Or, what strategic advantage might this potential future present to our enterprise, and how might we capitalise on it?

In part III we explore how an enterprise can foster curiosity, nurture hunches, and develop an acuity for exploring and identifying potential options.

Hypotheses

Once we have accumulated a portfolio of options—potential future scenarios that offer an enterprise the opportunity for strategic growth, or enable an enterprise to mitigate and navigate through strategic risk—we need to ensure the alternative options we collect are viable. This, then, gives us the opportunity to generate worthy *questions*.

Worthy questions are what make up a quest, and the majority of pioneering work.

Remember, a quest is the search for an alternative that meets cognitive criteria. The cognitive criteria we place on a quest relates to the viability of an option. So we ask questions. Is there merit in pursuing this option further? Do environmental triggers suggest we need to act on this soon? Or can we afford to wait? Is this option something our business model can leverage, or is it too far afield from our current efforts?[4]

And so, in order to determine if options are viable, we identify the questions that need to be asked, and we develop testable statements (hypotheses) to explore.

Experiments

Here is where pioneering *thinking* shifts into pioneering *doing*. Armed with the right questions and hypotheses, we proceed to determining the viability of different options.

The only way we can answer the questions inherent in our hypotheses is by conducting experiments. Experiments are also what build momentum — enterprise strategy is unlikely to pivot on the basis of a mere hunch.

And so, experiments are what provide the evidence and insight required to augment strategic decision-making. Experimentation is science, in its purest form.

At its heart, science consists of three factors: reason, observation and evidence. By generating a portfolio of options, we also generate sound *reasoning* as to why certain things are worth exploring. We translate this

---

4| For example, a car manufacturing company ought to be very interested in exploring alternative fuel sources, autonomous vehicles, collaborative ownership, cloud computing, artificial intelligence, gamification, quantum computing, network integration and complex adaptive systems (among other things). They might explore how cities are evolving, how demographics are shifting, and what new technologies are emerging. But … in among these explorations, there may be some options that don't carry a sense of urgency or relate as directly to the current business model or capacity to generate value. The growing trend toward microbreweries and the rise of new-world whisky distilleries, for example, may not have immediate relevance to a car manufacturing company.

into more worthy questions and testable hypotheses. Experiments then allow us to observe things. It's by observing things that we recognise new patterns and learn. With enough experiments and observations, we may then accumulate enough evidence and insight to inform strategy.

Insights

This is where we begin to shift from pioneering work to operational work. And it's at this intersection that the value of pioneering work is realised.[5]

The options we have identified and explored, combined with the experiments we have conducted, mean that we now have *viable* alternative options with which strategic decision-making can be augmented and enriched.

And, because we have tested things, we have some degree of precedent to play with. Our tests have been at a small and relatively safe scale, so now the question is not so much if this can work, but *how* we can make this work on a larger scale. Our initial tests mitigate the risk of new pathways — making it easier for both opportunity-driven and operationally driven leaders to get on board.

And so, do we choose to progress with these viable alternative options?

Strategy

Let's just remember what the default version of strategy looks like within an enterprise cursed with efficiency. It looks like busy executives looking for quick fixes, easy answers and boxes to tick. You have familiar, easily measurable goals, and the appropriate peppering of jargon and buzzwords to make a strategy seem robust and relevant. The outcome of this strategy work will contain all the usual suspects, won't rock the boat too much, and will provide the delightful delusion of progress.

With Quest-Augmented Strategy, things are different.

Here, our default thinking is challenged — we have viable alternative options to consider. And these are not merely spontaneous 'ideas' generated within strategy meetings on a whim, or whimsical 'me-too' bits of tangential strategy or tactics ('Hey! Let's build an app!'). Rather, these

---

5 | At this point in the hero's journey we return to the ordinary (operational) world, with the boon of insight that could make a profound difference to the path we take.

are genuinely viable alternative options for decision-makers to consider. These pathways have been explored, experiments have been conducted, and things are primed to scale.

And so, when considering Quest-Augmented Strategy, leaders will ensure ample time is dedicated to considering a diverse range of options. Cognitive biases and distortions will be checked, assumptions will be challenged, and quick fixes will be resisted. Rather than avoid the paradox and tension of good strategy, here we embrace it. The 'too hard' basket doesn't exist.

Decisions

If our objective is *meaningful* progress, the intersection of strategy (the thinking work) and execution (the doing) is critical. At this point we begin to shift the focus of the triangle—from strategy, to leadership, through to culture.

To 'decide' means to kill off other options.[6] Deliberation is liberation, freedom follows focus, and sequence gives you the freedom to focus. Hence, this is where good implementation and operational leadership can play important roles.

Of all the things we *can* do, we ask, what do we choose to progress? What strategic pathways will yield the most enduring relevance and value for our enterprise?

Progress

Meaningful progress is the ultimate intention of Quest-Augmented Strategy—the antithesis of stagnation and decline.

An enterprise is making meaningful progress if it is moving towards an improved or more advanced position, one of enduring value and relevance.

It's meaningful progress that sees an enterprise outfox the Inevitable Kraken of Doom—by not only identifying new potential growth arcs, but by having the pioneering leadership and the adaptive work culture to pursue them.

6| In Quest-Augmented Strategy, these 'killed off' options don't die. But, akin to the ghosts in Pac-Man, they return to the portfolio of options until such a time as they are needed to be called upon again.

Missions

Missions occur at the other end of the quest spectrum. Whereas a quest is infinite, and encourages thorough thinking and asking better questions within the context of uncertainty, a mission is finite, and is focused on executing operational excellence towards a certain objective. We use missions — with due consideration — to progress our most important projects.

'CHANGE IS THE NEW NORMAL'

That's a line I hear from the leaders of the more savvy organisations I've been working with. It's not 'we need to innovate' or 'it won't be long until we get through this change process'. No; pioneering leaders know that change is eternal. Our approach is not about successfully executing a strategy just so that we can dust our hands and return to business as usual. There is no 'business as usual' anymore — there's only default thinking, and the risk that we may be missing out on meaningful progress.

It's possible to look at this Quest-Augmented Strategy framework and think, *Ah! Okay, that's not so bad. I can see the formula here, and there seems to be a logical sequence. If I just follow the steps, all will be fine.* No. No, it won't. All is not fine, and it never will be.[7]

If you're seeking a neat and orderly way to ensure the enduring success of your enterprise — a nice line of boxes to tick, or a foolproof template to work from — then I'm afraid you've underestimated the cunning and patient intelligence of the Inevitable Kraken of Doom. Disruption is ripe, and your tears of impending irrelevance are like salty-sweet nectar to the Kraken.

No easy answers or proven formulas can guarantee enduring relevance and meaningful progress.

But if you dance through the Quest-Augmented Strategy framework, recognise that the path to meaningful progress is non-linear, requiring courage and the diverse input from pioneering heroes. Then maybe — just maybe — you'll be ready to face the dragons that lie ahead.

7| I'm doing this deliberately (to encourage perpetually constructive discontent) — just play along.

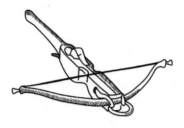

6. Here be Dragons

C artographers in the 1700s (and earlier) would often mark uncharted territory with depictions of dragons, serpents and other sea monsters.[1] 'Here be dragons', some maps would warn. Now the saying is used metaphorically to warn people away from unexplored areas, or pathways that haven't been tested.

In coding, the expression is sometimes used to warn folks about particularly complex or obscure passages of open source code. In version 3.5 of the Mozilla Firefox browser, for example, 'Here be Dragons' appeared when users typed 'about: config' into the address bar.[2] By Firefox placing a warning like this, other coders knew that if they proceeded, they needed to act wisely and with care. While many avoid tinkering within such passages of code, more adventurous coders prefer to explore these areas. Indeed, by proceeding through this more challenging code, they may be able to clarify elements of it—and therefore make the path safer for others.[3]

And so, this chapter is my warning to you: there be dragons ahead.[4]

---

1 | This is, in part, where the metaphor of the Inevitable Kraken of Doom comes from. But mainly because Krakens are cool.

2 | In somewhat simple speak, this opens up the configuration of the browser.

3 | Also known as pioneering.

4 | I also use 'Here be Dragons' at certain points through the rest of the book, to warn you of impending paradox.

BYO LANTERN

The path to meaningful progress is frequently non-linear, uphill and against the grain, full of doubt and uncertainty, and fraught with dead ends, setbacks and failure. Why on Earth would anyone want to take that path?[5]

Pioneering leadership enables and empowers folks to find a way through, shining a light on the path for others. But losing your way can be easy. And taking this path is infinitely more challenging than simply perpetuating default thinking and building incremental improvements to the status-quo. It is very much a hero's journey — not for the meek of heart or the short of wit.

You can't place your hope in distant goals or objectives in order to stay motivated, because you don't know what the future holds, and if they'll even be relevant then. You don't have the answers.

And so, instead of squinting into the future, you need to shine a light on the path in front of us, and celebrate small wins along the way.

What constitutes a meaningful sense of progress? What wins are worth celebrating? And how do you know if you're even on the right track?

This is where rituals come into play, something we explore in much more depth at the end of this book (see chapter 21).

Rituals are the routines that we hold sacrosanct. They put the spotlight on the work that matters, to find meaning in the progress made, and to recalibrate your approach where needed. Such rituals also integrate the opportunity to reconnect with the greater purpose in your work, witness your developing mastery, and provide more insight for autonomy.

But, even with good rituals in place, losing your way can be easy.

You're going to buck up against the Curse of Efficiency. And you're going to come across influential folks who'll cross their arms and say things like, 'that won't work', 'we can't afford to muck around' and 'show me the evidence'.[6]

5| This is actually a good question. Why?

6| To which we'll reply, 'really?', 'agreed!' and 'gladly — let's experiment'.

Quest-Augmented Strategy offers us clever ways to circumvent, enrol or navigate through the nitpickers, naysayers and guardians of the default.

But, even then, things can get dark — and your light may dwindle.

They say that when you stare into the abyss, the abyss stares back. Well, I say you do so at a safe distance.

DECOUPLE YOUR WORK FROM YOUR SELF

We talk about dragons in this chapter, but perhaps the biggest threat to meaningful progress is *ourselves* (and the internal demons we harbour).

An essential element of pioneering leadership — and the navigation through doubt and uncertainty — is the keeping of curiosity[7] as a constant companion. This is where we keep asking questions, rather than drawing conclusions. The very process of asking these questions places us in a state of dissociated metacognition.[8] Our perspective is removed from the playing field, so we can assess things from a different vantage point.

This is very important for resilience and enduring motivation. By assessing things from a more objective/observer/helicopter perspective, we are less likely to personify failure or draw premature conclusions. The alternative is to be caught within the game, and to make failure personal. Thomas Edison had a good frame for this, apparently once saying, 'I have not failed — I've just found 10 000 ways that won't work.' This highlights Edison had a very clear distinction between his self and the methodology he was employing.

Anything that helps you engage in dissociated metacognition is to be encouraged. Simple activities, like keeping a journal or a blog for your thinking and progress, enable you to view your thinking from a dissociated perspective (and see progress along the way). When these activities are anchored to a daily or weekly ritual, you create a buffer for some of the insidious threats to pioneering leadership.

---

7 | Not to mention the other superpowers: imagination, wonder and doubt.

8 | *Metacognition* refers to the awareness or understanding of your own thought processes. It's like self-reflection. Dissociated metacognition is where we can review our current and past actions from outside of our immediate first-person perspective.

For example, self-doubt can become crippling for anyone attempting to engage in pioneering work. All sorts of cognitive distortions[9] happen within our heads at the best of times, but combine self-doubt with the imposter syndrome (refer to chapter 4), uncertainty and a lack of discernible progress—and it becomes tempting to just give up.

But with good rituals for dissociated metacognition, doubt can truly become a wondrous companion. From this perspective, we aren't doubting ourselves, because we've decoupled our selves from our work. Instead, we are asking critical questions about the methodology we've used, and the reasoning we are using to inform our decisions.

This process is also a chance to mitigate or address the many forms of self-sabotage available to indulge in.

THE SIREN CALL OF SELF-SABOTAGE

Sirens are another form of sea monster one must be wary of. In Greek mythology, sirens are dangerous yet beautiful creatures that lure sailors to steer their ships into rocks with their enchanting music and charm.

Self-sabotage works like this too—except in this case, it's an alluring and insidious call within our heads.

We are all profoundly adept at getting in our own way, and the higher the anxiety, the more likely it is that self-sabotage may be at play. This is concerning, because most pioneering work is laced with anxiety.

It happens like this: unbeknown to our conscious mind, we create stories about our reality that nest alibis to excuse ourselves from poor performance. The most common forms of self-sabotage I've observed among leaders (and many other folk) are:

◊ **Procrastination.** The classic. Here we believe that we work better under pressure—so that's the story we use. And we probably have a glistening track record that

---

9| Cognitive distortions are exaggerated or irrational thought patterns that mean we perceive our world inaccurately (usually in a less-useful and more negative light). They include things like personalising, catastrophising, jumping to conclusions or taking a binary view of the world (right/wrong, good/bad, and so on).

suggests we can leave things until the last minute and still execute them brilliantly.[10] The risk, of course, is that something may happen at the last minute that prevents this brilliance from occurring. You might get a migraine, a connecting flight may get cancelled or the internet may drop out. And then, as a result, the work you produce is substandard. But lo and ahoy! You can blame that *thing* that happened. 'If it weren't for that migraine, this would have been much better,' you say, in all seriousness. And so, your alibi works—you are excused, and live to fight another day.[11]

◊ **Perfectionism.** The other classic. This one is drenched in cognitive distortion. Here we believe that we cannot begin to make meaningful progress until we have more information, or until conditions are more favourable. And so we focus on clearing our inbox and attending to other urgent matters first, in order to create a more favourable environment to make meaningful progress within. But it's never enough—we always need more information, and more can always be done to improve things. Eventually we are forced to execute/ship/submit our work—much to our lament—but we can comfortably say we 'just didn't have enough time'. Perfectionism is, in many ways, a wonderful thing—it means you hold yourself to high standards. But it ceases being useful when it gets in the way of meaningful progress.

◊ **Being busy.** When faced with uncertainty, getting stuck into the busywork is easy. This is the Curse of Efficiency (refer to chapter 2).

10| And, to be fair, this could be clever leveraging of Parkinson's Law—the notion that work expands to fill the time available for its completion. Make a smaller container for the work, and it takes less time.

11| Procrastination is, in some situations, a benefit to pioneering work in that it enables you to take on multiple threads of input at any one time (encouraging greater lateral thinking). But the biggest threat it poses is that by leaving things until the last minute we encourage faster thinking and there's a higher likelihood of defaulting to our defaults and the Delusion of Progress.

◊ **Disorganisation.** Pioneering leadership requires a healthy level of organisation — within your own mind, and within your collective team. For the pioneering work in Quest-Augmented Strategy, you'll be holding many hunches, concepts and threads active and in suspension at once. Without organisation, they'll quickly unravel — and you'll lose the opportunity to leverage the diversity of input from your team. For operational work, disorganisation is even more pronounced. The alibi in all instances is usually, 'I didn't know.'[12]

◊ **Choosing difficult circumstances.** This is where we choose to work in an environment or manner that does not support meaningful progress. This is usually accompanied by an 'open-door policy', which sounds good, before you examine it more fully. The most valuable resource a leader has is their attention, which means you need to guard it. This translates into creating dedicated time to engage with your team, staff and stakeholders, rather than leaving your door open and waiting for them to come to you.[13] It also means crafting dedicated time, in the right contexts, to make meaningful progress. Otherwise, we'll catch ourselves using the alibi, 'It was non-stop at the office today. Meeting after meeting — I barely had time to work on [meaningful progress].'

◊ **Physiological self-sabotage.** Go on, have an extra coffee. And have that cake too. You deserve it, right? Then, later, 'Oh!' *Gaping yawn.* 'I'm so tired. I might just work on this later tonight…'

◊ **Over-commitment.** This the most noble form of self-sabotage — and another element of the Curse of Efficiency. This form of self-sabotage is very common among leaders, and it's kind of a good thing. It happens when people say yes to new challenges. I do it all the time. You probably do

---

12| Or 'I don't recall receiving that email' or 'I think my calendar has syncing issues' and so on.

13| Some leaders I know choose to do their most progressive thinking work at home, or at cafes or co-working spaces outside of the main office (knowing that it's a distraction factory).

too. To all outward appearances, you are the hero! Saving
the day, yet again. But what can be happening is that we
work hard to fulfil other people's priorities. In exchange
for their attention/acceptance/validation/praise/esteem/
whatnot, we sacrifice meaningful progress. 'I've just got
so much on my plate. I mean, just look at everything I'm
doing: *[insert default busywork, the Curse of Efficiency,
and the Delusion of Progress]*.'

Obviously, plenty more forms of self-sabotage are possible—the siren's
call is as diverse and melodic as it is tempting.

But you can resist the siren's call in two main ways—or at least steer
your ship away from the rocks before you sunder it.

The first is to ensure you integrate daily, weekly, monthly, quarterly
and yearly rituals into your life. By creating a sacred space to think,
you'll be able to assess your activities from the perspective of dissociated
metacognition. From here, you'll be able to identify self-sabotaging
behaviours, and integrate new experiments to mitigate them.

The second is to share the hero's journey with others.

IT'S DANGEROUS TO GO ALONE

I've written this book for you: the individual reading this. Pioneering
leadership must start (continue and flourish) with someone—and that
someone may very well be you.

But it is my hope that your colleagues—fellow leaders and intrapreneurs—
may read this book too. And that together, equipped with a shared
understanding, you may rally around shared rituals to explore and identify
viable alternative options (to inform and enrich enterprise strategy and
make meaningful progress).

It's much harder to self-sabotage when you are part of a small team.
It's also harder to succumb to cognitive distortion or the more crippling
elements of doubt.

While it's romantic to think otherwise, no great change or meaningful
progress was affected by a lone individual. A small, diverse team keeps
things in perspective, and keeps things moving.

WHAT IS THE RIGHT SIZE FOR A TEAM?

When I refer to a team, you may wonder how large the team is. Are we talking a couple of colleagues, or the whole enterprise?

There's no easy answer to this, but for a reference point I'd suggest that the ideal team size is 7±2. According to Jeff Bezos, the CEO of Amazon, if a team can't be fed with two pizzas, it's too big.

Now, I've eaten pizzas in Chicago and New York—they're huge. If we're to go with the thinner base of a wood-fired pizza, I'd suggest that the ideal number of pizzas for a team is three or four. But then, pizza is my one true weakness[14]—I can happily eat one-and-a half pizzas in one sitting. So let's just call it three.

In any event, somewhere around 7±2 people is the ideal team size. Naturally, bigger teams can harbour smaller teams, but when I refer to your team, I'm talking to the 7±2 that work with you closely.

Spotify, the commercial music-streaming enterprise, uses the 7±2 team as the main unit of organisation in their (agile) organisational structure. They call this unit a 'squad'—it's multidisciplinary, self-sufficient and autonomous, and it acts like a mini-startup focused on one core problem. Squads that share the same strategic focus are grouped together in 'tribes', and people who share the same discipline are organised into collaborative 'chapters'. 'Guilds' are also formed around special interests that aren't specific to chapters.

The strength of this approach—squads, tribes, chapters and guilds—is that it allows one person to be a member of several different groups within completely different functions. This enables all individuals and groups to benefit from diverse perspectives, and ensures that they do not lose sight of the bigger purpose and meaningful progress.

14| That, and tiramisu. And burnt-butter and salted caramel crepes with fresh double thickened cream too, for some reason.

Other benefits of keeping teams small include the minimisation of:

◊ **Social loafing**. This is the phenomenon whereby motivation is decreased with the realisation that you belong to a group. When teams get larger, individuals can experience less social pressure, and feel less personal responsibility. This is because their individual performance becomes much more difficult (or even impossible) to assess amid a crowd.

◊ **Relational loss**. This is where you feel as if you are receiving less support as a team gets larger. Smaller teams are more likely to have each other's backs, and to help each other when and where needed (in terms of problem-solving support, information support, or emotional support).

◊ **Latency and friction**. This refers to the delay in obtaining feedback, and the obstacles that exist between team members. With smaller teams, communication and feedback is much more frequent and frictionless.

Keeping teams to 7±2 also keeps team meetings, huddle-ups and other rituals feasible. People can chime into team meetings remotely, and things won't be lost. You can also comfortably book a table at a restaurant or cafe and converse well.

So: keep teams small, and keep them networked.

IF IN DOUBT...

... it probably means you are pioneering. Good. But don't get lost in the darkness—for there be dragons. Let this one question be your beacon: *Are we making meaningful progress?*

If not, then what are we doing?

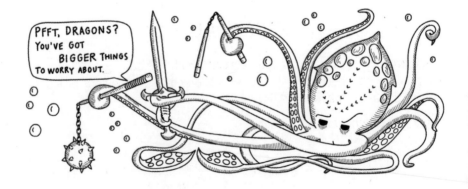

Summary

Part II

◊   A quest is the search for an alternative that meets cognitive criteria.

◊   Business strategy can be viewed from at least two different perspectives: one finite, the other infinite. From a finite perspective, we treat business as a game to be won. From an infinite perspective, we never declare victory. Instead, we focus on progress and the creation of enduring value and relevance. This book embraces the latter philosophy.

◊   To adventure means to take a risk in the hope of a favourable outcome. Three elements are required to make this happen: a progressive strategy, an enterprise culture that values learning, and leadership that values new thinking.

◊   To pioneer means to open up a new area, and to lead in the development of new and better ways. Through pioneering leadership, enterprises enable meaningful progress and secure enduring relevance.

◊   At least three major paradoxes exist within pioneering leadership. First, to gain certainty, we must embrace the fuzziness of uncertainty. Second, to build conviction, we must harness the benefit of doubt. Thirdly, to make meaningful progress, we must avoid success. Victory is never declared.

◊   The benefit of doubt is often underestimated. Doubt makes ideas stronger, leaders better, and life more wonderful.

◊   Within every large enterprise exist intrapreneurs—people who seek to leverage their influence to create new value within an enterprise. Savvy leaders foster intrapreneurship, creating startup-like environments in which it is safe to innovate.

◊   Quest-Augmented Strategy is a framework for meaningful progress. Like all models, it's flawed. But it's also very useful—particularly for enterprises seeking to unlock meaningful progress, new value and enduring relevance.

◊   This framework maps the distinction between pioneering work (uncertain, unprecedented) with operational work (predictable, precedented). It also maps the distinction between 'thinking' as the primary focus, and 'doing'. It's the doing that generates progress, but it's the thinking that makes it meaningful. And vice versa.

◊   In its simplest form, this framework enables the enrichment of strategy through the creation and capturing of 'options'. Options represent potential new pathways for an enterprise, and are validated through experiments.

◊   This process ensures that enterprise leaders have viable alternatives to consider (beyond the default). The pursuit of these viable alternatives can then enhance the likelihood of meaningful progress, new value, and enduring relevance.

◊   Pioneering leadership is not easy. The path to meaningful progress is frequently non-linear, uphill and against the grain, full of doubt and uncertainty, and fraught with dead ends, setbacks and failure. In order to stay motivated, pioneering leaders don't fixate upon distant goals, but instead develop rituals to review learning, reconnect with purpose and recalibrate their focus. Through dissociated metacognition, pioneering leaders are able to mitigate the effects of cognitive distortion and self-sabotage.

◊   This is further enhanced when part of a small team. The ideal size of a team is 7±2. At this 'mini-startup' size, the meaning of people's work is not lost in the crowd, support can be provided to teammates, and communication latency and friction is minimal. It is easy to engage in team rituals, and to connect in more relaxed, social contexts.

◊   The one overarching question to guide you through pioneering leadership is, *Are we making meaningful progress?*

Part III

Cultivating Options

Optionality [noun]: a state or quality in which
discretion or choice is available.

Quest-Augmented Strategy is our elegantly 'flawed-yet-useful' framework for meaningful progress. We're going to plunge right into the abyss, and start with the pioneering thinking required to cultivate options.[1] After all, without viable alternative options, we simply default to our defaults.

But generating alternative options that are of genuine strategic benefit to an enterprise isn't simply a case of gathering senior leaders into a room for a few hours of brainstorming. Nor is it about simply replicating the strategy of competitors, or outsourcing this process to an expensive agency to come up with all the answers for you.

No—to truly cultivate options, we must build the capability to explore uncertain futures, to seek out potential incoherencies, and to foster acuity for the hunches that may harbour options worth pursuing.

---

1 | Those potentially viable alternatives that could influence and enrich strategic decision-making.

7. An Intuitive Reckoning

I n chapter 1 we briefly explored a crude explanation of how learning occurs, and how our default thinking is formed—through the observation and codification of patterns (repeated phenomena).

A similar and yet altogether more mysterious thing happens with our *hunches.*

Hunches are the precursor to any potential idea or realisation. They are our intuitive reckonings that an alternative possibility, explanation or way may be available to us. They are the threads of patterns yet to be codified into learning.

We experience at least two forms of hunches.

The first could be described as spontaneous. An intuitive notion comes to you, seemingly out of the blue. It feels as though it's true, even though you have not applied any conscious reasoning to it.

A spontaneous hunch may strike you at any moment—like in a conversation with a friend. *Something's not right*...you find yourself knowing, before you've figured out why. Maybe it was the waver in their voice as they spoke with you. Maybe it was a micro facial expression you noticed, or some sort of incongruence between what they were saying and how they were acting. It's the subtlest thing. And so you ask, 'Is everything okay?' ... and your hunch may or may not be validated.[1]

---

1 | 'Ha! Yes, everything is fine. As we were talking I thought I had something stuck in my teeth, and I was trying to be subtle about checking. Oh, and I was busting to pee. But yeah, all good!'

We're in dangerous territory here. Hunches are immensely powerful ways to connect with intuitive insights. And yet, we need to ensure we are not merely seeking to confirm our default assumptions (preferences, stereotypes and biases—see chapter 14). Fostering your acuity for spontaneous yet accurate hunches—and developing the courage to act upon them—is a delicate art, and something I am still to striving to develop to a higher degree.

But it's the second form of hunch that I can comment on with an element of authority.

The second form of hunch could be described as nagging. It's that persistent hint that things aren't right, or that things could be better.[2]

Now, what we frequently do with such hunches is ignore them. And this is perfectly valid. Sometimes our mind simply seeks distraction from the task at hand—a new idea to liberate us from the crappy work in front of us. Resisting the temptation to become distracted, and instead remaining focused on the work that matters, is an important discipline—and something that makes up the bulk of operational work.

But if a hunch is persistent—if you repeatedly intuit the same nagging feeling—you'll want to dedicate time to exploring it.[3]

One of my more inspiring clients is Suncorp Group—a large finance, insurance and banking corporation based in Australia. Mark Milliner, the CEO of Suncorp Personal Insurance, championed the integration of a dynamic strategic innovation system into the personal insurance portion of the business. This system was incredibly effective. As Milliner explains in *Understanding Strategic Risk in Suncorp Personal Insurance*, 'this process came about not because of a crisis or a reaction to the latest management fad but because of my growing, nagging sense that the number one risk to our business could be the status quo. The risk that we could wake up one day after a long winning streak and realise we were irrelevant.' In a book documenting their approach to strategic innovation, Milliner further describes that the things keeping him up at night are no longer operational issues, but rather the 'invisible forces' of change that

---

2| Or that we're missing something. Something that might either mitigate a significant future threat, or allow us to capitalise on a significant opportunity in a timely way. If only we knew what that missing element was!

3| This requires liberating yourself from the Curse of Efficiency.

threaten the status quo—changes that can reshape industries, and our world as we know it.

Milliner was able to take a nagging hunch and—with the input of diverse and talented folk—work it into something significant. This is the thinking of pioneering leadership.

But where do you start? What's the first step to pursuing a hunch?

We can answer this in at least three ways.

Given that a hunch may be the fragments of a yet-to-be-codified pattern, you could seek to observe more patterns (thereby learning and understanding this nagging phenomenon in greater depth). In part IV we'll explore the role experiments play in helping to progress our learning.

In any event, this processing requires time—time for slower and much more thorough thinking than we are typically used to. The time invested in good thinking[4] enhances the quality of the experiments we conduct. But even then, we can become lost in the infinite possibilities of the future. You can only open so many tabs before your browser crashes.

And so, perhaps the best place to start is with self-awareness— understanding your current enterprise identity, business model and the context in which you operate. This then enables you to contrast your current state with potential future states, to see where potential incoherencies may lie.

WAIT, WHO ARE WE?

And what do we stand for? And for whom?

Every enterprise forms and exists to serve a need in the market. But it's surprising how frequently we can forget what that need is. Or, as an enterprise grows, to find that we can no longer articulate it succinctly—it is instead wrapped up in bloated, meaningless corporate-speak.[5]

4| Which, by the way, is not just about staring out the window. That's useful, but good thinking also involves the immersion of diverse perspectives within the tension of intriguing incoherencies—something we'll explore in the next chapter.

5| We synergistically integrate extensible meta-services while utilising next-generation growth strategies to produce world-leading collaborative quality vectors among multi-modal e-services in diverse sectors.

If you're in this situation — if your enterprise has forgotten whom it serves, and why — then you need to have a deep leadership conversation with your colleagues.

This conversation is both urgent and important, but it's not something that can be rushed. Together with your colleagues, you need to be able to develop an effective representation that captures the complexities of your business model and the nature of the need it serves within its current context. And this needs to be sufficiently succinct and relatable that it can serve to influence strategy and pioneering work.

One of the first stumbling points in realising an enterprise identity is the distinction between what we do, and why we do it. It's very easy to simply list the key activities your enterprise engages in[6], but this does nothing to capture the value generated, or the market need it meets.[7]

Attempting to refresh, rediscover or reconnect with the purpose of your organisation — the guiding *why* — should reveal some challenging assumptions among your team. If time is allowed for such a conversation — and if it is facilitated in a way that encourages thorough thinking and open debate — hidden needs may also be identified. Additionally, differences in perspective among leadership about current or emerging needs may also manifest. This may be angsty conversation. But, if we stay within the tension and work through it (exploring assumptions and negotiating through differences in perspective), we may generate a valuable and refreshed sense of identity for the business.

Here be Dragons. It's easy to get lost in this process, or to create bland, generic identities that say nothing, and are impossible to share with a straight face with a friend at a barbecue.[8] If you feel like you are going around in circles, return to *need*. What is the need that exists in the

---

6| For example, 'We manufacture, sell and distribute home and office furniture.'

7| For example, Ikea doesn't simply make furniture. 'We create a better everyday life for the many people.'

8| 'So, Microsoft eh? What are you guys about?' 'Well, our mission is to empower every person and every organisation on the planet to achieve more.' 'Cool story, bro. So, what does that actually mean?' 'Uh, we're focused on creating a family of devices and services for individuals and businesses that empower people around the globe at home, at work and on the go, for the activities they value m — hey, wait, where are you going? Hello?' (I shouldn't be teasing Microsoft. They're a client and they do brilliant, pioneering work. It's just the Apple snob in me. Disregard this!)

market that your enterprise is currently serving? What are the factors within this, and what is most important?

The identity of your enterprise is a concept core to strategy work. It is the 'why' banner under which the 'how' of your business model operates.

AND WHAT IS IT THAT WE DO, EXACTLY?

It's difficult to ensure the enduring relevance and value of a business model if you don't know what your business model is.

Perhaps one of the best tools available to chart out a business model is the 'Business Model Canvas' (as described in the brilliant book *Business Model Generation*). Developed by Swiss business theorist Alexander Osterwalder and strategic consultancy Strategyzer, this canvas explores nine essential elements of any functioning business.[9]

The nine elements identified by Osterwalder and Strategyzer can be split across four main functions (the first of which is most important):

◊ **The offering.** This is the value proposition, which relates to an enterprise's identity. It is the collection of products and services that an enterprise offers to meet the needs of its customers. Ultimately, it is the value proposition that distinguishes one enterprise from another.

◊ **The customers.** A business's activities and value proposition must connect to customers. (Otherwise, what's the point?) This portion of a business model is divided into three key sections:

1. *Customer segments.* Good businesses are able to clearly identify who they serve, what their distinct needs are, and who their ideal customers are. Some business models serve a mass-market approach (one size fits all); others serve diverse markets; and others focus on serving one niche market. Knowing who your business model delivers value for is critical.

9| The Business Model Canvas is available under a Creative Commons license at businessmodelgeneration.com/canvas/bmc

2. *Customer relationships.* An enterprise must identify what
   relationship they have with their customer segments.
   Is it supported self-service (as is the case with some
   software companies), totally automated, or more personal
   and direct? Or does your enterprise create and foster a
   community platform to gather and nurture customers?

3. *Channels.* This refers to how an enterprise delivers
   value to its customers. Does your enterprise have its
   own channels (a shopfront or website), or do you rely
   on major distributors or other partners to reach your
   customers? Or both? The best channels will distribute
   value to customers efficiently.[10]

◊ **The infrastructure.** This covers the moving parts of an
   enterprise—the stuff that enables a business to acquire
   and transform resources into value. This portion of a
   business model is divided into three key sections:

1. *Key activities.* This refers to an enterprise's most
   important activities—the essential things your
   enterprise must do to create and deliver value.

2. *Key resources.* Every enterprise requires resources in
   order to generate and deliver value (and to support and
   sustain this process). These resources can be physical,
   intellectual, human and financial.

3. *Key partnerships.* This describes the network of suppliers
   and partnerships that serve to optimise the business
   model, reduce risk or acquire resources. Partners may
   undertake key activities within a business model.

◊ **Finances.** This covers both the costs (the monetary
   consequences of the business model generating and
   delivering value to customer segments) and revenue
   streams (the way an enterprise obtains value from each
   customer segment, in exchange for value delivered).

10| Enterprises that rely upon outdated or inefficient distribution channels will find
themselves ripe for disruption. This is what Uber has capitalised on in the taxi industry, and
it's why entertainment industries suffer so much piracy—it's so much easier for some people
to illegally download movies in some countries than it is to wait for its official release.

By investing time to discuss each element of the Business Model Canvas (and how they interact), a clearer picture of your enterprise business model will emerge.[11]

The picture that emerges can be confronting. The discussion might reveal that your enterprise is lacking in essential competencies.[12] It might reveal that the business model is currently overly focused on a less valuable customer segment (ignoring a more valuable customer segment). Leaders might also realise that their distribution channels are creating unnecessary friction between customers and value—and so they may wish to review alternative approaches. Or, the discussion might also reveal that the business model is heavily reliant upon one key partnership (either for a key resource or activity). If that partner decides to withdraw from the arrangement, the integrity of the business model would be at threat.

Such revelations bring about immediate tactical consequences, which operational excellence would (rightly) demand we address without delay.

But, in the rush to fix the existing business model, it can be easy to forget to address the bigger question—*will our current business model and identity remain viable in the future?*

A CONTEXTUAL HUNCH

Here be Dragons: things are about to get meta.

'Context' refers to the multitude of circumstances that form the setting within which an enterprise operates. The identity of an enterprise—and the business model that serves it—is formed to meet the needs of customers within a given context.

To engage in dissociated metacognition is to think contextually. And so, when a leadership team are reviewing a business model, they are doing so from a contextual perspective.

11| This is something enterprises should review frequently (yearly at an absolute minimum—constantly is better).

12| In running this activity with the senior leaders of a large multinational organisation, for example, the senior leadership team realised that they had zero digital or technological savvy—and yet they were deciding upon the strategic direction of the enterprise within this context.

Some may view a business model with reference to past contexts. But nostalgia is of zero benefit to enterprise strategy.[13] And so, strategy is usually tackled from within our current context. Such an approach is severely limited, however, and reactive at best.

The *only* contexts that matter for strategy are the myriad complex and as-yet-unknown future contexts.

There is no present tense. The benefits and consequences your enterprise is experiencing *right now* are the result of strategic decisions made previously. And these strategic decisions did not benefit from the knowledge or insight we have today.[14]

Which brings us back to the focus of part III and the top-right quadrant of Quest-Augmented Strategy—how can we leverage *pioneering thinking* to create the most strategic value to an enterprise? How can we venture beyond our default thinking and preference for precedent? And how do we even begin to make sense of the possible future contexts ahead of us?

Particularly given that we have this *nagging hunch* that our current business model may not be viable in certain future contexts...

13| 'Back in the day, people would do business eye to eye, belly to belly! You could judge someone's character by the firmness and duration of their handshake. There was none of this Spacebook or MyFace nonsense! Bah!'

14| Eh? Eh? See where we are going here? Let's dial up the insight we have today, so as to make better strategic decisions for the future. Quest-Augmented Strategy, ftw!

8. Intriguing Incoherence

So, the first step of pioneering thinking is to *know* your current business model and identity, and the context in which you operate (covered in chapter 7).

CURRENT CONTEXT

BUSINESS MODEL & IDENTITY

When a business model and identity are coherent with their current context, magic happens. There is a clear purpose and relevance: an enterprise generates value to serve market needs. The business model and identity *make sense* within this context.

But what happens if the *context* changes?

Will your current business model and identity remain coherent within this context? Or will this new context render things incoherent?

COHERENCY IN CONTEXT

Kirsten Dunlop and Luca Gatti—strategy consultants and authors of *The Strategic Risk Framework*—suggest that this coherence is the true object of strategic thinking and decision-making. This elegant framing of strategy is simply profound, and has influenced my own thinking and approach to strategy immensely.

Dunlop and Gatti highlight that this simple approach—framing strategy in terms of the coherence between a business identity and its context—has the effect of empowering decision-makers to deal with extremely high levels of complexity.

Within this perspective, strategy becomes something much more dynamic and emergent—a relationship between current and emerging contexts, rather than a fixed document or plan. Dunlop and Gatti's approach also shifts the conversation about strategy from a quantitative focus (which tends to work in terms of probability) to that of a qualitative focus (which instead focuses on possibility).

Sometimes, this is a straightforward activity. An emerging new context may be known and predicted. With this knowledge, an enterprise can make strategic decisions to capitalise on opportunities and/or mitigate risks inherent within this anticipated new context.

AN EXAMPLE OF MITIGATED INCOHERENCE
WITHIN AN ANTICIPATED FUTURE CONTEXT

NOMOS Glashütte would have to be my favourite watchmaking company. Based in Germany, NOMOS specialises in manual-winding and automatic mechanical watches. The context of their business ecology includes the Swatch Group—a Swiss designer, manufacturer and distributer of watches, movements and other components—which holds a lot of power over smaller manufacturers like NOMOS. This power is particularly felt when it comes to the critical escapement and balance components of mechanical watches, which they sell to nearly every watch manufacturer. These are the components that help the watch to keep the 'tick-tock' of its heartbeat regular. They are the most costly and complicated part of the movement, and there's no room for error. One might assume that all watchmaking brands that claim to have in-house movements would have their own versions, but these components are actually something very few brands have the capacity to make, especially the balance spring. The Swatch Group have, therefore, been required to sell these components to every manufacturer—but it has been known for some time that, as of 2016, they will no longer have such an obligation.

(continued)

AN EXAMPLE OF MITIGATED INCOHERENCE
WITHIN AN ANTICIPATED FUTURE CONTEXT *(cont'd)*

Naturally, should the Swatch Group decide to stop selling these components to companies outside of their group, or if they decide to hike their fees to ridiculous levels, companies like NOMOS would be in struggle-town.

But NOMOS anticipated this new context and the strategic risks it posed to their business model and identity. With this future incoherence in mind, they saw an opportunity to form a new identity and business model—one that was freed from the shackles of the Swatch Group. And so, over five years this small company quietly worked in collaboration with the University of Dresden, investing over €11 million into the development of their own in-house swing system and escapement. When this new innovation was revealed in 2014, it was heralded as a declaration of independence in the watchmaking industry—and a move that will help ensure the growth of NOMOS for years and decades to come (keeping the Kraken at bay).

Not all futures are clear and recognisable, and nor do all futures have a clear date at which they will come into effect. Rather, the 'invisible forces' that threaten the future viability of your enterprise (and the latent opportunities that accompany them) are fuzzy and hard to discern, and could manifest and disrupt your enterprise very quickly.

The future is complex and uncertain, and it harbours an infinite range of possible contexts that could render your business unviable. But fear not, for this territory can be explored.

FINDING FUTURES

To find futures, we need to venture into the angst of uncertainty, and systematically and collectively use our *imagination* to explore what's possible.

Ha, I imagine that, right now, some gruff, hardcore, old-school, traditionally minded and operationally driven leaders have just stopped reading. They're probably looking for an evidence-based approach. That's fine—let them go.

But, if you're still with me, good. This is important.

Many folk shy away from exploring possibility within the complexity of an uncertain future. Instead, they seek the safety of familiar, evidence-based approaches, and solid numbers from which to assess the *probability* of certain futures manifesting. Such an approach does little to address the infinite complexity of the future. Akin to setting forth 'a clear goal' or 'vision for the future', a focus on probability (rather than *possibility*) simply creates the delusion of certainty while reducing the range of possible future contexts leaders are inclined to explore. The result of such a conventional, evidence-based and probability-biased approach is that we're left with a set intelligence similar to that which anyone else can develop or access. Therefore, such an approach does not generate any sort of distinct strategic advantage—it merely produces the same set of options your competitors have.

Quest-Augmented Strategy is not simply about generating the same set of options that any conventional approach might offer. This is about equipping enterprise leaders with new, viable alternative options to augment default strategy. It's only through this approach that we can unlock new value and new growth arcs, and maintain enduring relevance.

To find these options, we must be able to imagine futures that exist beyond the realms of likely probability.[1]

---

1 | Dare I point out how much has changed in just the last decade? And how much of this change was unexpected and unprecedented? And how much will change in the next decade?

FACT OR FUTURE?

Futures cannot be represented through facts. Facts, like evidence, can only exist by being observed. This means that, by the time the fact has been observed, it has already happened. Don't look for facts or answers—look for better questions. It's the questions we ask, and the meaning we explore, that will generate the insights most useful to strategy.

I've already mentioned Einstein's belief that imagination is more important than knowledge. And certainly, when it comes to anticipating possibility and new future contexts, this is the case. Knowledge only serves to reflect the sum of what we know. Imagination is the gateway to that which is not yet known.

But enough philosophy! Here are seven almost-practical perspectives you can use to explore complex and uncertain futures.[2] All of these perspectives encourage *divergent* thinking and exploration.

Here be Dragons: The goal here is to enrich our understanding of diverse possible futures. At this stage, we're not trying to fix anything, and we're not trying to make strategic decisions about our current business model or identity. Not yet. We are simply seeking to understand what possible future contexts might lay ahead.

While you'll want to be careful not to constrain your focus, it is good to start the process of pioneering thinking with some sense of the changes believed to be of strategic significance to your enterprise. Generally speaking, these aspects will include things like technology, the economy, society and the environment (and the structural changes inherent within them).

So, let's get into the perspectives you can use.

Reverse assumptions

This is a very useful perspective to embrace early in any process that encourages divergent thinking. Thanks to the Curse of Efficiency, one of the first things we naturally do in an explorative session is seek to

---

2| We'll unpack individual and team rituals in part VII. Such rituals form the contexts in which pioneering thinking can occur. The following list of perspectives will help to ensure these rituals are more effective at generating strategic options worth considering. We can adopt plenty of other, useful perspectives in this space, but these are the main ones.

conclude it. To find the 'right answer'—to tick that box, be done and move on to the next challenge.

But explorative thinking—and the envisioning of complex, uncertain futures—doesn't work like this. There are no right answers.

And so, rather than charging in with what we think are the best answers to the most probable scenarios, a good *trip-wire* to default thinking is to reverse our assumptions.

Here, we write down what we suspect to be true about the future. For example, if we're thinking in terms of retail, we might imagine possible future contexts where all shopping is done online, a universal digital cryptocurrency is at play, and many items are delivered digitally to your 3D-printer at home (saving consumers money and minimising waste).

Now, these may be valid elements of possible future contexts. And you could feel quite smug coming up with these ideas—so smug that you remain closed to other possibilities. Which is not useful, at this point.

So, to prevent this from happening, look at the assumptions you have about the future, and reverse them. What new possibilities exist?

Maybe in the future hacking becomes so sophisticated, and people are so fearful about identity theft and unsolicited data acquisition, that online shopping actually diminishes (or is more frequently performed via a proxy). This leads to a return to more 'traditional' forms of trade.

Maybe a universal digital cryptocurrency does emerge—but maybe a range of company 'loyalty' programs also provide the equivalent effect of digital currency. By participating in research and allowing access to personal sensors, for example, one can accrue currency that can be used for any goods or services of a particular corporation and its partners. Maybe these 'loyalty' wars become so intense that customer loyalty 'points' become the new currency?

Or maybe 3D-printing actually turns out to be a short-lived fad. Thanks to the meta-web, people actually find they don't need to shop for physical items anymore, because most of their time is invested online. Digital items and artefacts become more important. Homes are fitted out with complex holographics, and so on.

All of these future scenarios are equally possible and valid—but we may not have got to them if we hadn't reversed our assumptions.

Resist solutions, conclusions and judgements

While 'solutions-focused' and 'outcomes-orientated' might appear on the resumes of the desperately bland corporate folk, such notions should not contaminate pioneering thinking. Training ourselves out of the need to jump to quick fixes, and to remain in the angst and tension of uncertainty, takes a while—but doing so almost always leads to better thinking.

Similar to our desire to find the right answers, it is natural for us to seek to ease the tension of uncertainty with quick solutions. But, at this point in our pioneering thinking, we are not seeking to solve anything. We're exploring. Anything that draws this process to a conclusion robs us of further exploration. Likewise, judging something to be correct or incorrect—before we have conducted any experiments to validate it—is also of little use.

Scott Belsky, author of *Making Ideas Happen*, suggests that teams create a backburner for new ideas. In the same way as a cook might use the backburners of a stove for a pot that doesn't require his or her immediate attention, a backburner for ideas is a place to keep them warm but out of the way, so that we can avoid being distracted from the mission at hand.[3]

But if we are engaged in pioneering thinking, we almost need the opposite of a backburner—a place to store potential actions, missions or projects, so that they don't distract us from the exploring that is ahead of us. Let's call it the fridge. If you're engaged in pioneering thinking with your team and want to identify possible future contexts, put distractions in the fridge.[4] Create a safe space to capture this thinking, so that you can stay with the task at hand.

Explore trends

Each year Gartner, the information technology research and advisory firm I mention in chapter 3, publish a branded model called the 'Hype Cycle'. This model represents the maturity, adoption and social application of specific technologies, tracking them through the various stages of hype.

3| This backburner looks like a box on a whiteboard, a section at the bottom of a page or at the back of a notebook, or a special folder within a team's project management software.

4| And, just like your own fridge, it's probably worth regularly checking in on the things that are collected here. Some things might still be fresh, some will have expired, and some will require immediate attention. 'Hmmm, this mouldy cheese is either really, really good or really, really bad.'

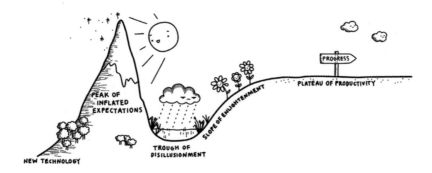

The first part of the cycle is the initial innovation, proof of concept or technological breakthrough. This is what pioneering organisations want to be keeping an eye on. At the time of writing this book, technological triggers such as quantum computing, bio-acoustic sensing, virtual personal assistants, 3D-bioprinting and brain–computer interface technology are emerging. Media fall in love with the 'newness' of this technology, and things quickly get hyped up.

Technologies such as the Internet of Things, wearable technology and cryptocurrency are already at the second phase, which Gartner describes as 'the peak of inflated expectations'. Early adopters and fast followers begin to play with the new technology. Negative media publications begin.

Next in the cycle comes the 'trough of disillusionment', where the reality of the technology does not meet the hype generated by media. One can currently find things like gamification, augmented reality and mobile health monitoring in this part of the Hype Cycle. In my experience, this is where some of the slower enterprise leaders hear about things for the very first time.[5] At this stage, less than 5 per cent of the potential audience have adopted fully.

5 | Unless they've got good rituals happening, or have startups and intrapreneurs working within their enterprise, it might be a case of too little, too late. Larger organisations may be able to acquire startups in this space—but you'll need to be switched on. A much better approach is to have been monitoring these technologies earlier, and building them into pioneering strategy.

What follows next is 'the slope of enlightenment'. More enterprises understand how the new technology can be used, and further iterations mean that some of the awkward elements of the early prototypes have been smoothed out. Gesture control, in-memory analytics and 3D-scanning are examples of technologies currently in this phase.[6]

Finally comes the 'plateau of productivity', where 20 to 30 per cent of the potential audience has heard of the innovation. Things enter a crazy growth period, and larger enterprises attempt to jump on the bandwagon (following progress, rather than leading it).[7]

The Gartner Hype Cycle is one of the quickest ways to get a rough initial sense of what technologies are emerging, and it can be a great starting point for discussion and enquiry into possible futures.

But the Gartner Hype Cycle only represents the major technological trends.

Technology will always be a great catalyst, but when you start to combine these trends with sociodemographic trends, consumer trends, geopolitical shifts and other such movements, the real magic emerges.

For example, take the emerging trend of wearable technology, combine that with virtual personal assistants, throw in a workforce shift to more remote and/or freelance work, and what do you get? Or, combine remote health monitoring with the fact that some countries are now producing greater numbers of qualified medical practitioners who are happy to work for a fraction of the fee of their counterparts in higher-taxed countries. What future do we have here?

Exploring the overlaps and gaps between trends is a very useful way to generate a richer perspective of possible futures.

Establish feeds

Pioneering leadership requires our hunches to be kept well fed. We do this by being mindful of our feeds—the channels we have established to feed us information.

6| Some conservative organisations will have heard about this technology by now, but they'll still tend to hold off on any sort of adoption until more evidence accrues.

7| Which is fine, if it's not your domain that is being innovated. Still, you don't want to only hear about new technologies influencing the potential future context of your enterprise after a third of your competitors have already adopted it.

In my experience, few leaders are aware of their information diet. They have often formed habitual routines that see them receive information from a small range of familiar sources—the newspaper in the morning, for example, maybe a few key news websites during the day, and then maybe the news on the television in the evening.[8]

At best, the default information diet serves to validate existing world views and default thinking. At worst, it's addictive, amplifies cognitive bias, and diminishes mental health. Rolf Dobelli, author of *Avoid News: Towards a Healthy News Diet*, suggests that news is to the mind what sugar is to the body—that it is overly negative, distorts reality, and amplifies insecurity, pessimism and fear (which tends to lead to a more conservative and myopic outlook).

But what's the solution? Abandon news altogether?[9]

As Mark Twain once said, 'If you don't read the newspaper, you're uninformed. If you read the newspaper, you're misinformed.'

The solution, as is often the case, lies somewhere in-between. And, it starts with self-awareness.

Remember—as a leader, your attention is your most valuable resource.

So, here's an actionable insight for you. For one week, see if you can track your information diet. Identify where your attention is placed. It'll be kind of like a food diary—but instead of trying to creatively categorise peanut-butter brownies, here you are focused on what information you consume (and, more importantly, from where).[10] The timing of your information consumption can be insightful for you too.

What you may find is that you rely on only a few information outlets. If you also overlay this with your natural energy shifts throughout the day, you might discover some interesting opportunities. For example, mornings are an incredibly productive time for me. But, in the past I would start my day with social media and email, which diminished my capacity to capitalise on my most productive time.

8| I know, right? There are still people out there who watch television.

9| Actually, abstaining from consuming any news is better than consuming most of the news stories on commercial stations and sponsored websites.

10| Like any experiment, you're going to perform better while you are self-aware, thanks to the Hawthorne Effect, which describes the way people modify or improve an aspect of their behaviour if they know they're being observed.

Maybe you have a similar thing going on. Maybe you read negative news *before* you plan your day in the morning. And maybe the media you consume is having a subtle, influential effect on the way you think, and the decisions you make.

In order to envisage complex and uncertain futures, we need to expose ourselves to diverse new information feeds. And this can easily be established in a few simple steps.

For starters, use a curated and adaptive news aggregator to keep abreast of key trends. Several simple options are available nowadays, and they'll work across your devices. The best thing about this is that you'll be able to specify the key trends you wish to monitor, new technology key words, and other future shifts. Then, each day you'll be fed new information from diverse fields within the diverse frame of reference you have provided. Even better, the cleverer apps will learn your reading habits — providing you with more relevant information over time.

If you want to take this to the next level, you can create opportunities to discuss new ideas with colleagues.[11] The savvier organisations I've worked with have a thriving and dynamic internal social network. Leaders model pioneering behaviour, and the enterprise benefits from the diverse collective input of its employees. Discussions are started around new ideas, and a growing database of intelligence is gathered around key themes. Books are discussed, conference notes are shared, and learning is an actively valued part of every day.

Dial up diversity

We tend to surround ourselves with people who think like us. This makes for cognitive ease, because our default world view is unlikely to be challenged or confronted. This might be fine for very small teams doing formulaic work in tight parameters with predictable outcomes. But if you're leading, thinking or pioneering, a lack of diversity is woeful.

I'm not simply talking about gender diversity[12] but the full spectrum: age, culture, expertise and experience. The more diverse thinking styles and

---

11| We'll explore potential rituals for pioneering thinking in part VII.

12| Although *urgent* work needs to be done to support gender equality in enterprise leadership.

perspectives you can access, the better your ability to think strategically and consider complex future contexts.

Now, I fancy myself as quite the progressive person: I'm pro science, equality and diversity. But I still make an effort to keep abreast of folks who offer bizarre points of view.[13] The reason being that we all run the risk of creating our own filter bubble — a scenario by which we only expose ourselves to perspectives that support, validate and reinforce our default world view. This is usually how we make friends — we get along with them because they share similar interests, values and political outlook. But our life (and our thinking) is *much* richer with diversity.

Find the friction

The areas ripe for innovation and disruption are those in which unnecessary friction exists. Friction is the stuff that slows things down. Thanks to our inherent laziness (and the Curse of Efficiency), we are always seeking faster and more efficient ways to do things. This asymptotic[14] need for efficiency is the primary driver for most of the innovation we see in the market today. If your enterprise is not helping to reduce the friction between the value it generates and customers accessing it (your channels), you can bet someone else is thinking about disrupting this space.

When exploring complex futures, a common thread may be that a key element of friction has been removed — and this has changed things dramatically.

Here's an example. Imagine you've recently entered a midlife crisis and bought yourself a 'cafe racer' motorcycle. Life is good — you're still a bit scared to ride it, but you like polishing it and taking Instagram selfies with it. After its second service, you're informed that a small part is missing. Your mechanic can order it in, but it's going to cost a fair bit of cash, and it'll take a few weeks to be delivered.

In a not too distant future, the mechanic would instead be able to download the schematics of the missing part and use a 3D-printer to

---

13| Like folks who deny anthropogenic climate change, for example. It's really intriguing — some folk genuinely believe it's all a big conspiracy concocted by scientists.

14| Asymptotic graphs are the ones in which a line curves ever closer to an axis, but never quite reaches it.

print the required component as part of the service. Hence, a big piece of friction would be removed.

What if a key element of the ecology in which your enterprise exists were rendered frictionless? What might that future look like?

Carve out time for exploration

So far we've explored things that can happily happen in your own time, without directly encroaching upon the existing default work of an enterprise. This might be due to my own bias towards introversion, but the reality is you've got to make this a reality at work. Leaders need to lead this, and demonstrate the kinds of pioneering behaviours you want others to emulate. If curiosity and thorough strategic thinking are important, you need to ensure that the time dedicated to these activities is not consumed by the urgency of default operational work.

In chapter 21, you'll find a set of actionable insights for different time intervals. Keep in mind that obtaining a rich sense of what's possible—piercing through the complexity of an uncertain future and moving beyond default probabilities—takes time.

And remember: the purpose behind exploring possible futures is to generate new thinking—which, in turn may stimulate new pathways to competitive strategic advantage for your enterprise.

FRAMING FUTURES

Using diverse perspectives to identify possible futures is one thing. But then we need to be able to *frame* them appropriately if their meaning is to be conveyed.

And the best way to do this is with *narrative*.

Since the dawn of civilisation, narrative has been used by our species to develop and share our understanding of complex phenomena—everything from ethics and philosophy, to physics and ecology.[15] Being able to use

---

15| Science fiction has informed our curiosity and scientific enquiry since as early as circa 2100 BC (when Sumerian texts included epic and fantastical poems).

narrative to describe possible futures is the quickest way to cut through complexity.

Consider this simple example narrative of a possible future:

> For the first time, earnings from the New Zealand livestock industry have officially been eclipsed by VegaVat—a single scientific Benefit Corporation that specialises in the creation of 'vat-grown' meat products. Heralded as both an environmental and an ethical boon for New Zealand and the world, VegaVat produce synthetic vat-grown meat with enhanced nutritional qualities and taste. Not only does this meat come at a fraction of the cost of regular meat, part of the VegaVat's profits is funnelled to the genetic preservation of endangered species. 'While we can currently grow 'living' tissue and simple organs, it is our hope at VegaVat to be able to bring back some of our most-loved yet extinct species,' a spokesperson from VegaVat informed us.

Upon reading that story, your mind will instantly create a web of assumptions in order to manage the complexity of the concept. The result is a future context that we can relate to and understand fairly quickly.

Here's another narrative:

> The Australian Government has just signed a license agreement with Onikage Corporation to leverage the shackled Japanese Artificial Intelligence entity Saibankan. The Government intends to lease access to this intelligence to all country, district and magistrate courts. According to sources, 'Jurybot' will soon be handling the majority of court cases. 'This new agreement is a significant boon to the justice system in Australia,' a Government spokesperson said.

This narrative suggests a similar and yet very distinct future context—a context in which artificial intelligence has enough widespread acceptance that it can be utilised to adjudicate human affairs. And that such an entity could be developed and leased by different corporations.

And now here's a rather different narrative:

> A new education policy requires students to read books—but parents are not happy. 'It's archaic,' one parent said. 'When my daughter logs in to attend class, she learns in a thriving, massive virtual world. She

chooses projects and learning challenges, and works collaboratively with other students from all around the world, creating her own learning adventures and thinking for herself. Why on earth would we want her to sit in social isolation — disconnected from the world, from creativity, collaboration and play — to simply "follow the plot" of some author?'

This last narrative is happening right now, and will manifest to a much greater extent in our near future. By reading this, we get a sense of this future context. We can perceive some of the complexities of this future, through the power of narrative.

You'll notice that in each example, I adopted the newsreader persona. This was deliberate. When framing future worlds, it's easy to get lost in the infinite complexity and possibility of it all.[16] The newsreader persona allows us to capture glimpses of these future contexts in a way that is compelling — the better news stories are good at capturing attention and conveying meaning with an economy of words.

So! If you're leaning into the collective challenge of pioneering thinking and envisaging potential future contexts, an easy framework to adopt is that of a newspaper or news bulletin.

This idea comes from a variety of sources — my friend Dr Amantha Imber, author of *The Innovation Formula*, teaches a similar technique as a way to convey ideas succinctly and meaningfully; Luca Gatti and Kirsten Dunlop also advocate this approach in their *Strategic Risk Framework*; and the Association of Professional Futurists uses frameworks akin to a weather forecast. You too can create a narrative context to frame potential futures.

If you're running this activity remotely, or asynchronously (as may be the case across multinational organisations), you may even want to adhere to

---

16| Farseers — beings of an Eldar race gifted with the ability to see into the fabric of the future — need to be very careful not to succumb to the inherent chaos and uncertainty of that future. They do so by adhering to strict rituals and clear frameworks. Well, at least that's the impression I get from some of the science fiction books I read.

a 'newspaper' template.[17] This is quite simple: imagine what the front page of a newspaper (or news website) might look like if it were to come from this future context.

Include the following sections: headlines, a major story describing a representative effect of a major disruption, a snapshot on world news, a local/personal/everyday interest story, and a category relevant to your enterprise.

If you're running this activity with a group, together in the same room, you may also want to use a 'news bulletin' template. Here, teams deliver short news bulletins that feature a set of stories from the future across a range of news categories.

Ideally, this is both an ongoing activity (forming a small part of weekly and monthly rituals for individuals and teams), and a specific event (like a three-day immersion). At the end of such an event, you'd hope to have between twelve and twenty different future contexts 'captured' and expressed in narrative form.

NOTHING IS TRUE

Remember: the role of stories and narrative is to help us conceptualise and comprehend infinitely complex possible future contexts. The point of a story is not to convince or convert others to a 'truth', but rather to offer a vision of a possible truth. 'Storytellers invite us to return from knowledge to thinking, from a bounded way of looking to a horizonal way of seeing,' philosopher James Carse beautifully observes.

17| Yes, I'm suggesting you default to a familiar template. Enough cognitive burden is going on here already!

Alas, the only way to determine if a possible imagined future is true is to observe it. But that means waiting until it has happened, which is hardly proactive or strategic. And so, to reconcile the fact that no story is true (yet)—and to avoid simply subscribing to probability (like anyone can do)—we hedge our bets and work to capture a wide range of possible future contexts.

Here, the breadth and diversity of this range of possible futures is more important than the depth and detail of the narratives that represent them. With more possible futures, our pioneering thinking is stretched even further—enhancing the likelihood of future contexts that are surprisingly different. The variety of these future contexts might serve to test our current business model and identify refreshingly new and useful ways of doing business.

And so, with such futures mapped out, we can explore the third and final part of this puzzle—incoherence.

SEEKING INCOHERENCE

When we begin to seek out possible incoherencies, we're looking for the state at which a possible future context may render your current business model and identity unviable.

These are always the things that seem obvious in hindsight. Today, people scoff at Kodak scoffing at the thought of digital cameras disrupting their industry. At the time (despite having dabbled in digital cameras themselves) Kodak saw their identity as a *producer of photographic film*—the arrogance of their past successes and growth saw them dismiss the threat of digital cameras (a capability they had already demonstrated).

If Kodak had engaged in Quest-Augmented Strategy—if they had pioneered beyond default thinking and imagined possible future contexts in which no-one would want to use fragile and expensive film (or wait for their photos to get developed)—then maybe they would have realised that their identity and business model needed to be refreshed. They might have re-imagined their identity as *preservers of memories* and, in so doing, opened up new avenues of relevance and growth.

But alas: arrogance and the Curse of Efficiency saw this once great enterprise meet the Kraken. Let's ensure that doesn't happen to you.

To find possible pathways and alternative strategic options for an enterprise, we need to *contrast* our existing business model and identity against the possible future contexts we have identified.

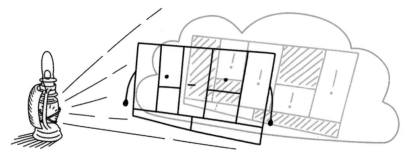

Here, we go through and ask the same questions we asked when establishing our understanding of our current business model and identity, going through similar components — such as the market need, our customer segments, channels, and key partners and activities. But this time, we explore these elements from within this *new* future context, noting down where our business model may be rendered incoherent or unviable.

For example, if you were in the insurance industry, a possible[18] future might be one in which identity theft[19] is a real and common thing — so much so that people seek out enterprises that may be able to protect them from such risk (or at least mitigate its effect). More so, individuals may seek greater protection for their own privacy, and the security of their data. And within this future, it may be possible that new identities

---

18 | Probable?

19 | A scenario that's happening today — hackers can adopt people's online identities, make purchases and engage in fraudulent activities that can potentially demolish a person's career and reputation.

are available for purchase—thanks to clever algorithms and an army of bots who can mimic an individual's online activities. If you were to look at your current business model from within this context, you might find some significant gaps—or that your primary value proposition is no longer relevant.

If this is the case—rejoice! For now you have a new, optional strategic pathway to monitor and consider. Do this across each of the imagined future contexts, and you'll have a range of alternative options to consider.

9. Pathways of Possibility

As a result of pioneering thinking, we have a bunch of intriguing incoherencies—possible future contexts in which our current business model and identity may be unviable. We've even explored where potential opportunities may lie. Maybe a gaping opportunity exists to serve an otherwise unconsidered customer need in a new way? Or maybe you've identified a glaring dependency within your key partnerships? Or maybe current delivery channels are rendered obsolete in a possible future context?

Upon discovering specific incoherencies—particularly when these incoherencies share *commonality* across multiple distinct future contexts—you might experience an 'a-ha!' moment. This is the point within pioneering thinking where suddenly a clear pathway seems to emerge. This is usually accompanied by an individual (or, even better, collective) physiological response—it causes some people to snap their fingers, clap their hands, or literally bound out of their seats. Within the mind, we have just 'clicked' a set of dissociated patterns into a newly combined pattern. It can be electrifying.

Prior to this point, the process may have seemed nebulous. But now, the path forward may seem *so obvious* that you'll wonder why it took you so long to see it, or why other folks aren't pursuing it already.

Hold your horses. Remember: the point of Quest-Augmented Strategy is to enrich decision-making and counter default thinking with *viable* alternative options. Just because you've identified an option, doesn't mean it's viable. And besides—some pathways don't become immediately apparent in a beautifully coalesced 'a-ha!' moment. Some persist as nagging hunches in the background.

We don't just throw all of our effort towards the first seemingly viable option that strikes us. Instead, we note down these options, and through repeated forays into the overlapping incoherencies of possible future contexts, we start to build a *quiver of options*.

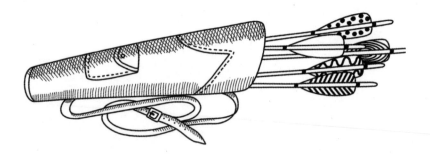

A QUIVER OF OPTIONS

A *quiver* is a case for holding arrows—but now the word is also used to describe a collection of surfboards (or snow/skateboards) of different lengths, thickness and/or design. By having a quiver of boards, a surfer (or board rider?) can choose the right board for the context.[1] For example, I have a small quiver of skateboards, consisting of a longboard (for smooth roads and less traffic), a cruiser (for busier streets) and a double-kick board (for awkwardness, injury and regret). 'What's in your carry quiver?' was a question asked of me by the Chief Storyteller from Bellroy—an enterprise that engineers wallets, bags and better ways to carry—when I worked with them. Here, she was referring to the different bags/wallets/satchels I own, for use in different contexts.

And so a good question to ask any pioneering leader is, what's in your options quiver? Because if you're doing well, you'll have a bunch of them—different strategic decisions and pathways your enterprise may be in a position to execute, relevant to emerging contexts.

An advertising agency, for example, might have options that include potential strategies for emerging technologies and/or new media platforms (including, possibly, more bizarre options that live within the convergence of virtual and augmented reality, the quantified self and the Internet of Things). By monitoring emerging platforms and the drivers of change, an option from within the quiver may show potential viability.

But remember: we're on a quest to generate *viable* alternative options to augment and enrich strategic decision-making. How do we know if something is viable? We test it.

---

1 | Like a short board for smaller, choppier waves, and a longboard for bigger (longer?) waves. Yes this is me trying to sound cool.

A GROWING ACUITY

It's difficult to un-see a potential incoherence in an imagined future. And this is wonderful.

This means that, after engaging in pioneering thinking and exploring possible future contexts (and their inherent incoherencies), your leadership team[2] will develop a growing capacity to develop and foster nagging hunches around these potential incoherencies. You'll begin to notice common incoherencies that exist across multiple possible futures. And it's these common incoherencies—the ones that keep emerging—that ought to give us cause for concern.

Much like our actions when we experience cognitive dissonance— whereby we naturally seek to minimise the inconsistencies between our thoughts and our behaviours—we will also naturally seek to resolve these potential incoherencies. An unresolved question is a beacon for curiosity. Your mind will start actively scanning the environment for more information in this field. You and your team will begin to notice new threads of evidence. As you attune more deeply into relevant feeds and discussions around this potential future context, more 'a-ha!' moments will occur. You'll attend conferences, host meet-ups and follow the development of key players on social media. You'll listen to podcasts and you'll debate new ideas as they relate to your enterprise strategy.

At some point you'll have an abundant quiver of *alternative options*—dozens of potential strategic pathways that may unlock new value and enduring relevance for an enterprise. Then, after collectively monitoring these options, gathering new intelligence, observing key

---

2| And anyone involved in strategic innovation in your enterprise—which can be everyone, depending on how you structure it.

drivers and identifying key triggers[3] in the environment, you'll arrive at a point where you need to consider translating your pioneering thinking into pioneering *doing*.

But—unless you're a CEO with an incredibly supportive team, a trusting board and an enterprise culture that thrives on change—chances are you'll need to prepare for chooks.

IN ANTICIPATION OF CHOOKS

Chooks (or 'chickens', for folks outside of Australia and New Zealand) can make a grumbly type of clucking that almost sounds like *'yes-but-but-but-but-but...'*. Committees also make a similar sound.[4] When confronted with a new idea or alternative ways of doing things, our default response is to say 'Yes—but [insert reason this won't work]'. And this is perfectly reasonable—every enterprise needs to maintain a healthy immune system to protect itself from new ideas, lest its focus become diluted.

Another classic challenge on the path towards pioneering growth is those key decision-makers (or peers) who fold their arms and say, 'Show me the evidence.' This is also quite reasonable. After all—these incoherencies haven't manifested yet, have they? And some of the things you're suggesting might require *fundamental* changes in an enterprise's business model. Potentially thousands of jobs and millions of dollars are at stake. It's far too risky to embark upon an untested new path.

We may have optionality, but it's still too early to integrate a potential new pathway into the existing enterprise strategy. And besides—confirmation bias may be at play. And so, to ensure things aren't being collectively distorted, and that the options we have for an emerging future are viable—we craft and conduct *experiments*.

3| Indications that things are shifting towards an imagined future—for example, the expensive acquisition of a key piece of technology, or the passing of an unprecedented court case in another country might be a triggers for imagined future contexts.

4| I know 'chook' is usually associated with the female of the species, but this kind of grumbling in committees can come from men and women equally.

Summary

Part III

◊ Pioneering is largely concerned with the generation and exploration of viable alternative options—potential strategic decisions that may unlock new value, strategic advantage and enduring relevance for an enterprise.

◊ To best explore viable alternative options for enterprise strategy, we must first understand our current enterprise identity, the market need we meet, and how we go about meeting that need. The Business Model Canvas is a good way to review this. Within this framework, our understanding of the enterprise's finances, infrastructure, customers and value proposition can be refreshed.

◊ The business model review may reveal discrepancies, gaps or issues that require immediate tactical attention. Such items need to be addressed to ensure the business model is optimised within its current context.

◊ 'Context' refers to the multitude of circumstances that form the setting within which an enterprise operates. The identity of an enterprise—and the business model that serves it—is shaped to meet the needs of customers within a given context.

◊ The benefits and consequences your enterprise is experiencing right now are the result of strategic decisions made previously. The only context that matters for strategy now is the future context. But until it is observed, the future is unknown.

◊   In order to augment default strategy with viable alternative
    options, we need to enhance our awareness and
    understanding of possible future contexts. By contrasting our
    current business model and identity against these possible
    futures contexts, we may identify strategic opportunities
    and risk.

◊   We naturally seek the safety of familiar, evidence-based
    approaches to assess the probability of certain futures
    manifesting. But this does little to address the infinite
    complexity of the future—it only serves to reduce the range
    of possible future contexts we are inclined to explore. This
    means that a conventional, evidence- or probability-based
    approach can only generate the same set of options your
    competitors have (bringing no distinct strategic advantage).

◊   Quest-Augmented Strategy requires exploration of possible
    future contexts that exist beyond likely probability. Such
    futures cannot exist in 'fact'—to find them we must
    systematically leverage our collective imagination.

◊   Several perspectives can assist us in the exploration of diverse,
    complex and uncertain futures. By reversing our assumptions
    and resisting quick fixes and neat conclusions, we can stay in
    the space of uncertainty for longer. If we then start monitoring
    trends through various and diverse information feeds, and
    if we begin to build conversations that invite diverse input
    around possible futures, our imagination can go further.

◊   The most effective way to cut through the complexity of
    a complex possible future context is to use narrative. A
    useful persona to adopt when telling such stories is that of
    a newsreader, using the framework of a newspaper or news
    bulletin. This ensures our stories capture attention, are
    compelling, and are economic with words.

◊   Once you have identified a diverse range of possible future
    contexts that may be of strategic relevance to your enterprise,
    you are then able to place your current business model and
    identity in those contexts. By doing this, certain incoherencies
    may become apparent, which draws into question the future
    viability of your business model and identity.

◊   You will likely find that specific overlapping incoherencies
    exist across multiple possible future contexts. Across these
    incoherencies, dozens of potential strategic options may exist.
    But, at this point, whether these options are viable is still
    unclear. And so, two actions are now required: the continued
    monitoring of the drivers of change for possible futures, and
    the use of experiments to address and determine the viability
    of specific options.

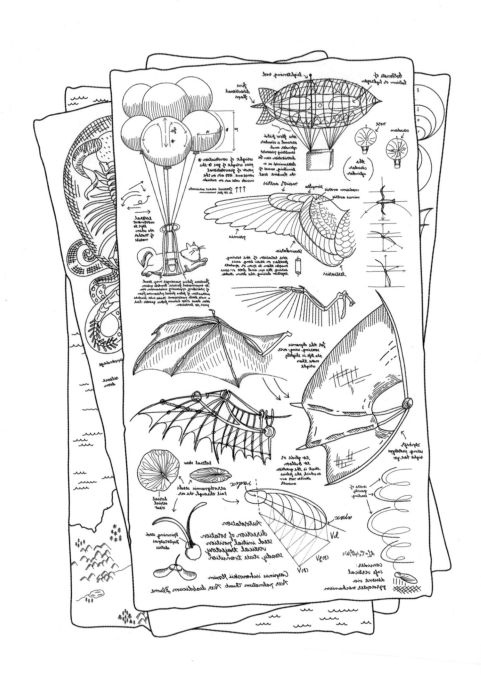

Crafting Experiments

Experiment [noun]: a course of action tentatively adopted
without being certain of the outcome.

Assuming that you're maintaining an active quest towards relevance and new value—and that you've been monitoring common incoherencies across various possible future contexts—you'll have a quiver of options. If signs suggest that a particular future context is likely to manifest, we then must seek to ensure that the strategic options we have generated are *viable*.

So far, Quest-Augmented Strategy may seem as though you're just postulating about the future. It almost conjures an image of wizards debating from within an ivory tower (which has a telescope and astrological charts), goblets of brandy in hand, stroking beards and harrumphing verily. And while the wizard in us might find this quite admirable, our inner rogue knows that we can't stay still. At some point, we need to shift from exploration to *experimentation*.

Experiments translate pioneering thinking into pioneering doing. They enable us to begin to validate these potentially uncharted and unprecedented pathways, to ensure that they are viable. They also enable us to tackle the legitimate questions and concerns that we anticipate our peers and other decision-makers will have. Through ongoing experimentation and learning, an enterprise is primed to execute pioneering strategy.

This process is much akin to scouting out a new path. In ye olde war times, pioneering leaders would utilise scouts, rangers and pathfinders—folks who would advance ahead of the troops in order to ensure that the way forward was clear and safe.[1] In modern business times, pioneering leaders have internal experiments and embedded intrapreneurial hubs (code for 'startups') to explore and test the validity of strategic options.

We are about to enter interesting territory.

Some enterprises still have an unhealthy obsession with 'ideas' and cherrypicking buzzwords. Before you know it, people will be espousing lean pivots with agility while looking to build the next killer app, iteratively putting the customer at the heart of the experience, and so on. Many shiny objects and convenient, pre-packaged solutions can distract us from good thinking. And so, in part IV, we navigate through this mess to find the options most viable.

1| Bah, I can't even pretend to be a war historian. This analogy is mostly informed by fantasy novels, war games with miniatures, and a healthy dose of D&D.

10. It's Not About Ideas

T he most important question to ask ourselves—in any moment or context—is, *Are we making meaningful progress?*

In the 'Experiments' quadrant of Quest-Augmented Strategy, meaningful progress is determining if a strategic option is viable. You might be wondering why this is not about coming up with cool ideas. In fact, we've leapt straight from exploration to experimentation while barely mentioning the 'i' word.[1]

This is not to say that ideas aren't important; they are. They are an essential component of how we think and learn. But if you're doing this right, ideas should be happening most of the time as a result of good thinking.

The word 'idea' is a combination of its Greek meaning of 'form and pattern', and its base 'to see'. So, in other words, ideas are patterns we've sensed or detected. If we have established a diverse and stimulating feed, and have allowed ourselves to be immersed in challenging new future contexts, it's very likely we'll have woven a few patterns together into ideas.

These new ideas are certainly not part of our default thinking,[2] but some might make up some of the strategic options in our quiver. If so, great! When a particular future seems likely to emerge, we can pull these options from our quiver and start testing their validity.

---

1 | Both ideas and innovation.

2 | For this to happen, we'd need to observe these ideas manifest a heap of times, over a long time, in a context in which said idea-manifestation was the norm.

We do this testing by taking a science-based approach (see chapter 11). But before we can do this, we need to get over the mystical reverence in which we hold ideas.

COMING UP WITH THE 'BEST IDEA' IS THE WORST IDEA

An element of my work involves speaking at conferences and events. Whenever we get a request of this nature from an enterprise, the first thing my team attempts to do is get a sense of the strategic *intention* behind the event. Sometimes the event has a real strategic imperative, providing a chance to rally folks together and shine a light on the path ahead. From here, we focus on the *effect* of the event—what we want people to *think, feel* and *do* as a result. Next, we can work out the relevant motivation strategy and design for before, during and after the event, and I can then tailor my contribution to serve this.

But sometimes no strategic imperative is apparent. The organisers are busy, and doing the best they can with the limited time and resources they have. And so I tend to get the default briefing—for example, 'We'd really like you to challenge their thinking, to get them motivated, to think outside the box, to be more innovative' (and so on). Not satisfied with this, I probe and begin to challenge their thinking within the briefing call—encouraging them to think beyond the default conference scenario, to lift their sense of what's possible, and to begin to co-create something brilliant.

In one such briefing call, the organisers revealed that their conference theme was 'innovation'. 'We're hosting a festival of ideas,' they told me.[3] And so I frowned (over the phone), and began to probe further. They soon revealed they were intending to run a competition to reward the 'best idea' generated during the event. Throughout the event, participants would break up into teams to workshop new ideas. The process would then culminate in a short pitch from each team on the last day of the event; ideas would be judged and a prize would be awarded to the team that came up with the best idea.

3| This is almost as bad as when someone tells me they're making their event really 'Fun'. Capital 'F' fun usually involves some sort of forced engagement combined with tacky gamification. Fatiguing awkwardness ensues.

This is not an uncommon approach. In large enterprises, senior leaders often share a certain frustration — a yearning for fresher thinking and practical ideas that will enable them to be more innovative. They often also perceive a lack of time to dedicate to this, thanks to the Curse of Efficiency. And so competitions, much like goal-setting, become the go-to for busy executives — they are an easily implementable, nicely visible box to tick that says, 'See, we're doing something about this.'[4]

But true innovation exacts a toll. This toll might be time, relationships, comfort, money, or some combination thereof. Unless you're willing to invest in it, you're only going to get lukewarm results. Or worse — results that sabotage the very thing you're trying to achieve.

Let's return to our 'competition'. You might be thinking that a competition for ideas is better than not doing anything for innovation, right? Maybe, though I have my doubts. My issue is not with the intention to engage people in the process of innovation but, rather, with the shallow, default way in which many seem to go about it.

Here's list of issues associated with competitions to find the 'best idea':

◊ **Define 'best'.** Searching for the best idea glosses over the importance of a clearly defined problem. And is this idea we are searching for required to solve a problem in our current context, or an emerging future context? In other words, are we reacting to a problem, or are we being proactive in our strategy?

◊ **Best, according to whom?** What agendas are at play here? Seeing as we are not taking an objective, scientific approach but, rather, relying upon the subjective judgement of others, we must ask: who does this idea serve? If we want to win this competition, what's more important: something that may secure new value and relevance for the enterprise (or business unit), or something that will appeal to the short-term priorities of those who are judging the merit of the idea?

4| Perhaps the only thing worse is the 'suggestions box' or the 'folder on the intranet' — which almost always offer no feedback loops or sense of progress to people who submit ideas (which effectively communicates that their ideas aren't valuable and that innovation is not as important as business as usual).

◊ **Okay, great: here's a simple, easy-to-implement
'tactic'.** Real progress and change is the result of many
ideas combined, woven, tested, unravelled and rewoven
together until they work. To host a competition for the
'best idea'—and to treat ideas as single units—means
anything established is, at best, tactical. This may be
useful in the context of a clear, present challenge. But if
we're looking to build for the future, we require strategies
that harmonise several tactics and many ideas. Such work
is much bigger than simply coming up with the best idea.

◊ **And, oh look—time's up.** Generating great ideas
requires thorough thinking. Certainly, working together
with a diverse team in a tight time-frame can help to
generate creative thinking—constraints are useful in this
regard. But doing this in one single session will favour
fast thinking and ideas that are easy to comprehend. The
classic divergent–convergent approach in a group context
may also mean that consensus kills the best ideas (leaving
us with a bunch of default ideas everyone can agree on).
What's more: it's hard to decouple ideas from identities
in this context. Here, we run the risk of people claiming
ownership over ideas. If consensus or group-think sees an
idea not make it to the pitch phase, the message to the
individual is clear: don't stray too far from the norm. Stick
to the default.

◊ **Too bad, losers.** And so, people pitch their set of
predictable and fairly lukewarm ideas. Voting (judgement)
is conducted and a winning team is chosen. They
are awarded with a prize: an extrinsic reward that
contaminates any intrinsic motivation the team may have
had towards innovative, strategic thinking. Did they
participate because they care about the future relevance
of the enterprise, or did they just want to win a cool
prize? Hard to tell. Maybe both—but the unfortunate
message is clear: we value that which gets rewarded. And
where does the balance sit for most enterprise scorecards?

That's right: the default, business-as-usual stuff. For the
90 per cent of folk who didn't win a prize, the message
is also charmingly clear: your ideas weren't good enough.
Thanks for trying, but better luck next time. And they
will wait for a next time. That's right—wait. Is this the
effect we want? To have our people wait to innovate, and
to only engage in the process if an appropriate reward
is offered? Or do we need to integrate this into how we
work? I think the latter, and parts VI and VII share some
thoughts on how to do this.

Many of the issues outlined in the preceding list can be extrapolated to
the flawed notion of searching for the 'best idea' in the first place. By
seeking ideas, we gloss over the importance of exploration—instead
latching on to notions of 'best' from within our current context. We treat
innovation as though it is a finite game to win, rather than the infinite
game of delivering value and staying relevant.

Steve Jobs, the founder of Apple and Pixar, was once asked by *Business
Weekly*, 'How do you systemise innovation?' His answer: 'You don't.'

This answer may have disappointed those looking for a neat and easy
system to adopt—a magical solution to liberate folks from the uncertainty,
angst and paradox inherent in pioneering innovation and growth. But
the truth behind innovation is that no neat, proven systematic approach
makes innovation happen for you today, or into the future. The approaches
taken by others in the past may not work for you today.[5]

Rather than seek fancy new systems, let's instead focus on the one
approach that's proven the test of time: science.

A SCIENCE-BASED APPROACH

Science, like everything, is flawed. But of all the flawed approaches one
can take to pioneering through uncertainty, to advancing knowledge and
discovering new pathways of possibility, it is the least flawed.

5| And some of the things you've tried unsuccessfully in the past *might* work for you
today. Ah the infinite paradox!

Of course, some argue that science can't prove anything. They'd be correct. For example, science cannot prove that the sun will rise tomorrow. But, thanks to a vast amount of evidence combined with sound reason, we can be almost 100 per cent certain it will. A scientific approach, when leading any pioneering strategy, is infinitely more preferable to a crystal ball, blind faith, a gut-feel or strong belief.

Many folks turn to science for certainty and conclusive evidence—but such an approach is an anathema to good thinking. Any conclusion closes the gates to curiosity—it's imagination, curiosity, doubt and wonder that drive scientific discoveries. Rather than trying to prove we are right, science seeks to find where we may be wrong.

Nearly everything we once thought true about the world has been proven to be wrong, thanks to science. We once thought the Earth was flat, but then discovered it was round. We once thought the Earth was the centre of the universe, but then discovered that we are just a blip in a vast and possibly infinite universe.

Again, science doesn't seek to prove things—rather, it seeks to disprove.

How does this work in the context of Quest-Augmented Strategy?

Well, take a look at your quiver of options and think about the most important emerging context. Consider which strategic option might be most valuable to your enterprise, given this emerging context. Pull said option from thy quiver, consider it, and then come up with a declarative hypothesis.

A hypothesis is a supposition, made on the basis of limited evidence, as a starting point for further investigation. It takes the shape of a testable- statement. Here's a relatable example: 'If we replace email with an enterprise social media or communications platform for all internal communications, we will see an increase in staff productivity and collaboration, and engagement with cross-functional initiatives.'

Now, I've chosen an example that should be relevant to any enterprise leader *today*. This isn't a future thing. Email is the worst. But, also, if an organisation were to see that the retention of talent and the move to a more entrepreneurial culture is critical for ongoing agility and relevance, then this might also be a strategic option to serve that future.

FORMING A HYPOTHESIS

If the internal email example is a bit tame for you, think about the experiment Netflix undertook. Originally, this company made money by renting DVDs via mail (actually sending out physical discs for people in the post). Things were going great — by 2007, over a billion DVDs had been delivered. But rather than simply follow the default growth arc, in the same year they invested in a new, tangential growth arc: streaming videos online. This was well before the practice became mainstream[6], and it has subsequently seen Netflix become one of the dominant players in this space (revenue from online streaming is now more than double that of mailed DVDs, and has allowed Netflix to easily branch out internationally). The early hypothesis for this experiment may have simply been, 'People will consistently pay good money to stream online content'.

This hypothesis has yet to be disproven in Netflix's context, and subsequently the company has conducted further experiments (including the hypothesis that 'People will pay good money to stream online content that has been produced in-house' — something shows like *House of Cards* are yet to disprove).

You may have even more daring hunches in your enterprise. Say you're a high-level executive in a pharmaceutical enterprise, and you've been monitoring several possible futures and key trends like the Internet of Things and the Quantified Self. This may lead you to the hypothesis that people will pay good money for embedded biomedical devices that can regulate blood glucose levels (and other key factors) on their behalf, and/or via their smartphone (or wearable device). People seem particularly interested in being able to review their internal health metrics (and having accurate historical and real-time data shared with their doctor). Such technology may also be used to connect to the devices of close friends, serving as an early-warning measure for anyone who finds themselves in trouble.

6| Pun alert!   *(continued)*

FORMING A HYPOTHESIS *(cont'd)*

Naturally, developing such devices is a big experiment, involving many facets (Who will pay for this? How will we create this? How does it get 'installed'? How frequently does it need to be refreshed? Will people feel comfortable with this? And so on). But it's through answering these new questions that viable alternative options are potentially discovered. And, from there, new growth arcs are born.

A third example might relate to farming. With the increased environmental and economic costs associated with livestock (not to mention increasing ethical concerns among the market), some farmers may wish to explore insect-farming as a viable source of protein production. Here, the hypothesis may be 'Key sectors of our market will pay good money for protein harvested from insects'. And so, experiments in more ethical and potentially more economically and environmentally efficient protein sources may commence.

In any event, through each of the provided examples we have a testable statement. We don't just jump straight to wide-scale execution — we need to see if this approach and our reasoning are valid.

And so, using the three pillars of science — observation, evidence and reason — we proceed to experiment. Figure 10.1 provides an overview of this process, along with a legend. We'll discuss each element in the following sections.

Figure 10.1: The experimental approach

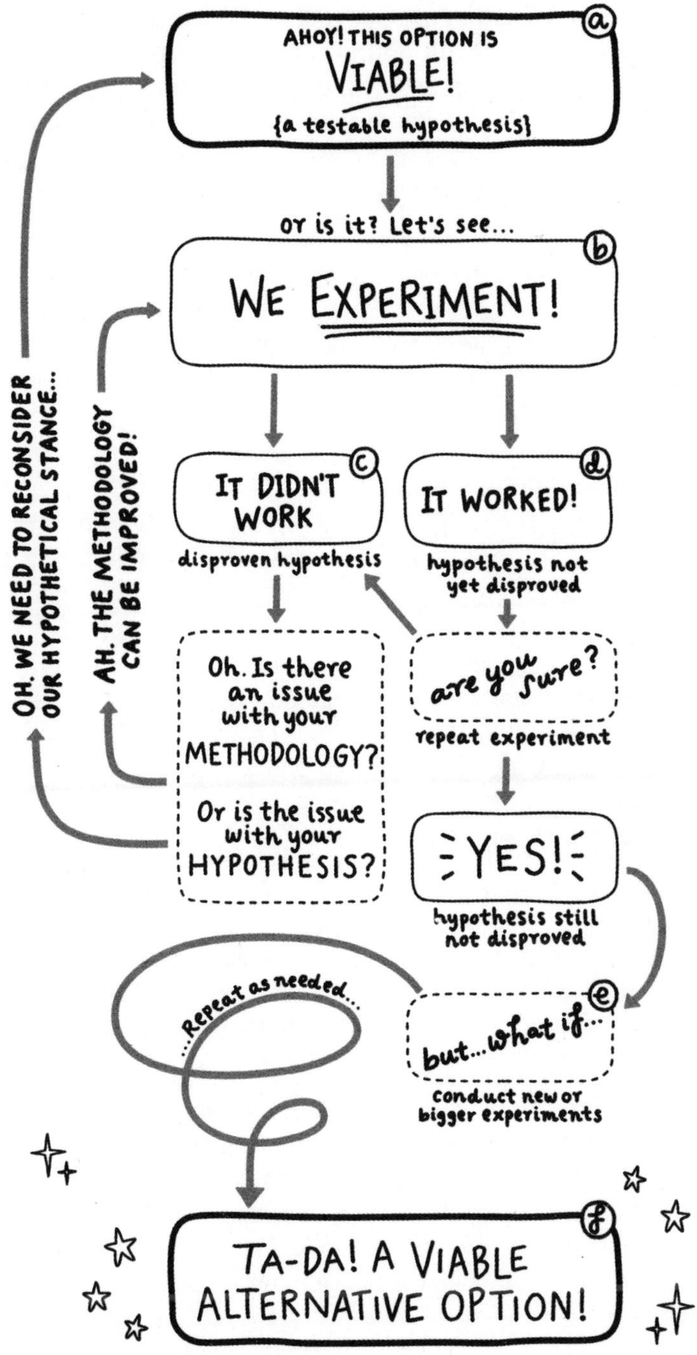

A | The testable hypothesis

This is the starting point of experimentation. When an option is pulled from a quiver, it carries with it the weight of a heap of conversations, overlapping possible futures, and the intersection of established and emerging trends. Getting lost in the complexity inherent within a strategic option can be very easy, and so a clear hypothesis helps to clarify and focus our enquiry. As ever, the overarching context here is to determine if this option is viable.

Part of this phase will involve looking at the literature and reference material accumulated as part of the exploration phase. Because we are at the edge here, it may be difficult to consult peer-reviewed publications (as a scientist might do), but by engaging with relevant peer authorities, we can clarify our experimental approach.

B | Crafting and conducting an iterative experiment

Small, safe, smart, cheap and fast—this is how we start our experimentation. At the simplest level, pacing through a hypothetical will allow you to rapidly experiment (or prototype) an option. Here, much like the personas and pathways we adopted in chapter 8, we map out and adopt the personas of the customers/users and stakeholders engaged with this experiment. We pace through how this option might work if we were to implement it—and through empathy and future-pacing, we identify a bunch of snags, pitfalls and traps we otherwise wouldn't have been aware of. These insights further help us to refine the design of our experiment.

At the next level, we might shift to wireframes and paper mock-ups—cheap props and other tools that might help us understand the user experience within the experiment. We anticipate resistances, and the questions or concerns other senior leaders may have about the option. We also seek constraints early, so we can enhance and improve the design of the experiment.

Next, we begin to understand the things we might measure. You'll note that we haven't asked the market what it wants yet. Keeping our customers and end users in mind throughout all elements of our experimentation is important, but at this stage we also need to factor internal stakeholders into the mix. What questions will they have? What 'evidence' will they need to see in order to feel that the option is viable?

Evidence, of course, is always contextual.[7] Evidence-based practice in medicine takes a long time to establish, because the population is so vast, and the risks are so high. But, within the context of an enterprise, a comfortable level of evidence can be obtained more quickly because (for many options) you are not creating new medicine that could have nasty side effects. Rather, you're mitigating strategic risk or unlocking strategic advantage—and waiting is the riskier option.

And so, we gather evidence relevant to both our internal and external stakeholders, so as to assess the validity of our strategic option.

At this stage, we may be experimenting with real people. If you recall the hypothesis example I provided earlier—a 'future of work' cultural experiment where we have *no email for internal communications*—we might be working with a small group of people over a short period of time. Again, think small, safe, smart, cheap and fast. Maybe we start with a small business unit of 30 and hold the experiment over a week. This experiment may include the adoption of a new internal social media or communications platform, combined with a new weekly work ritual. What do we find?

Or, if you recall our slightly more edgy 'internal biometric intervention agent', our initial efforts might include analysing existing continuous glucose monitoring devices available in the market (along with similar devices), and mapping out the friction points and opportunities available. Then, a prototype app might be created—just a rough set of wireframes—to better understand how users might interact with the system in everyday life. Later, these experiments might include working with folks who have type 1 diabetes, and monitoring their blood glucose levels with the app. 'Intervention' might be simulated at this stage, and plenty of learning may occur, but if the evidence suggests that people may be able to integrate this app into their everyday lives, research can shift to the development and early prototyping of the embedded 'sensor'.

---

7 | A lot of books reference clinical studies of relatively small sample sizes—extrapolating the implications of the evidence collected. While this is fine, scientific reasoning is perhaps more useful than relying on evidence collected in a different past context. The alternative is to wait until a vast bulk of evidence is collected, and a new theory is formed—but, by then, the world will have changed, and your competitors will have moved on.

Or, in the case of our pioneering farmer, initial experiments may include overcoming the 'brand' perception of insects. A 'pop-up' restaurant in partnership with a celebrity chef might be created along with an 'insect-only' menu. Such an experiment might help to determine if a viable market exists among gourmet restaurants.

At this point, we are not looking to create the perfect experiment. We're looking to create an opportunity to accelerate our learning and understanding of the viability of an option.

C | It didn't work!

How interesting![8] Your hypothesis being disproven may be due to one of two things. Either:

◊   your methodology could be improved

◊   your hypothetical stance needs to be reconsidered.

If, upon reflection, you believe your methodology was flawed, great! You're now wiser than before, and can design a better experiment. The enterprise context will always have complex variables at play—some of them you can control, and many you cannot.

In the 'no internal email' experiment, maybe miscommunications occurred, or expectations weren't clear. Or maybe unanticipated frictions were encountered in the process of the experiment. Or maybe some assumptions were revealed to be incorrect. Or, heck, maybe the internet dropped out or some firewall got in the way. In any event, it's back to the drawing board for the next iteration.

Likewise, if the pop-up gourmet insect restaurant turned out to be a flop, maybe it was due to a lack of adequate marketing? Maybe people are actually comfortable with the notion of eating insects for protein—they just don't see it as gourmet. And so, exploring the viability of this option among other customer segments may be prudent.

If you're keeping experiments small, safe, smart, cheap and fast, the ramifications of setbacks should be low. You're not putting all your hopes

---

8| And, actually the experiment did work. Remember: we're seeking to disprove a hypothesis. This brings us more learning and insight.

into 'one shot', and so you should be able to get onto the next iteration quickly and with relatively little fuss.

If, upon reflection, you believe your hypothetical stance needs to be reconsidered, great! In our context here, this means that a strategic option may not be viable after all — and so back to pioneering thinking you go (enriched with this new insight). And guess what? Thanks to your experimentation, you may have just saved the enterprise from making a bad strategic decision.

In any event, you've got options for meaningful progress and learning.

D | It worked!

Or, maybe...maybe it was just good timing, luck, an unanticipated positive variable or a quirk within the sample group. We're not sure if the option is *viable* at this stage — we just know that our hypothesis has yet to be disproven. Have we discussed the results with peers? Have we thrown enough at it? Have we accounted for all cognitive biases?[9]

Perhaps you can repeat the experiment with a different group, or different variables, and get different results? Or maybe it's time to scale up the experiment with a slightly larger group? This might be a bit more expensive, and a tad more risky, but if we're smart about it we can still keep it safe (and minimise the ramifications of what might go wrong).

Unless you have a very clear mandate from the CEO and senior leadership that communicates that experimentation, curiosity, learning and relevance are valued (as much as 'business as usual' activities), chances are you'll need to do some 'stakeholder management' here. This naturally gets easier the more influence and authority you have.

If you're an unofficial intrapreneur working with a small team looking to make a difference, you may need to reach out to senior leaders in your organisation to 'sponsor' your efforts. This introduces a whole heap of potential complexities, though, depending on how savvy they are with Quest-Augmented Strategy. Be careful that you don't end up proceeding to simply fulfil their own needs — being instrumental is important if

---

9 | See chapter 14 for a list of the main ones to watch out for.

you want to gain traction with those who hold influence, but being instrumental to meaningful progress is more important.

Let's say that you're able to repeat your experiment and scale up your efforts. One of three things may happen. You'll realise that:

◊   your methodology needs to be improved

◊   your hypothetical stance needs to be reconsidered

◊   you are now ready to throw some 'what ifs' at your hypothesis.

We're familiar with the first two options (back to the drawing board), but the third option gets really interesting.

E | What if...

At this stage, we start exploring the peripheries and 'what if' scenarios the chooks may consider.[10] Let's start with peripheral experimentation.

In my early days as an academic, I lectured at three different universities, simultaneously. I would find myself lecturing in different units—some of which I had no real expertise in.[11] One such unit was ecotoxicology. Now, I'm no ecotoxicologist, but I can tell you, having to lecture in this stuff did make me learn a thing or two. One element of ecotoxicology relates to the safety measures designed to protect 'average people'. These will include guidelines for the allowable limits of chemical products or pollutants in the environment. However, because they were designed for 'average people', these guidelines don't protect the more susceptible population groups that exist on the edges of the bell curve—for example, infants; the elderly; people with particular sensitivities; and people whose occupation exposes them to higher or more persistent doses, synergistic effects (such as when a cleaning agent is combined with hot water and inhaled via steam) or accumulative effects. All of these groups add to a hefty precautionary element—which is very important in the context of human health.

---

10 | I say 'chooks' affectionately. We need to be able to consider legitimate concerns, and possibly address or mitigate them through our experimentation.
11 | At the time, my PhD thesis had been submitted, but I was in limbo. The universities didn't have any other candidates, and I needed the work. Crazy, in hindsight.

In the context of enterprise strategy and pioneering leadership, the precautionary principle needs to be tempered with *risk-mastery*. With technology catalysing change faster than ever before, hesitation can be just as dangerous as proceeding blindly.

And so, in our experimentation phase, we consider what might go wrong. Where may this become stuck, and how might we test (and learn) for this now?

If we think in terms of our first example—*no email for internal comms*—we may be able to anticipate some of the resistance, concerns, friction, snags, traps, tar pits and pitfalls along this new path.[12]

So some of our questions might include: How will this work for our frontline sales staff? Will this create extra burdens or friction for them—if, for example, they're emailing communication with clients but then having to switch platforms internally? What about security risks? What is our backup or contingency plan if something goes wrong? What if important communications get lost among the chatter? What if the Gen Ys jump on board and fill our feed with lol kittehs? No, seriously: how are we going to bring our more stubborn folk on board?

If experimental design can factor in these considerations (and if you're inviting real users into the process) you will—through repeated experimentation—be able to iron out many (but certainly not all) kinks in the option.

The result?

F | A viable alternative option!

Hurrah! Here, we've used progressive reasoning to observe new patterns, and evidence suggests that this option may be viable. Wootus maximus! This is the handover piece—the ultimate output from pioneering thinking and doing. One of the many Holy Grails we may find by questing into the unknown. Packaged intelligence to enrich, augment and inform strategic decision-making.

12| Like a scout—or, if we're exploring a dungeon, a rogue. A rogue with lock-picking and trap-disarming skills.

Is it guaranteed to work? No! But, just like science can't prove anything but can make confident predictions, by this point we can be confident it will work. This confidence, in turn, can allow enterprise strategy to be more courageous and pioneering.

IT'S ALSO NOT ABOUT SUCCESS

Just as this process isn't about 'ideas', we also don't want to focus on 'successful outcomes'. We want to get to a point where an enterprise can generate its own intelligence to stay ahead of the game and unlock new growth arcs and enduring relevance. But when an enterprise has a history of incentives and weighted scorecards geared toward short-term wins, and a management culture that comes down heavy on compliance, it can be hard to get this type of experimentation happening. The more we celebrate 'success', the more we communicate what we consider to be worthy—successful outcomes.

But this only leads to more of the same outcomes—outcomes that serve our current context and not the effort that goes into securing new value and ongoing relevance.

Remember: in science *failure*, *truth* or *success* doesn't exist. There are only disproven hypotheses, learning and progress.

Let's explore how we can rethink failure to make more meaningful progress in your enterprise.

11. Planning to Fail

Before we get carried away, it's worth remembering that all phases of the Quest-Augmented Strategy model ought to happen concurrently. Futures are continually monitored, informing the experiments that matter. Unanticipated results from experiments may yield further questions worth exploring (meaning things flow between the four quadrants of the Quest-Augmented Strategy model — refer to figure 5.1 on p. 60). Likewise, the resulting intelligence from experiments informs strategic decision-making, and vice versa.[1]

All of the elements of Quest-Augmented Strategy interact with each other (see figure 11.1, overleaf). It's not a linear, step-by-step process.

1| For example, experiments may yield intelligence, but decision-makers may still have questions before they are willing to commit wholly to a new strategic path. And so, we conduct more experiments, and make more observations, to yield more insight to better inform strategy. It's all one delightful web.

Figure 11.1: The non-linear flow of Quest-Augmented Strategy

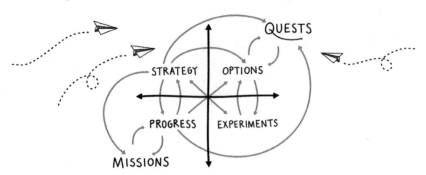

One thing that *is* consistent with this new way of working is *failure*.

But many organisations are woeful at handling failure. Failure becomes personalised, and career-limiting. In some cultures, it carries a stigma — *'Two bad quarters and you're out!'* The existing feedback loops only serve to reinforce compliance and non-thinking conformity. Any mistakes that do happen are quickly and quietly covered up — preventing the opportunity for shared learning. Curiosity is quashed — staff are simply there to slot into their cubicles and do their jobs. Customer feedback and complaints don't reach decision-makers, and the enterprise coasts along into the Inevitable Kraken of Doom.

Of course, I'm painting a somewhat extreme picture here. But another extreme has also crept into the vernacular — that of celebrating failure. I'm guilty of espousing this message. It's certainly preferable to the alternative, in which failure is shameful, but *celebrating* failure might be taking things a bit too far.[2]

You see, failure is a spectrum.

---

2 | The real thing to celebrate is *learning*.

FAILURE, AND THE NINE LAYERS OF HELL

I should probably point out that I wasn't raised within any particular religion, and so the word *Hell* doesn't carry much weight for me. I read it almost as though someone got distracted while saying hello. (I once played a Dungeons & Dragons module called 'A Paladin in Hell', which was fun.)

In the Inferno (the first part of Dante's 14th-century epic poem *The Divine Comedy*), a protagonist ventures through nine circles or layers of Hell—from limbo to lust and gluttony right through to fraud and treachery.

You might be (quite rightly) thinking this doesn't seem like a barrel of laughs—but let's work with the 'nine layers' bit. Also, if the word 'hell' makes you feel uncomfortable, just replace it with another word. 'Failure, and the nine layers of bad' perhaps? No... that doesn't work. Hmmm. While watching people choose to be offended by perspective is a secret hobby of mine, I think we're on the edge of something cool here. Let's abbreviate 'failure-Hell' to 'Fell'.

Yes! Fell works because this is what happens when you have fallen. It's also used to describe things of terrible evil or deadly ferocity (*'Fell beasts haunted her every step'*). So, cool bananas: failure+Hell = Fell.

The point here is that there are varying degrees of failure—some warrant a celebration of the learning achieved, some require changes to be made, and some, well... some suck (see figure 11.2, overleaf).

Figure 11.2: Failure and the Nine Layers of Fell

'CELEBRATE' THIS

IMPERFECTION

CONSIDERED QUITTING

FAILED EXPERIMENTS

CHANGE THIS

LACK OF ABILITY

PROCESS INADEQUACY

DISTRACTION

DON'T CELEBRATE THIS

PESSIMISM & WILFUL IGNORANCE

APATHY

CORRUPTION & DEVIANCE

Let's start with the deeper layers. Don't celebrate stuff here.

Corruption and deviance—the ninth layer of Fell

This is where people are found to be wilfully sabotaging enterprise strategy, or are operating in conscious and deliberate violation of enterprise values, ethics and integrity. Here, I'm talking about corruption and folks who put the enterprise at obvious risk just to line their own pockets. This is the worst type of failure, and demands immediate inquisition—into not just why and how an individual or team did this, but also why and how they were able to. If this shit is happening, big and immediate cultural and leadership intervention is needed.

Let's look at an example of this type of failure. In 2013, evidence emerged that a group of men within the Australian Defence Force had engaged in activities that involved the creation of highly inappropriate material that was demeaning of women within the ranks. The response from the Chief of Army, Lieutenant General David Morrison AO, was swift, direct and ruthless. In a video addressing all troops, he clearly stated that such actions are in direct contravention to every value the Australian Army stands for.

The Lieutenant General had stated, categorically and many times, that the Army needed to be an inclusive organisation. 'I will be ruthless in ridding the Army of people who cannot live up to its values. And I need every one of you to support me in achieving this,' he explained. 'The standard you walk past is the standard you accept.'

I could quote more, because this remains one of the greatest examples of clear and direct leadership in action. (A search using the Lieutenant General's name brings up the video of his address to the Australian Army.)

Suffice to say: if anyone has failed you at this level within an enterprise, your leadership response needs to be just as swift and effective.

Apathy—the eighth layer of Fell

This is perhaps the most insidious and common failure among enterprises—and it can extend from frontline staff right through to senior leadership. Apathy is the non-participation in meaningful progress. It's often masked with sound reasoning (at best) or *'computer says no'* reasoning (at worst).[3]

---

3 | In either event, people are clearly not even *searching* for an alternative way.

Apathy is a bigger risk to large enterprises than failed experiments and projects. Apathy occurs when people are not even trying to deliver meaningful progress—they're simply going through the default motions. I've seen this happen in some organisations where senior leaders know they only have a couple of years left before they retire. Rather than rock the boat, or embrace the cognitive burden that comes from pioneering growth, they simply exist in a holding pattern—waiting it out until they retire.

This also happens at the frontline too—especially if staff have minimal visibility of meaningful progress (and no rituals to draw this into focus). Teams can figure out the minimum effort required to coast below the radar. Such laziness could be quite clever if channelled appropriately—but at this layer of Fell, it's not.

Pessimism and wilful ignorance—the seventh layer of Fell

This is only slightly better than apathy. Pessimism is where people prejudge something before collecting or reviewing the evidence. They are closed to possibility and any evidence that may challenge their perspective. They put the burden of proof upon others—magnifying the effort required to make meaningful progress, while ignoring it when it arrives. A pessimistic senior leader with influence can be catastrophic to the enduring relevance of an enterprise. If viable alternative strategic options are blocked or burdened with pessimism, any meaningful progress or growth will be stunted.

A far better approach—and something that is encouraged throughout a quest—is scepticism. Here, we reserve our judgement until we have reviewed the evidence. With scepticism, we are still engaged in the process—we're asking questions, and leveraging doubt effectively—but we're not blocking the path to progress with our own stubborn ignorance.

Note: you might think that optimism is the solution. But we need to be careful with this, too. Blind optimism — the automatic 'yes' to new ideas and initiatives — can be just as dangerous as pessimism (the automatic 'no'). This is because we may expose ourselves unnecessarily to risk, and put our trust in the faith that everything will work out (rather than the science of accumulated observation, evidence and reason).

Sceptical optimism is perhaps the ideal state to embrace. In this state, you can maintain an eye for what's possible, with an optimistic outlook, while still being grounded in curiosity and reason.

Righto — now let's shift to the middle layers of Fell. Here, things aren't so bad, but they still need to be changed.

Distraction — the sixth layer of Fell

This is only slightly better than apathy. Here, at least, people are busy doing the work. It's just that they're focused on the wrong things. They're busy being busy, ticking irrelevant boxes. Are they bad people? No. Are they doing this deliberately? Probably not.

But there is an issue here. If important projects aren't being completed, or if meaningful progress isn't happening, something needs to happen. Something needs to change.

It could be that unreasonable expectations are placed on leaders and their people. In retreat from the anxiety that is often inherent within challenging new work, they instead succumb to the Delusion of Progress by focusing on the default (and more familiar) activities.

It could also be that the scorecards by which your people are assessed (in terms of performance) — and the incentives that go with this — are heavily skewed to 'business as usual' activities. If this is the case, people focusing on the activities that yield the most reward is only natural. As

I explained earlier, incentivised goals are incredibly powerful. They'll create all sorts of behavioural distortions if we're not careful.

I remember working with one large enterprise that wanted to become 'world leading' in customer experience. But, when reviewing their progress in this regard, they were surprised to see that no-one had engaged in activities to enhance customer experience. The reason? These activities were inefficient, and took time away from the bulk of their 'balanced scorecards'. Part of any enterprise strategy requires being clear about the 'lead wheel' that drives decision-making and culture. You can only choose one. You can't have it all, with equal priority given to customer intimacy, operational efficiency and product leadership. Something has got to be the lead wheel, and this will be reflected in the structures that influence your enterprise culture.

If people are getting distracted from the work that creates the most meaningful progress, something has got to change.

Process inadequacy—the fifth layer of Fell

Now here's another failure we may buck up against. It appears to be quite common, and relates to the previous *'computer says no'* element, but in this case, your people aren't apathetic—they're frustrated.

I see this happen where enterprise leaders want to collect more intel on their customers—which means having staff keep their customer relationship management (CRM) software updated. But if this software is clunky to use—if staff encounter issues entering, saving or searching for useful information—its uptake is highly likely to be patchy at best. The intention will become fragmented as people switch to their own spreadsheets or preferred CRMs.

Is this a failure? Yes! But it's not necessarily the fault of the user—and, in any event, searching for someone to blame is never the way to go about this. Instead, we get curious: how can we change this to make it work better? Where can we remove the friction? Is there a *viable alternative option?*

My guess: probably! Why not embark upon a quest to find it? Because I daresay that this will become an incoherency across *many* future possible contexts.

Lack of ability — the fourth layer of Fell

As you can see, the 'failure' is lessening as we ascend each layer of Fell. Here, we encounter failure due to the fact that some folks may not have the skill or ability required to demonstrate desired behaviours or execute an intended course of action. Is it their issue? Partly, yes. But the solution is pretty simple — learn.

If a lack of ability is getting in the way of meaningful progress, we can either ensure that our people have access to the appropriate learning, or we can hire those who already possess the skills we need.

This gets interesting when we review the digital literacy of senior leadership teams and boards — which in many enterprises (but not yours, surely) is almost tragic. However, the opportunity to learn is *right there*. Thanks to the internet, learning has never been so easy, immediate and accessible.

A lack of ability is an understandable failure — the world is changing fast, and we are required to learn faster than ever before. But it's an easy thing to change.

Righto! Now we can start considering the learning from failures in the upper three layers of Fell, and whether these can actually be celebrated. Mind you, the introvert in me has an instinctual aversion to celebrations that involve loud music, balloons or forced participation. So, rather than summon the brass band, let's treat our celebration of *the learning* that comes from the following three failures as more of a quiet, reflective sort.

Because the reality is failure of any sort still kinda sucks. But these failures are the least sucky (in fact, they each harbour great good).

Failed experiments — the third layer of Fell

You won't need to flip back many pages to see that failure is a natural part of the experimentation process. The worst failures at this point are flawed methodologies or unanticipated biases. For example, when reviewing the evidence you have collected after observing an experiment, you may identify that the results suffered from confirmation bias. When you look back upon your focus group interviews and observations, you might see that questions were asked in a manner that could be considered *leading*—the question: 'Why do you prefer using the new communications platform?', for example, assumes that people actually prefer it when, possibly, they detest it. Encountering such biases in experiments sucks, because you then need to review data with a caveat and a bigger note of caution.

However, reflecting on such mistakes only makes us better, and improves the quality of future research. This is why the peer-review process is so brutal in science — it makes for better research.[4]

Considered quitting — the second layer of Fell

If you have collected enough evidence to suggest that 'You know what, this ain't working', then quitting is a very viable option.

In fact, quitting is, in many ways, admirable.

This is not to say that perseverance isn't important — it is. But that applies to a higher order of things — like persevering in a quest towards enduring relevance.

But conventional motivational folklore would have you believe that 'quitting is never an option'. It is. It always is.

And so, if something is not working for you — and if you've tried enough ways, and collected enough evidence to suggest it's not working — quitting

---

4 | Though one could argue that occasionally scientists forget that they are people, too. I've worked in some challenging research cultures where harsh critical feedback is delivered personally, under the veneer of 'science'. Doing feedback well is a critical element of any culture — most are terrible at it, which is why we have to use anonymous 360° surveys. But nailing this means only great things happen.

is a smart move. Quitting is not about stopping—it's about letting go, so that you can progress.

A good scientist will engage in 'considered quitting' if presented with enough compelling evidence. A good enterprise leader will also engage in considered quitting if a particular product or market—despite much effort and exploration—is not yielding the desired results.

Evidence-based quitting is very important when the thing you are striving for becomes no longer relevant. If we don't quit, we risk investing too much of our *identity* into the achievement of a particular goal. We ignore mounting contrary evidence and persist dogmatically in a doomed pursuit towards an increasingly irrelevant and unachievable goal (as per the seventh layer of Fell).[5]

Oliver Burkeman, author of *The Antidote: Happiness for people who can't stand positive thinking* (it's great, btw), points out that 'theodicy'—the effort to maintain belief in a benevolent god, despite the prevalence of evil in the world—is occasionally used to describe the effort to maintain any belief in the face of contradictory evidence.

We don't want this sort of nonsense happening in enterprise leadership so, all things considered, considered quitting is something to be celebrated.[6]

A lack of perfection—the first layer of Fell

If you don't believe this is a layer of failure-Hell—just try writing a book. Imperfections everywhere! This has been my world. Heck, what am I saying? This *is* my world. And I'm sure that, at many times, this is your world too.

This type of failure happens when things don't happen perfectly. You publish a book, only to find it has typos (like this one inevitably will—even after several rounds of personal and professional editing

---

5| This dogged persistence has been seen among mountain climbers. In 1996, fifteen climbers died on Mt Everest during the climbing season. Of those deaths, eight took place on a single day—a disaster attributed to the stubbornness of an expedition leader, and the fixation upon a goal related to internal identity.

6| Mildly. But what's most exciting is that the resources considered quitting frees up can be invested into other meaningful pursuits—which is something definitely worth celebrating.

and multiple proofreaders). You launch a website and make a big announcement—only to find that one of the links is broken (even though you and your team checked Every Single Link multiple times). Or you only realise after working ridiculously hard to integrate new, user-requested features into the latest version of your software—getting the design right and smoothing out the user experience—that the software has a bug in it. Ugh!

You can look at this in several ways. Life is perfectly imperfect. Perfection is asymptotic and, therefore, unachievable. 'You did your best, and that is enough' (*bah!*). Here's what I like to bring it back to: constructive discontent.

If you're making any meaningful progress, you *always* have more to do. Progress—and the game we're playing—is *infinite*. When we make peace with the fact that a discrepancy will always exist between where things are and where things could be, we become a bit more open to this kind of failure.

But perpetual discontent—even if it's constructive—is hardly fun. This is why rituals play such an important role. We'll explore these in part VII, but one ritual can be useful in celebrating the learning that comes from a lack of perfection, and so is worth mentioning here. In fact, it's the one thing that makes constructive discontent bearable—gratitude.

When all you are seeing are the incredibly small mistakes and minor stuff-ups—and when cognitive distortion is blowing these out of proportion—gratitude pulls us back into perspective. This is helped further when we ritualise it, and have others to draw our focus to it. I'm incredibly lucky to have my partner, Kim, my business manager, Bianka, and some of my professional colleagues and friends to pull me up on this. I hope I do the same.[7]

I wonder—who on your team calls your focus to gratitude?

7| I also start each day with gratitudes (it's the first thing I do on my computer—see chapter 21).

YOU WILL BE TESTED

Pioneering is hard work. You (and your people) will be tested. The good elements of failure — failed experiments, considered quitting and imperfection — will occur. Regularly, if you're doing well.

If you've set up an intrapreneurial hub or a strategic innovation unit, or are running an embedded startup with a remit to generate viable alternative strategic options for possible future incoherencies, you'll need to help ensure that it is safe to fail in this critical work. If you try to impose default enterprise structures on these processes, you'll end up crushing the very magic of pioneering work.

Don't let this new work suffer from the Curse of Efficiency. Protect it.[8]

Remember: pioneering leadership is about exploring, finding and unlocking viable alternative strategic options. But this occurs within the context of an enterprise that is focused on executing the existing business model — today.

Some will see this exploration as a threat to their personal interests. Great companies like Apple, Google and Facebook know that if you're not prepared to cannibalise your own business, someone else will. Indeed, some of the viable alternative options we find upon our quest might mean cannibalising elements of our own business. These are the very things we worked hard to establish in the past — and some folks will be quite attached to them.

And so, a friction will always exist between these two worlds — between the pressing need to be efficient today and the imperative to stay relevant tomorrow.

Default thinking is the goliath with the home-ground advantage.

---

8 | We'll explore establishing a 'bimodal' culture in part VI.

It has familiarity, predictability and precedent. It easily allows people to feel 'in control' and alleviates the angst of uncertainty. It generates quick wins and clear results. With default thinking, we can tick boxes, and feel a sense of progress.

Don't be deluded. Pioneering leadership is the single most important imperative for all enterprises today. It's a hero's journey. It takes courage, and the ability to persist through failure, but the results are worth it—viable alternative options, and the promise of meaningful progress, new value and enduring relevance.

12. Viable Alternative Options

I f our default is *the option we choose automatically in the absence of viable alternatives*—and if default thinking is what leads us closer to the path of decline and the Inevitable Kraken of Doom—then the fruits of our quest become the very antidote and salvation.

But before we hand our gathered intelligence over, we need to ensure it is packaged appropriately. Akin to not serving 30-year-old whisky in a polystyrene cup, we don't want to simply deliver a viable alternative strategic option as a PowerPoint presentation attached to an email.

PACKAGING INTELLIGENCE

This book is a form of packaged intelligence. I've taken great pains to convey the paradoxical complexity of leading a quest in a way that's practical and actionable. Some will say that I should 'dumb it down' and provide more 'top tips' and 'practical, how-to steps'—but that's just the Curse of Efficiency speaking, looking for quick fixes.[1] Now, I could have done this; in fact, I could have presented this intelligence as a simple, prescriptive list of what enterprise leaders must do if they want to secure enduring relevance. But, such an approach is both patronising and

---

1 | Still, you can tell this is a raging insecurity of mine. As an author, I hope this is all making sense to you!

arrogant. It doesn't inspire thorough thinking and nor does it allow the reader to own the process. Instead, they are simply following instructions, like a robot.

When you're thinking about *how* you present viable alternative options to strategic decision-makers, you need to consider some vital points.

Firstly—is the timing right? Have your fellow enterprise leaders been kept abreast of developing insights, or will they be ambushed with this new insight? Have they been invited to participate in and contribute to pioneering thinking (exploring uncertain futures and identifying incoherencies)? Or is this stuff all new to them? Have their questions and concerns been addressed in the experimentation phase? Or are you encountering these for the first time only now?

As you can see, I'm hinting at something here. The more inclusive you can be in your quest, the more likely it is your leadership peers will be receptive and on-board. Where possible, provide updates on progress and learning frequently. Involve them, so that when viable alternative options are discussed in strategy meetings, they don't come as a surprise.

If you're the CEO or senior executive of a large enterprise, you may have a strategic innovation team reporting directly to you. Or this team may take the form of an embedded startup or intrapreneurial hub. If you're in such a hub—or are looking to start one—know that the most important value you can provide as a result of leading a quest is *insight*, in the form of viable alternative strategic options.

Which brings us back to packaging (and your second main consideration). At some point, you'll need to deliver this insight. It could take the form of a report, or a presentation. It could be that time is dedicated to exploring alternative options as part of an offsite strategy development retreat. In any event—you'll need to present this intelligence.

It would be nice to pretend that strategic decision-making is a rational process, but it is often just as flawed by cognitive bias as anything. As Scott Berkun explains in *The Myths of Innovation*, 'Innovative ideas are rarely rejected on their merits; they're rejected because of how they make people feel.'

Gosh, feelings?! How do we factor this in?

COMMUNICATING IN FULL SPECTRUM

When transitioning from academic research to business consulting, I needed to learn how to 'de-academify' the way I communicated ideas. Because I had spent ages going deep into the research, I had become too close to what I knew. This resulted in me rushing through fundamental concepts I (incorrectly) assumed everyone knew. The result was, I imagine, confusing and somewhat overwhelming (in a disempowering way) for folks who listened to me. It was only when I met Matt Church — a good friend and mentor — that things began to change.

Matt is the founder of Thought Leaders Global and the author of *Amplifiers*. He runs a business school for expert consultants along with another mate of mine, Peter Cook (author of *Implement*). Very early in my transition, Matt introduced me to one of the fundamental elements of thought leadership — the ability to capture, package and deliver world-class thinking in a way that has integrity. The result? People get it, and you become known for what you know.[2]

Give the viable alternative option a name

We can't keep calling multiple viable alternative strategic options viable alternative strategic options! It's a mouthful. And it's a slippery slope if we start using acronyms.

Instead, you want to create a name to hang stuff onto. This could be a codename, like 'Operation Lazydog' or 'Operation Moonshine' — something unique and memorable. Or it could be ultra-relevant: 'The Bitcoin Option' or 'Emailbane'. Whatever it is, give it a catchy name. You'll have multiple viable alternative options within your quiver, and they each need to be discernible and memorable. If you lose people with an ultra-technical name early on in the piece, winning them back may be hard.[3]

2| Thought Leaders Business School runs today, and I've been known to mentor folks within it. Check it out at www.tlbusinessschool.com

3| A lesson many academic researchers could reflect on when delivering — for example, here's the title of a legitimate PhD thesis: 'Detrital Zircon Evidence for Mixing of Mazatzal Province Age Detritus with Yavapai (ca. 1700–1740 Ma) and Older Detritus in the ca. 1650 Ma Mazatzal Province of Central New Mexico, USA' (aka: 'A Study of Old Rocks').

Start with (their) why

Even if we are doing strategy well—with thorough thinking and due consideration—time will always be of the essence. You may be tempted to jump to the cool bits but, just as I have done with this book, you need to establish the contextual relevance and need for this strategic option.

So, explain the incoherence. Unpack the mismatch between your current identity and business model, and that of an emerging set of future contexts.[4] Identify the specific problem inherent to the emerging context. Then bring it back to why. Not your why, but *theirs*—the strategic decision-makers'. Hopefully this is one and the same: the biggest why, in an enterprise context, is enduring relevance.

Frame the problem

Having established the why, you now want to dial up the imperative—contrasting the viable alternative option with the default 'do nothing different' option. What are the implications of doing nothing? What's our window of opportunity? Where will it hurt us if we don't act?

If a photo is placed in a dark frame, the colours are perceived to be brighter. Likewise, if a viable alternative strategic option is framed in the context of an emerging incoherence, its validity will shine the brighter.

Our intention is not to manipulate but to influence. To convey the thinking that has occurred in a condensed, concise and compelling manner, so that decision-makers can grasp the bigger strategic opportunities and implications of this new alternative pathway.

Ultimately, we need to remain non-attached—strategy is complex, and we often cannot be across every facet. But if we are presenting a viable alternative option, we want to ensure that we frame it appropriately—so we have people's attention, and they are primed to listen.

4| Remember: by the time you are considering viable alternative options, you'll have been monitoring the drivers of change and signs will indicate a particular future is more likely to manifest. Therefore, the time for strategic investment—if we want to obtain advantage—is now.

Unpack the option

This is where full-spectrum thinking (and communication) comes to the fore. In fact, it should influence all facets of how we communicate important ideas and concepts. This type of thinking comes with the recognition that two important spectrums exist in how we think and communicate.

The vertical spectrum allows us to think and communicate in terms of big picture (contextual) through to detail (concrete). And the horizontal spectrum means we can think and communicate with an emphasis on logic, or an emphasis on emotion.[5] See figure 12.1.

Figure 12.1: Full-spectrum communication

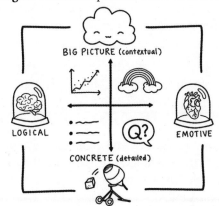

Any viable alternative strategic option will carry its own set of complexities. And so the best place to start when unpacking this option is with a big-picture, logical framework. This can take the form of a model, a grid, your business model, or some sort of diagrammatic representation of the option. At this stage, the point is not to get bogged down in detail, but to map the territory. By establishing this context, people will be able to associate any detail you share within the puzzle of the bigger picture.

---

5 | This was the gold Matt Church shared with me early in my career. Matt provides much more depth to this, however — check out his work to learn more.

After establishing a contextual framework, you'll then be able to drill down into detail. It's similar to what you're experiencing now[6] — in chapter 5 we established the model for Quest-Augmented Strategy, which provides context for the sixteen chapters that follow it. If ever you are lost, you can return to the contextual framework to get a sense of where we are. Likewise, if you feel that people are getting lost in the details of your option, you'll be able to return to the overarching framework to decontextualise things.

The details you provide include the case studies from your experiments, and the intelligence you've gathered through the exploration and monitoring of diverse feeds. Throughout this, you'll want to humanise the data. Rather than simply parroting facts, you can bring insights to life through the power of story. As we've explored, narrative is a powerful way to convey compelling complexity in a short amount of time. You may wish to integrate the 'newsreader' perspective into how you present this option.

Finally — after moving from a big-picture, logical framework, through to detailed studies and descriptive stories — you'll want to return to the big picture, and the emotion behind the decision-makers' big why.

This is what it's really all about. If you want to ensure this option remains memorable, link it to an analogy.[7] Answering the question 'what's it like?' for the viable alternative options you present will help ensure that everyone has a grasp on it.

Of course, all of the above is more like a dance than a set of sequential steps.

Provide a path

By now, you'll have presented a clear and compelling overview of a viable alternative option.[8] Ideally, this all comes as no surprise because many key decision-makers have been involved and kept updated with the progress of your quest. It may have already been covered, but a key element

---

6| Albeit you're not writing a roughly 70 000-word book!
7| I have attempted to do this with the Inevitable Kraken of Doom (it's just an analogy for insidious decline — or is it?). I've also used the analogy of a 'quiver' — heck, analogies are scattered throughout this book.
8| It would never occur this neatly or sequentially in real life, but this is a good reference point.

of pioneering leadership is shining a light on the path—highlighting the way forward through what is otherwise relatively uncharted and unprecedented territory. Here, you deliver your scout's report—the things you've learned on the path so far.

Chances are, if you've been building a momentum of evidence through experimentation, the next steps will be relatively clear: continue scaling up the experiments. Bring more enterprise focus and support to the pursuit of this new alternative strategic option.

In fact, let's not call it the alternative anymore: let's integrate it into our enterprise strategy! New rainbows of growth and relevance, here we come!

Maybe ... Just because it's a viable alternative option, however, it doesn't mean it will be progressed. Our role in Quest-Augmented Strategy is not to replace strategic decision-making, or to make all the decisions ourselves. Rather, our role is to augment, enhance and enrich this decision-making.

In part V we'll take a brief look at the domain of strategic thinking, and the tension of balancing pioneering growth with the demands of operational excellence and stewardship.

Summary

Part IV

◊ Experiments allow us to establish the viability of alternative strategic options. They are a means by which we can scout out potential new pathways, and learn about any potential issues we may encounter.

◊ It is important that we focus on learning—and not simply the generation of novel ideas. Ideas are an important element of leading a quest—they are the by-product of good thinking. But one of the quickest ways to kill strategic innovation is to create a competition for the 'best ideas'. This only serves to gloss over the important process of thorough thinking and exploration, and at best only generates tactical ideas to serve our current context.

◊ The least-flawed approach we can take is a science-based one. Here, we start with a hypothesis—a supposition made on the basis of limited evidence that serves as our starting point for investigation. This takes the form of a testable statement.

◊ Once our hypothesis is formed, we craft a series of iterative experiments in an attempt to disprove our stated hypothesis. Our starting premise is always small, safe, smart, cheap and fast.

◊ From an initial set of rapid prototypes, we can get a grasp on the most important elements of our experiment, our measures and our methodology.

◊   Our hypothesis might be disproven. This could be due
     to a flaw within our methodology, or an issue with our
     hypothetical stance. In either case, through experimentation
     we have now obtained new insight that can be used to
     enhance the experiment, or our understanding of a particular
     option. We go back to the drawing board, and repeat.

◊   If experiments reach a point at which a hypothesis cannot
     easily be disproved, we repeat the experiment, and scale it up.
     If our hypothesis continues to remain valid, we then start to
     throw new questions at it—actively seeking to disprove it in
     relevant new ways.

◊   If our hypothesis survives this, we may have ourselves a viable
     alternative strategic option.

◊   Failure is an inevitable part of the process—but there are
     varying degrees. The worst forms of failure are corruption,
     deviance, apathy, pessimism and wilful ignorance. These
     failures require immediate intervention from leadership, and a
     review of enterprise culture.

◊   Distractions, process inadequacies and gaps in capability are
     another set of failures. These are not ideal, but they are easy
     to address through structural changes and direct intervention.

◊   Failed experiments, evidence-based quitting and a lack
     of perfection are the least-worst failures. They still aren't
     enjoyable, but these failures are the result of good work, and
     offer rich new learning and insight. Because of this, these
     failures ought to be celebrated.

◊   When experimenting and persisting in pioneering work,
     enterprise leadership will be tested. The biggest threat to
     pioneering work is default thinking, the Curse of Efficiency
     and the Delusion of Progress. Keeping on track requires
     constant, wilful effort.

◊ The antidote to default thinking takes the form of viable alternative options. The intelligence inherent within a viable alternative strategic option needs to be packaged appropriately, and communicated across a full spectrum — from big picture to detailed, including both logical and emotive frames. The evidence yielded from experiments combined with effective narrative will help ensure that the viable alternative options generated by quests are considered in the best light.

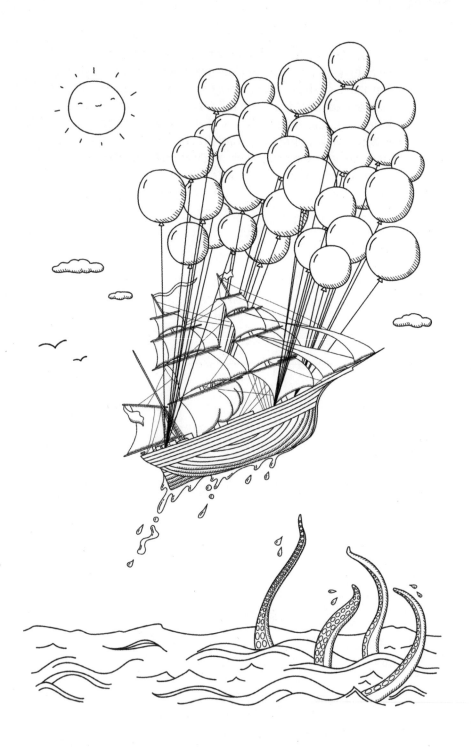

Part V

Augmenting Strategy

Strategy [noun]: a course of action designed to
achieve a long-term or overall aim.

Well, ahoy! If you've led a quest into infinitely complex and uncertain possible futures, and returned with profound insights that could serve to augment our strategic decision-making today, welcome back.

Likewise, if you've established a strategic innovation team or an embedded startup and supported them in the exploration, experimentation and validation of alternative strategic pathways, brilliant.

Here is where we harvest the insight we've gathered to augment, enrich and enhance our strategic decision-making. In part V, we'll explore how you can make the best decisions — balancing the urgency of operational needs with the imperative for pioneering growth.

13. Back to the Future

So far we've encountered a few nasties on our journey, but the two main villains would have to be the Curse of Efficiency and the Delusion of Progress. It's thanks to these two that we find ourselves locked into default thinking, which—if we're not careful—will see us descend into irrelevance and meet the Inevitable Kraken of Doom.

Of course, we need default thinking—it's how we learn, and life would be ridiculously inefficient without it. In fact, our defaults would serve us brilliantly in all facets of business and life, if only things were static and never changed.

But stuff does change. And in a strategic context, the biggest opportunity and threat facing any enterprise today is the sheer complexity of our dynamic and uncertain future. It's the fact that an *infinite* number of possible futures exist within and beyond reasonable probability—and any one of them may render your current business model and identity unviable.

But! Thanks to the fact that our strategy is augmented by pioneering leadership and an ongoing quest for enduring relevance, we have a sense of what lies ahead. What's more, we have a range of viable alternative strategic options to consider in addition to our defaults.

TOWARD COHERENCE

When we catch ourselves progressing within our defaults, the most important question we can ask ourselves in any given moment is, *Is this contributing to meaningful progress?*

We can find plenty of opportunities to delude ourselves with *meaningless progress* — but what constitutes meaningful progress? What does it look like? And how do we know if we're making it?

In the context of strategic decision-making, we can consider meaningful progress to be anything that serves to optimise coherence within emerging future contexts. Coherence is where our business model and identity make sense within a context.

Once upon a time, advertising on the television and in physical phone directories made a certain kind of sense. But now the internet renders such approaches incoherent. Such outdated approaches don't make any logical sense in our current context. They are incomprehensible.

The trouble is, without Quest-Augmented Strategy, people only have the past and their current context within which to make decisions. Sure, some folks might have some guesses as to what may come about in the future, but the picture will be patchwork, and it's hardly an enriched way to go about strategy. In fact, this is what strategy can look like without the enrichment of a quest.

UNENRICHED STRATEGY

So! Things are humming along, and everyone is busy. At some point you realise it's been a while since the team got together to discuss strategy. But that's okay — all of the right key performance indicators are being met, and your leadership colleagues can be trusted to look after their respective units. The current business model and organisational structure is optimised to support this.

Then, on a flight you happen to read an article that describes a new startup seeking to 'disrupt' the industry you're in. You scoff at it, and shake your head — but you keep the article. Maybe it's something to bring up at the next strategy meeting. Speaking of which, when is that?

You shoot an email out to your team asking when everyone can get together to review the strategy. It quickly becomes a mess so you get your assistant to try coordinate timing. Your colleagues question the need to meet in person and suggest a teleconference instead. You're busy too, and a teleconference does seem a lot easier—and so it is organised. Most of the team make it, but time is short and everyone seems to only be concerned about elements of operational efficiency. When you mention the startup, you are met with arrogant dismissal. And so the meeting continues—everyone defends their accountabilities and talks about inefficiencies in the enterprise software. You all agree that alternatives should be explored, and someone agrees to get their team onto it.

Things resume back to business as usual. It's still busy, and you're still generating wins—but you still have this nagging sense that you're missing something. You follow up on that startup you read about, and it turns out they were acquired by a larger company. *Interesting*, you think.

Months later, you attend a conference which features a futurist speaker. Normally you're dismissive of such folks—anyone can play a set of videos to dazzle us about fancy things in the future. But the things she is talking about trigger that nagging hunch you're harbouring. *We're missing something here…*

After the conference, you take another look at what's happening in your business and notice that a couple of key customer accounts have moved. You have a good relationship with one of them, so you give your contact a call—only to hear they're now using that new technology you scoffed at nearly a year ago!

After the call, you immediately contact your team for an urgent strategy meeting. This time is must be in person. Figuring out a time is challenging—and everyone makes a point of highlighting to you how busy they are—but you make it happen.

Knowing the opportunity cost of bringing your leadership colleagues together from across different cities—not to mention the actual cost of flying and accommodating them—you work up an agenda to ensure you make the most efficient use of the time. You also send through some reference material—a scattering of articles—so that your team can come 'prepared'.

(continued)

UNENRICHED STRATEGY *(cont'd)*

The team arrive. You know you've only got a day so you get right into it, explaining that key customers are beginning to adopt this new technology, and that your enterprise is not doing anything about it. The immediate response is defensive downplay and denial. You suspect that your colleagues were too busy to read the briefing notes in detail—they likely only skimmed the surface. After spending time explaining the problem, you realise that it's morning tea time already. Your colleagues are already ducking out to make calls, and some are working on email.

When they come back in, you decide to rally everyone together to focus on solutions. The team jump in with a range of quick fixes and short-term tactics. People offer differing perspectives, and things get angsty. Someone says, 'Let's build an app!'—which prompts someone to remember that the enterprise software issues still haven't been addressed. The leader responsible cites legitimate reasons for the delay—and now the conversation shifts into familiar territory: how can we upgrade or innovate our software, so that we can be more efficient?

Lunch time comes, but this renewed focal point has alleviated the angst. Your leadership colleagues are now working on the features needed within this software. People are chiming in with 'cool factoids'—'It's gotta be responsive,' someone says with a nod. 'Make it sync with wearable,' someone else one-ups.

You look at the time and—crap! It's now mid-afternoon. You bring people's attention back to the original problem—'The business landscape is shifting, and we're not prepared,' you stress. But rather than explore the problem, people resume offering predictable solutions. By the end of the day, you're staring at a set of goals not dissimilar to your existing strategy. These include: improve the efficiency of enterprise software, review offerings to re-engage existing customers (while expanding into new markets), and redouble efforts toward all existing goals and targets. Some clear accountabilities are established, and people leave the meeting feeling as though they've made some good decisions. Maybe.

But by then it's all a case of too little, too late.

Those competitors using newer technologies eat deeper into your market share. Steep discounts are required to retain customers, and diminishing margins put more efficiency pressures on leaders and their people. Your new enterprise software is deployed, but because everyone is so busy, no-one has the time to learn or use it properly—and so they default to the old system. Your team becomes even more fragmented, and seemingly more concerned with meeting their own individual targets than they are with working together to secure the enduring relevance of the enterprise. Some, you suspect, are just waiting for an opportunity to jump ship—they can see the shadow of the Kraken already...

...and so on.

Let's not take an approach like this.

Just because you lead a large and established enterprise does not mean you need to constantly be stumbling to keep up with the pace of change.

You could be leading it.

GET STRATEGIC ABOUT STRATEGY

Before we get into the process of reviewing options and making strategic decisions (covered in chapter 14), let's first ensure that the context for strategic thinking and decision-making is effective. The following sections outline a few things to consider.

Ritualise it

When everyone is busy, things like strategic development, review and decision-making can easily become haphazard and sporadic. But, when we make these a ritual—a routine held with reverence—they become an elevated priority, and part of the fabric of your enterprise culture. In chapter 21 we review the rituals of pioneering leadership—developing, reviewing and renewing strategy is one of the most critical.

Two days: the absolute minimum

If you're ever going to develop strategy, two days is the absolute minimum time you'll need. You can review strategy in a day, if people have their act together and good conversations have been happening in the lead-up to it. But to develop strategy, you need at least two days.

The reason for this is the dinner, and the sleep.[1] After the first day of previewing our emerging future context, the anticipated incoherencies and the strategic options available, you'll need time for non-rushed discussion. This conversation can extend over dinner — and the contextual shift from workshop room to non-rushed dining can do wonders for the discussion and the debate. 'Sleeping on it' also allows us time to reflect, and to let any tensions that may have emerged among the team to be placed back into perspective. The refreshed review of strategic options after an intense day of discussion and debate is always clarifying. Clearer decisions can be made and, thanks to the time leaders have had to connect with each other over a meal, team spirits are renewed. This can then translate into greater courage and support in the leading of pioneering strategy.

Invert learning and get into conversation early

In the past we would learn in the classroom together, and do our homework alone at home. Now the modern classroom is inverted — we do the learning at home (online), and our homework together in the classroom. In a strategic context, this means that discussions occur in the lead-up to any strategic immersion. This is an opportunity to share relevant insights about emerging futures and potential incoherencies, and to ensure that everyone is abreast of the viable alternative strategic options available. Rather than swagger into strategy meetings pretending to know everything — or using the time together to cover basic elements — people can ask these questions in the lead-up.[2]

This is particularly important if some leaders do not possess the literacy relevant to the options under review. For example, if senior leaders do not possess digital literacy or an awareness of emerging phenomena such as 'the sharing economy', they will be ill-equipped to make strategic decisions. But with an inverted learning process, they can be on-ramped. This also serves to prime collective acuity early — more folk will be more open to any learning or observations relevant to strategic development.

---

1 | Ideally these two days are held somewhere special, away from the normal context of work. This is so participants can gain better perspective, and also be better able to resist the insidious busyness that pervades most of our work. It's all too tempting to just 'pop back into the office' to finish some tasks (which flags that our attention is more focused on short-term urgencies, and not on longer term strategy).

2 | Ideally, these discussions occur via modern communication platforms or closed internal social networks, so that the conversation can occur asynchronously in a manner distinct from email.

Establish intention and pre-frame behaviour

Discussion during time set aside for strategic development can easily descend into debates around quick fixes for operational issues, or box-ticking activities in which we simply replicate existing thinking. But if you establish a clear intention and a contextual mantra[3] to go with it, your chances of staying focused can be increased.

Likewise, if you know that your team has the tendency to get distracted by emails or phone calls—or if you know of other specific, observable behaviours that diminish the efficacy of your meetings—you can pre-frame your expectations before they occur. With one team I worked with, the CEO simply declared that they were going to be running with phones off during the workshop, and that he trusted folks could manage their time and organise their work to be available and fully present for the workshop. This behaviour was then reinforced throughout the workshop.

Build space and slack into the agenda

In design, white space (or negative space) is important. If you're reading the physical version of this book, you'll notice the white space on either side of the body text. Even more white space is used when we introduce a new chapter. The reason for this is that white space helps to enhance attention, focus and comprehension. Apple does this very well in almost all of its designs—including its website and any keynotes. Google is pretty good at this too—compare google.com with yahoo.com and you'll instantly see what I mean.

The agenda for strategic development is much the same. In fact, it's probably one of the main things I find myself coaching my clients on before running any strategic workshop. The Curse of Efficiency and the size of the investment means that people want to get the most out of the time together. The paradox is that we get more by focusing on less. So, instead of trying to do everything (which achieves nothing), we focus on one thing (which achieves something). Rather than focus on content, we focus on context.

3| A mantra is a statement repeated frequently. 'Will it make the boat go faster?' was a holistic and powerful contextual question frequently used by Sir Peter Blake to help the New Zealand team win the America's Cup in 1995. Every decision was run through this lens. Likewise, you can create a contextual mantra or question to 'holistically focus' your time invested in strategic development.

The other thing we need to do when preparing for strategic development is build in slack. In project management, 'slack' refers to the amount of time that a task can be delayed without causing a delay to subsequent tasks or the overall project. In strategic development, factoring in slack allows us time to explore emergent discussions—important conversations we otherwise could not have anticipated, and that are too important to be rushed or steamrolled by the agenda.

With these principles in mind, we can proceed to review options and make sound strategic decisions.

———————————————

14. Choosing to Choose

And here we are—the crux of it all. The space in which we decide what to progress, and what to kill off. Ignorance may have once been bliss—but now, thanks to an ongoing quest, our strategic decision-making is augmented with the presence of viable alternative options.

Strategy has just got a whole heap trickier. And more effective.

Where we used to be able to simply proceed with default thinking—where we didn't even need to be conscious of our choice (it just happened automatically)—now we must deliberately choose which option to proceed with.

Deliberation is liberation.

And choosing to not choose is still a choice.

Whatever choice we make will have implications for the future relevance of our enterprise. So, let's get into it—no excuses, and no stalling.

MAP YOUR OPTIONS

The first thing we need to do—after re-acquainting ourselves with our current business model and identity (and the emerging incoherence of a future context)—is map out the options available to us.

Note that our focus at this stage is no longer exploration. Rather, it is the gathering of the viable strategic options available for us to choose from (including the 'do nothing' option), so that we can make the best strategic decision.

This is important.

When confronted with complexity, it's easy to feel overwhelmed. This overwhelm is often lessened if we get the complexity out of our heads and into a manageable format. In strategic development, this could take the form of index cards or sticky notes—things that can easily be moved, categorised and grouped.

What it does *not* look like is 300 PowerPoint slides, or an equally long document. That stuff is reference material—it cannot easily be moved, categorised or grouped and so should have been communicated and discussed in the lead-up to the strategic immersion. If we're viewing slides or pages on a computer (or projected on a screen) we are forced to work with one slide or page at a time, and we must move through the document sequentially. We don't get context. And besides—our attention should be on strategic discussion and debate, not fixated on a screen.

Also, we must strive to minimise decision fatigue. This is the phenomenon in which the quality and rationality of our decisions deteriorates in proportion to the number of decisions we have to make. 'Decision fatigue' can also lead to decision avoidance. A paradox exists here, of course: we think we want choice—and Quest-Augmented Strategy provides it—but too much choice can be disempowering.

This is where default thinking comes to the rescue.

Anything that does not require thorough, considered and pioneering thinking ought to be left to default thinking. President Barack Obama deliberately automates what he wears (the same suit, every day) and delegates other routine decisions (like what to eat) to his staff. He takes this approach in a deliberate attempt to minimise decision fatigue.

So, when the time comes for strategic decision-making—keep it simple and focused. By all means, have reference material on hand, in case it is needed. But do not let it get in the way of good thinking. Streamline. Use visual tools like the Business Model Canvas (mentioned in chapter 7; see www.businessmodelgeneration.com/canvas/bmc), and limit yourself to the range of viable options you have gathered.

An abridged conversation might look like this:

> Here's where we are now [business model] and here's what's on the horizon [possible future contexts]. As you all well know by now, here's where our current business model and identity might be rendered incoherent or unviable [specific elements of the business model at strategic risk] and here are the opportunities for new value, if we play our cards right. We have several viable options to consider...

And then, the discussions commence—or, rather, continue. But now we have space and time to dedicate to thorough thinking—an approach that just may see us overcome our individual and collective cognitive biases, if we have the acuity for it.

A BIAS TOWARDS BIAS

The work of psychologist and Nobel Prize Laureate Daniel KaÙeman highlights, in his words, 'our almost unlimited ability to ignore our ignorance'.

Typically, this manifests as cognitive biases—patterns of deviation in our judgement which see us make illogical or irrational decisions.[1]

Our own cognitive bias can be hard to catch in ourselves, because it is with us all the time. Much like default thinking, these are cognitive shortcuts we take without conscious or deliberate thought.

Only through thorough questioning and reflection, and shared group acuity, are we able to challenge the possibility of cognitive bias when it emerges. And it takes a mature leadership team to be able to do this—*particularly* in the midst of strategic decision-making.

Whether you like it or not, cognitive bias is going to happen. The question is, how severely will it influence the strategic decision-making of your team?

---

1 | Which is possibly the last thing we want to be doing with regards to enterprise strategy.

BEMUSING BIASES

Well over a hundred different cognitive biases affect the way we think and decide—you can easily search for them online. But here's a list of the main ones to watch out for in the context of strategic decision-making:

◊ **Ambiguity effect**—in which our decision-making is affected by a lack of certainty. We tend to select the options for which the probability of a desired outcome is known, over options in which the probability is unknown. This can result in people avoiding strategic options where information is missing. Gathering evidence through experiments can mitigate the effect of missing information—but never completely.

◊ **Anchoring bias**—in which we become overly reliant on the first piece of information we hear. This is particularly important in relation to the sequence of options presented.

◊ **Availability heuristic**—in which we overestimate the likelihood of events that are more 'available' (recent, unusual or emotionally charged) in our memories. For example, if someone on the team once lost a heap of data using a cloud-based service, they may warn heavily against using cloud-based services (perceiving that the risk of a similar event occurring again is quite high).

◊ **The bandwagon effect**—in which we adopt beliefs, ideas and fads the more they are adopted by others. I suspect this is where 'Let's build an app!' came from—people saw other businesses building apps and thought they ought to build one too. And so they proceed to build crappy apps of no strategic merit. Beware the bandwagon!

◊ **Base rate fallacy**—in which we jump to conclusions, ignoring available statistical data in favour of specific data to make a probability judgment. Repeated experiments should serve to mitigate this, but being mindful of this bias may help you avoid poor judgements.

◊ **Bias blind spot** — in which we easily recognise biases in the judgements of others, but fail to see the impact of biases on our own judgement. I frequently fall into this trap, and this is partly related to the **introspection illusion** — a cognitive bias in which we wrongly think we have clear and direct insight into the origins of our thoughts and our mental state (whereas others do not). The heartening thing to always remember is that we are frequently just as flawed in our thinking as everyone else.[2]

◊ **Confirmation bias** — in which we look for, interpret and recall information in a way that confirms our own hypotheses and beliefs. We need to watch for confirmation bias throughout our experimentation and strategic decision-making — you may favour a particular option to an unreasonable extent, for example.

◊ **Conservatism bias** — in which we believe prior evidence more than new evidence that has emerged. This can be a good element of the scientific method, in which we are sceptical of new discoveries and seek to disprove them with more rigorous analysis. But we can get carried away. People were slow to accept the fact that the Earth was round because they maintained their earlier understanding that it was flat.

◊ **The curse of knowledge** — in which we find it extremely difficult to think about problems from the perspective of folks who are less informed. Sometimes, because we are so close to our knowledge, we tend to undervalue it. We think, *everyone knows this, surely* — but they don't. Just because you've been monitoring feeds and watching the drivers of change for months in relation to a specific option, it doesn't mean that

---

2| 'Pah! Speak for yourself!' you say. #irony

(continued)

BEMUSING BIASES *(cont'd)*

others share your knowledge. The ability to overcome this curse is an important trait of pioneering leadership. Doing so re-opens the gates to cognitive empathy.

◊ **False-consensus bias** — in which we overestimate the extent to which our opinions are typical of those around us. We assume that our opinions, beliefs, preferences, values and habits are normal and that others also think the same way. This bias calls to attention the need to actively seek diversity.

◊ **The framing effect** — in which we react to a particular choice in different ways, depending on how it is presented. Loss is perceived as more significant than gain. For example, in research published in the *Journal of Economic Behaviour & Organisation* it was found that 93 per cent of PhD students registered early when a penalty fee for late registration was emphasised — but only 67 per cent did so when the same choice was presented as a discount for earlier registration. I've been using the framing effect extensively in this book to emphasise the mitigation of strategic risk within the threat of future incoherence. I also present the opportunity for positive outcomes — but focusing on this is unlikely to get cut-through. You'll also notice we use this framing effect (to good effect) when presenting viable alternative options.

◊ **Hindsight bias** — in which we see certain phenomena as predictable, despite having had little evidence or any objective basis for predicting it. This is where 'creeping determinism' sees people declare that they 'knew it all along'.[3] It's a complicated phenomenon that has even been found to cause memory distortion (possibly our own subconscious attempts to reconcile cognitive dissonance). You'll see this occur in your team.

The highly sceptical person will — after critiquing every step of the processes — declare that they always knew a particular strategic option was the best way to go.

---

3 | Well, why didn't you mention this earlier, eh?

◊ **Hyperbolic discounting**—in which we opt for immediate pay-offs rather than larger gains later on. This bias is further enhanced where short-term goals are incentivised and reported on in regular intervals. In this environment, people will choose pathways that result in quicker pay-offs—rather than explore less-certain pathways that may reap bigger rewards in the mid to long term.

◊ **Illusionary truth bias**—in which we believe information to be correct because we are exposed to it frequently. This is something to be mindful of when monitoring information feeds and the drivers of change. Chances are you'll be exposed more frequently to a particular phenomenon, and so may attribute more 'truth' to it than it actually warrants. At the same time, this is a bias you can exploit—by sharing information about emerging phenomena more frequently, others are more likely to believe it to be true.

◊ **Information bias**—in which we believe that the more information we can acquire to make a decision, the better. Even if that extra information is irrelevant to the decision. This is a good bias to check if anyone seems to be stalling in strategic decision-making—choosing to not choose until we have more information is still a choice. And it may be influenced by a distorted evaluation of the importance of more information.

◊ **Normality bias**—in which we underestimate the possibility of a disaster (and the effect it would bring). This can result in situations where we fail to adequately prepare for major disruption because, 'Well, since it hasn't happened before, it never will.' We tend to interpret warnings in the most optimistic way possible—seizing upon ambiguities in order to infer that the situation is less dire.[4] This can result in being unable to cope once such a thing does occur.

---

4 | Oh look, the Kraken. A sign of good luck I believe—friend o' the whales and whatnot, amirite?

(continued)

BEMUSING BIASES *(cont'd)*

◊ **Omission bias** — in which we tend to prefer inaction to action. We judge harmful actions (like cannibalising our own business) as worse than equally or potentially more harmful omissions/inactions (like doing nothing, and therefore allowing a competitor to eat into our business) because actions are more obvious than inactions. In the zombie apocalypse, this is a tough one — do we chop off a bitten limb to potentially save a victim, or do we do nothing? Omission bias would have us choose the latter.

◊ **Optimism bias** — in which we believe that we are less at risk of experiencing a negative event compared to others. Lovely as this is, this thinking is not prudent. An abundance of optimism untempered by scepticism can leave us more vulnerable to legitimate threats.[5] We need to be mindful of this bias — particularly when working with conservative peers.

◊ **The ostrich effect** — in which we choose to ignore dangerous or negative information by 'burying' our head in the sand, like an ostrich.[6] Thankfully, the effort we invest in Quest-Augmented Strategy serves to directly counter this effect. It's hard to ignore the uncomfortable nature of emerging incoherencies when you have invested considerable time exploring and monitoring them.

◊ **Outcome bias** — in which we erroneously judge decisions based upon their outcome, rather than exploring how the judgement was made in the moment. This is a very important bias to be mindful of — particularly in the context of embedding pioneering leadership into workplace culture. Berating people for 'poor decisions' based upon unfavourable outcomes is

---

5 | No matter how much the universe loves us.
6 | They don't actually do this, btw.

very easy. But we must remember: decisions made in a past context did not benefit from the information we have now. The outcome, at that point, was unknown. So, rather than fixate upon the outcome, instead seek to understand the reasoning that influenced their decision. You might find it to be quite sound and, therefore, something to be applauded.

◊ **Pessimism bias**—in which we believe that we are more at risk of experiencing a negative event compared to others. This is the less-desirable flip side to optimism bias and, again, sceptical optimism is the saviour.

◊ **Planning fallacy**—in which we underestimate how much time it will take to complete a task. In my experience, everything takes about 1.2 times longer than your worst-case estimation (but I may be exaggerating). The planning fallacy may set you up for relentless disappointment (where you always feel behind, or that you are not achieving enough). It can also lead to more time-crowding, which diminishes the quality of our thinking (as we seek out defaults and cognitive shortcuts in order to stay on track).

◊ **Social comparison bias**—in which we tend to have feelings of dislike and competitiveness with someone seen physically or mentally better than ourselves. Microsoft once stack-ranked employees, but this only served to amplify social comparison bias and created a *Game of Thrones*-like culture—whereby the highest ranked employees would avoid or undermine their fellow highly ranked peers, lest they lose their own rank and status. In any leadership team (and, indeed, in any workshop, conference, meeting or event), levelling is a much healthier approach.[7] This is where all people become equal within any given context.

7| When beginning a leadership or strategic development program with a diverse team, I'll often deliberately 'apologise' for not recognising if anyone in the room holds rank or is 'kind of a big deal' (to quote *Anchorman*). Instead, I'll emphasise we're all here to [*insert purpose and context*], essentially levelling the playing field.

(continued)

BEMUSING BIASES *(cont'd)*

◊ **Sunk-cost fallacy**—in which we justify increased
investment in a decision or an existing option based
on the cumulative prior investment. This is in spite of
new evidence that suggests that the cost of continuing
outweighs any expected benefits. The thing to listen out
for is when someone says something like, 'But we've
already invested all of this money in *x*—we can't just
pull out now!' Actually, you can. And it may very well
be the most prudent thing to do. This fallacy relates
to loss aversion, which in turn relates to the *framing
effect*. We would much rather avoid loss than acquire
gains—and this is perhaps why default thinking and
operationally driven leadership can be so hard to budge.
Where pioneering leaders are more concerned about
new value, future relevance and meaningful progress,
others are more concerned about the preservation of
existing value.

◊ **Worst-case thinking bias**—in which small deviations
from normality are interpreted as signalling impending
catastrophe and doom. This bias can see us making rash,
unbalanced and abrupt strategic decisions—latching on
to any quick fix or magic wand to ward off a potential
threat before it manifests.

So, there we have it. And that's just a few of the many biases that
influence our ability to make good decisions.[8] If your leadership team
have the discipline and acuity to monitor and question potential areas of
cognitive bias, you should be set to make sound strategic decisions about
which options to progress.

8| And guess what? My selection of these biases is possibly (probably) influenced by my
own cognitive biases! It's also worth noting that the busier we become, the more likely we
are to suffer from cognitive bias and distortion. Curse you, Curse of Efficiency! *shakes
fist at sky*

STOP, START, SAVVY-UP

Having arrayed the viable options available, strategy can be as simple as choosing which activities we must stop, start and savvy-up, if we are to mitigate the inherent threats of an emerging future while unlocking new value and enduring relevance.

What to stop?

Nature abhors a vacuum. In order to create space for new opportunities and ways of working, starting with the things we wish to stop is useful. These can be identified as the elements within your business model that will no longer be relevant or useful in an emerging future context. They may be small, tactical initiatives ('Let's not waste any more money advertising in these channels') to bigger strategical decisions ('Let's exit gracefully from this market — it's no longer relevant to our future direction'). In fact, if you recall the elements of the Business Model Canvas we reviewed in chapter 7, you'll find that any one of the elements can contain things which you can stop. You can axe relationships with key partners, key activities or the use of certain external resources, should they no longer serve your enterprise or business unit in the future.

By starting with the things you wish to stop, you create more space to focus on the thing you wish to start.

What to start?

This is where we review the viable alternative options available, considering them in light of the information we have about emerging future contexts, our potential incoherencies and the opportunities for strategic advantage. This is further weighed against our capacity and capability to execute the steps required to pursue these new pathways.

In many ways, this is not the 'flicking of a switch' but, rather, a 'dialling up of the knob'. Because experimentation has already begun, and because these experiments have been increasingly scaled up, the decision to proceed is actually less about starting, and more about choosing where to shift our emphasis. Experimentation, therefore, continues — just at a larger scale and with much more support (in terms of leadership and funding).

What to savvy-up?

If some things are stopped and some experiments are 'started' (in the sense that they become a part of the main enterprise strategy), we are left with things that are neither stopped nor started. Rather than simply persist with these activities with a business-as-usual approach, strategic development allows us a chance to review and renew the way we do things.

To be savvy means to show shrewd and practical knowledge, and to be aware of the realities of life. To savvy-up, in this context, means using the knowledge we have to ensure that these activities and strategies are being executed in the best way possible. Because these activities aren't 'new', they are easily overlooked in the strategic decision-making process.

Savvying-up these activities might include looking at how we service existing customer segments. Are we doing anything new to add value and nurture key relationships here? Are we surprising and delighting our best customers? Or are we slipping into efficient defaults?

PICK A PATH

Strategic development can easily conclude with one whopping big list of things to do. This list can be intimidating—and, if left unchecked, may see people avoid the anxiety of the challenge inherent in new strategy by instead investing effort in default activities and the Delusion of Progress. Also, we want to ensure that strategic development is enriching and empowering—leaders ought to be excited and empowered in the aftermath.

This can be achieved by creating a shared sense of sequence. Rather than a vertical list of priorities, we instead spread our focus horizontally across a relevant time spectrum. This might include:

◊ **Actions to be completed within the next 24 hours.**
  You know, those small things you said you'd get right onto. Map them out. These could include sourcing or providing supplementary information, securing new domain names and organising important meetings. It's prudent for everyone to schedule an additional half-day or full day *after* strategic development concludes to action

these items (while they are timely and motivation is high). This will help ensure collective momentum is generated after strategic development.

◊ **Tasks to be performed within the next week.** These include things that require a bit more effort—such as creating a summary report of key decisions and accountabilities, and working up a Gantt chart of key projects and initiatives over the coming year. Scheduling a teleconference one week after the conclusion of any strategic development session is also worthwhile. This is primarily to create shared visibility of progress for pioneering work, but will also ensure that all leaders are supported in executing the strategy. A week later, new and unforeseen challenges may become apparent, and having the team support each other through this early on is better than finding out about it later.

◊ **Milestones to be achieved within the next month.** Checking in together in a month's time will further ensure that new strategic initiatives have translated into action. More support can be offered, and various initiatives can be tested for alignment against the bigger strategy. Are things working as intended? Do any adjustments need to be made?

◊ **Projects to be completed within the next quarter.** Now, we switch our focus to your most important projects. In chapters 16 and 21 we discuss this notion in greater detail, but suffice to say projects are the manifestation of strategy. They differ from goals and good intentions in that they have a deliverable and can be clearly assessed as on-track or not. At this point—approximately 90 days after your strategic immersion—you'll want to rally the team back to review progress made. Here another important leadership challenge also emerges—how do you deal with failed projects and setbacks? And how do you support your peers in the pursuit of pioneering growth?

◊ **Initiatives to be implemented within the next
year.** The final things to map out at the end of strategic
development are the bigger initiatives that will—by
this time next year—be well and truly implemented
and underway. At this point, you may wish to
create a tentative placeholder for the next strategic
immersion—an activity that clearly communicates
that this is an ongoing, continuous and infinite process
(while at the same time creating a container for strategic
activities).

Freedom follows focus, and this sequence gives you the freedom to
focus. By taking this approach, we don't need to focus on *everything* all
at once—we can focus on the right things at the right time in the right
sequence. At the end of any strategic immersion, we don't just have a
list of additional tasks and projects to complete on top of our existing
work—we have a game plan for making pioneering strategy happen.

15. Strategy for Breakfast

It is commonly said that 'culture eats strategy for breakfast'. I daresay this is because breakfast is the most important meal of the day, and good strategy is so nourishing.

Just because we have a potentially brilliant strategy doesn't mean we can then simply make upward flapping gestures at the rest of the organisation and say, 'Make it so!'

Strategy needs to be communicated effectively—and frequently.

And just like you don't hide a good breakfast right at the back of the cupboard, you don't hide good strategy behind layers of hierarchy, or buried deep within bloated PowerPoint presentations or documents on the intranet.[1]

BUT CHANGE IS GOOD, RIGHT?

In theory, yes, change is good. But in practice—not necessarily. At least, not for everyone. Some of the 'stop' decisions from the previous chapter may mean making tough decisions, which could mean redundancies

---

1 | If this is the case—if people can't find a good breakfast—they'll default to whatever is easily available—like sticking a teaspoon into that dubious jar of peanut butter. Or that old set of performance metrics that is familiar and yet no longer aligned to the new strategy.

and a cutting back of investment in some business units. These tough decisions are normally dressed in corporate code—we use terms like 'downsizing', 'productivity' and 'working smarter' to explain what is also people losing their jobs.[2]

But—if you're playing your cards right—this type of thing should actually come as little surprise to your people. You'll have been openly communicating on internal platforms, and sharing learning and the collective hunches about where the enterprise needs to turn to. You'll be supportive of intrapreneurship, and will have been dialling up the efforts of internal experiments. When people hear of the new strategic direction, it will make a certain kind of sense (thanks to the extensive monitoring of the drivers of change, and the accumulation of evidence via internal experiments).

But! If people are ambushed by change—if they don't understand, appreciate or connect with the direction that is set, or the purpose informing it (the 'why')—that change will very likely be resisted.

When goals and targets shift autocratically, or when leadership is perceived to lack the conviction to truly lead courageous, game-changing and pioneering strategy, or when deep-seated cultural issues[3] have not been addressed, then we'll see people defaulting to their defaults. We have a finite amount of time, energy and attention each day, so investing our efforts in things that provide a sense of progress makes sense. If people can't find meaningful progress in their work, they'll try to find it in other things—like micromanaging direct reports, making spreadsheets, or playing Candy Crush.

John Kotter (Emeritus Professor of Leadership at the Harvard Business School) has identified some common dysfunctional patterns among leaders driving change. In one such pattern, leaders actually do a very good job of capturing a pioneering strategy and vision for transformation—but then they proceed to communicate this vision in a single conference or meeting, or through a single missive. 'Having used about 0.0001 per cent of the yearly intracompany communication budget, the group is startled that few people understand the new approach,' Kotter observes.

2| *Dealing with the Tough Stuff,* by Darren Hill, Alison Hill and Dr Sean Richardson, is a great book for these conversations, which are part and parcel of good leadership.

3| Things like a stigma around failure, distrust of leadership, and behaviour distortion from overly incentivised leaders and managers. Not to mention politics and tiny empires.

In another pattern, much more effort goes into meetings, newsletters, 'town hall' presentations, open Q&A sessions, and so on — but some very visible senior leaders still behave in ways that are incongruent with the new vision. The result is more cynicism within the workplace culture, and increased distrust in leaders and their communications.

When translating strategic decisions into meaningful progress, transparency, and authentic communication in leadership is critical.[4] Quest-Augmented Strategy thrives in a networked enterprise, in which communication can easily occur across all elements of the business.

NETWORKED ENTERPRISE GOODNESS

In 1992, anthropologist Robin Dunbar published a groundbreaking paper exploring the cognitive limit to the number of people with whom we can maintain stable social relationships. The optimal group size lies somewhere between 100 and 250 people (with the commonly used value being 150).

When the total number of employees in an enterprise grows beyond 150 people, this likely also comes with cultural implications. Things begin to take on more of a rigid, corporate feel.[5] It's insidious. New policies and procedures get introduced, and things begin to feel more 'structured'. For those who value operational efficiency,[6] this could be a welcome change.

But those who value connection[7] will lament the additional barriers and friction that begin to get in the way of communication and relationships. Where once the workplace felt like working with friends (your 'second family'), it now feels institutional and less human; less organic and more clinical.[8] At its worst, we have a risk-averse, rule-bound, lifeless and impersonal organisation in which people file in like drones to tick boxes, follow instructions and churn through default processes — and where

---

4 | Leadership behaviours congruent to strategy and desired culture are also essential. We explore these in part VII.

5 | Here is also where we may be shifting from the 'crazy growth phase' to the 'plateau of maturity' on the enterprise growth arc (refer to chapter 3 and figure 3.1).

6 | Something we should all value — but only to an extent.

7 | Something we should all value — to an infinite extent.

8 | And the trouble is, this feeling is insidious. It's hard to see, unless you have rituals to disrupt the pattern of default thinking and your default growth arc.

the only way to advance things is to play political games with those in positions of authority, higher in the hierarchy.

Translating pioneering strategy in this extreme would be ... difficult.

So what's the solution? Break down all silos? Completely flatten all hierarchies?

Maybe. But as hip as such an approach might sound in our current Zeitgeist, it's fairly dramatic, and could require *massive* reorganisation. And the risk of such an approach is that we'll end up in a similar predicament a few years later.

And besides: silos can be efficient (although 'hub' is perhaps a better concept to embrace).[9] Silos still have an inherent hierarchy within them—which can be fine, if the numbers are small enough and the leadership is good. But this can be equally terrible. A hub (like a silo) groups people according to their expertise/function/location. But, unlike a hierarchy, no barriers exist to informal relationships. Here, people turn up and pitch in to the work that needs to be done. They help each other out, discuss better ways to do things, and get on with the good work of making meaningful progress.[10]

HYDRA DOMINATUS

Here's another way to consider your organisation in a networked context. Have a look at your org chart. If it fits on a page, or if it seems to have a strong sense of order to it, you don't have a networked enterprise. Instead, your enterprise is likely too hierarchical and structured.

Your enterprise is possibly strong and robust—things that were of value during the factory era, in which the work was formulaic and operational efficiency was paramount. In this context, the default approach to organising the work of an enterprise was to create structure and rules to unlock economies of scale.

9| Much like the hub of a wheel—the central node into which spokes feed—hubs within an enterprise are nodes that exist among other inter-webbed nodes.

10| Here, hubs have their own team rituals to stitch the fabric of their culture together (see chapter 21 for more).

But in our current and emerging context, *robust* is actually quite fragile.[11] Like an iron sword, a robust enterprise can break.

The alternative is to shift towards a more 'antifragile' or responsive organisational structure. *Antifragility* is a term coined by risk analysis and scholar Nassim Nicholas Taleb to describe a state beyond resilience or robustness. Where resilient systems resist shocks and stay the same, antifragile systems get better.

Think of it like the hydra—the mythical multi-headed beast. Chop one of its heads off, and two grow back in its place. Even the Inevitable Kraken of Doom can't stomach the antifragile hydra.

Such systems *thrive* on disorder and change, thanks to an inherent bias towards learning and adaptability. They have in-built, non-linear redundancies and backup plans that only get better with exposure to more external stressors. They are *stronger* for being tested.

Naturally this is all very exciting, but does this mean we need to throw out all of the structures we have? And, if so, where do we even start?

Why, with a quest of course.

Any large incumbent enterprises ought to be exploring more responsive ways of working.[12] What does this involve? Gathering options,

---

11| And possibly one of the main incoherencies to emerge across multiple future contexts—something your team ought to review, if you aren't already. #hottip

12| It's an imperative. Tarry not.

conducting experiments and making strategic decisions that enable enduring relevance and growth. If you're savvy about the incoherence of an unresponsive organisation, it'll become a mighty important thing to monitor and explore.

The more progressive an organisation becomes, the more the distinctions between the quadrants in Quest-Augmented Strategy become blurred. This is part and parcel of a networked organisation.

Within networked organisations, you need to consider two main elements:

◊ **Clustering.** This refers to the degree in which you have hubs or nodes—tightly knit groups where collaboration occurs naturally, due to a shared proximity and/or focus. If the hierarchy is rigid, you might call them silos. But if you have distributed authority, transparent communication and minimal management, you might think of clusters as the (antifragile) hubs or nodes of your enterprise network.

◊ **Path length.** This refers to the number of links separating any two nodes within the network.

We frequently hear talk about 'breaking down silos'—but doing so might threaten the efficiency and power of our tightly knit collaborative hubs. A better thing to focus on is *reducing the path length* between hubs. This is where we seek to minimise the friction between disparate nodes and hubs. By doing this, we open up the opportunity for more informal relationships and connections to occur between nodes—and, as a result, the enterprise as a whole moves closer towards a state that is more responsive and adaptive to pioneering strategy.

The quickest way to do this? Through your internal communication platforms.

A good internal communications network will effectively punch holes between nodes. Where connections in a traditional enterprise might otherwise take weeks or months to establish (by the time you wade through hierarchy, permissions, time differences, and so on), an effective internal communications network could see that same connection happen almost instantly.

This allows intrapreneurial hubs to form organically, and to easily rally together (no matter their function or geographical location) in order to progress your most important projects.

Of course, such gains will only happen if strategic intent is translated into the leadership behaviours that matter (see chapter 19), and when coupled with rituals that transcend barriers (like conferences that pull folks together—see chapter 21).

These ideas bring us back to our quest, and the hero's journey.

THE BIGGER QUEST

Leading a quest ought not be restricted to a small pocket of pioneering leaders within an enterprise exploring alternative strategic pathways.

Sure, it might start like this. But if you recall the final element in the hero's journey, at some point the hero returns to the ordinary, default world, bringing with them special *insight* to inform and progress pioneering strategy and growth.

Part of this insight is the pioneering strategy. The other part is the pioneering leadership, in which we can create an environment in which *anyone* can embark upon meaningful quests.

Imagine one of your frontline staff hearing about a frustration from a customer. Instead of just being efficient—quickly dealing with the frustration and then carrying on with business as usual—they get curious. In a short time, they uncover a similar frustration from another customer. A hunch is formed, and they begin to explore. They discuss this with their team—turns out others have noticed a similar frustration. Now a few folks are on the quest, exploring what could be a minor opportunity for strategic advantage. After continued monitoring and many conversations via internal communications, the problem becomes quite clear—a big gap exists between the current offering (or modus operandi) and an emerging market need.

The team reaches out to folks in a similar role in different countries. A special-interest project is created—a virtual hub of activity within the internal network. Articles and ideas are shared, and the drivers of change are monitored. Strategic options begin to appear. Small, smart, safe and short experiments are conducted, and new insight is rapidly obtained. By now, other leaders within the enterprise are aware of this quest. Because curiosity and intrapreneurship is valued, they figure out a way to support increasingly large experiments—directed by those within group. The experiments continue; some 'fail', but all yield profound new insight and learning for the group.

Meanwhile, the time for a senior leadership retreat is getting closer, and potentially integrating the new strategic option (while dialling back other areas of the business) appears to be quite a viable alternative. And so key leaders (easily identifiable from the internal communications platform or network) are invited to contribute to conversations leading up to the strategic retreat. New concerns and 'what ifs' are thrown at them, to which they are able to quickly gather new intelligence and responses. By the time the leaders meet, the decision to integrate this new strategic option into the main enterprise strategy is pretty clear. A path is chosen, and a new default is formed.

Because this happened via a transparent communications platform,[13] the new shift comes as no surprise. And because this strategic pathway originated from the frontline, a whole heap of empathy comes with it. The result? Everyone wins, and meaningful progress is made.

Now imagine if that were the norm. Imagine if curiosity—and the gumption to pursue meaningful progress—was the default across all units in your enterprise. Imagine if authority and autonomy were distributed appropriately, empowering connected hubs to work together to pioneer new growth and unlock enduring (antifragile) relevance.[14]

Speaking of progress...

---

13 | Transparent? Yes! So much information is readily accessible that it's nearly impossible to determine what information might be useful, and who might be best placed to use it, and when, and so on. Rather than attempt to bottle it up and distribute this information in a careful, controlled manner, it is now much more prudent (for speed, agility and responsiveness) to allow our people the autonomy and authority to act on it as they see fit. The benefits of trusting people to do so far outweigh the alternative.

14 | I'm far from the first to imagine this. Check out responsive.org and join the movement.

IT NEEDS TO START SOMEWHERE

Quest-Augmented Strategy is a framework to enable better strategic decision-making and leadership. It enables a more pioneering approach to enterprise growth.

But this can originate at any level within the enterprise. Even if you feel as though you're currently just a tiny speck within the belly of a behemoth enterprise, ways to build and demonstrate pioneering leadership are available.

In part VI we shift our focus to progress—or, more specifically, to how we get on with the *doing* that's required to make meaningful progress.

Summary

Part V

◊ Quest-Augmented Strategy allows decision-making to be enriched with a range of viable alternative options. Without such options, strategic decision-making is limited to default thinking and premature hunches.

◊ The context in which strategic decisions are made is important. Ideally, strategic immersions are an ongoing ritual in which ample time is dedicated to thorough thinking (both in the learning leading up to the immersion, and in the space and time available at the immersion). Strategic decision-making is not served by tight timeframes and a packed agenda.

◊ Where possible, decision fatigue should be minimised. This means doing work beforehand to limit the focus and discussions to reassessing future contexts, incoherencies and viable alternative options. Any reference material needs to be streamlined.

◊ In addition to decision fatigue, we are all beset by myriad cognitive biases. This is inescapable — although with time, thorough thinking, diversity, good questioning and acuity for potentially flawed reasoning, we can limit or mitigate the effects of such biases.

◊   Once options are mapped out, strategy can be as simple as
    deciding what activities to stop, what to start, and what to
    'savvy-up' or improve. Experimentation means that many
    viable alternative options are less risky — we are not starting
    from scratch, and so to 'start' to integrate these into the main
    enterprise strategy simply means scaling up experiments.

◊   Before leaving any strategic immersion, people ought to be
    clear on any actions and tasks to be completed within the
    following days and week. Milestones and projects' deliverables
    should also be mapped out for the next quarter, and key
    initiatives should be identified for the next year. While you
    are together, placing a tentative schedule on next year's
    immersion is worthwhile (if only to anchor that this is an
    ongoing, continuous and infinite process).

◊   Once a new strategic pathway or direction is determined,
    it needs to be communicated effectively. Change will likely
    involve stopping some activities, which can involve leaders
    having to have tough conversations. The resistance to
    change is amplified if people feel 'ambushed' by it, or if little
    communication has occurred in the lead-up to and aftermath
    of strategic decision-making.

◊   Pioneering strategy is developed and disseminated much more
    effectively within networked organisations. As opposed to
    traditional, hierarchical organisation structures, a networked
    organisation consists of tightly woven interconnected hubs.
    When authority and autonomy is distributed, these hubs can
    become 'antifragile'. Such hubs only get better when exposed
    to external stressors and change. If your enterprise has an
    effective internal communications platform, communication
    between hubs can be further enhanced — resulting in a much
    more responsive organisation.

◊   A more responsive organisation can ultimately mean that
    more people are empowered to lead quests — exploring new
    options that may enrich strategic decision-making and enable
    the enterprise to unlock new value and enduring relevance.

◊   Quest-Augmented Strategy needs to start somewhere.
    Even if you don't currently hold a leadership role with
    influence or authority, you can still take steps to build and
    demonstrate pioneering leadership. This starts with identifying
    meaningful progress.

———————————

Making Progress

Progress [noun]: development towards a more
advanced or improved condition.

S o what are we to do with this new, pioneering strategy? Why, we
get on with the work of making meaningful *progress.*

This is the final quadrant of the Quest-Augmented Strategy
framework introduced in chapter 5 (see figure 5.1 on p. 60). Although,
as you might have noticed in parts IV and V (and figure 11.1 on p.
142), the lines between each quadrant can quickly become blurred.
The more your enterprise shifts to becoming a responsive organisation,
the more autonomy and authority are distributed across your internal
network—the less relevant the Quest-Augmented Strategy framework
will be. Why? Because it'll be part of the very fabric of how your enterprise
works.

Paradoxically, pioneering beyond default thinking will become the
default—if we allow it.

But such an advanced condition might be a while away for your enterprise.
In part VI we focus on how you can establish intrapreneurial hubs and
ensure that pioneering strategy is effectively executed.

16. Bimodal Beginnings

O ur transition from strategic decision-making to operational execution ought not be too dissimilar to how we shift from optionality to experimentation. If we are attuned to dissociated metacognition and have the ability to reflect on our own individual and collective decisions, progress and leadership, then *everything* becomes an experiment to progress and learn from.

But not everyone readily shares this philosophy and awareness. And besides, everyone is busy, and we still have the Curse of Efficiency to contend with.

We can't force change across a whole enterprise.[1] If we are to make headway and break new ground, we need to get bimodal.

WORKING ACROSS TWO MODES

Bimodal is a statistical term denoting a continuous probability distribution within two different modes. It's also a term IT research and advisory firm Gartner introduced to describe a scenario in which an enterprise splits its IT function into two distinct modes. *Bimodal IT,* they call it—where one mode could be described as traditional, emphasising safety, accuracy

---

1 | Or, we can. But it won't work well, and we may find ourselves back in a similar position in a relatively short period of time. Better to grow it.

and predictability, and the other could be described as agile, emphasising agility, speed and efficacy.

Both modes need to work in tandem. Trouble starts when we try to bring the thinking of the old (established) mode into the territory of the new (explorative) one.

I'm sure you can see the similarities here. What Gartner is essentially proposing is that we run with default modes while also creating space to build and grow more pioneering modes.

This approach can be extended throughout any part of your enterprise.

Some of the clusters/nodes/silos/hubs in your enterprise will need to stay focused on the default/established/conventional/traditional modes of business.[2] These may be the types of activities that allow very little tolerance for error or failure—such as manufacturing, distribution and workplace safety.[3] And so we let them do their thing, all safe, predictable and efficient-like.

But that same thinking cannot be applied to the more pioneering elements of your enterprise strategy. In order to progress and execute these elements, we need a different kind of team that works in a different kind of way.

NEW TEAMS

One of your early challenges will be identifying a small team—one that shares a similar strategic focus—and giving them more authority and autonomy to progress a key element of pioneering strategy.

Naturally, you'll want to assess their willingness and aptitude for pioneering work first. Don't choose a bunch of tyre-kickers and digital laggards; at the same time, however, don't underestimate people's ability to adapt to new ways of working.

---

2 | At least, for now.

3 | But … default thinking can be dangerous here, too, if it's done blindly. If we are simply taking cognitive shortcuts to maximise efficiency—defaulting to established ways of doing things—we may be missing something critical.

The formation (or mini 're-organisation') of this team might involve the inclusion of new talent—folks who have worked in startups outside the enterprise. Such folks won't have been indoctrinated into existing cultural norms, and will bring a fresh perspective that may mitigate the inclination to return to the now 'old' (default) ways of doing things. At the same time, the savvy folks who have been with your enterprise for a while will have enough understanding of the wider enterprise ecology to ensure that work is progressed effectively. They'll know what channels are most effective to pursue, and which stakeholders to be most mindful of.

Our intention here is to embrace (and lead) a new way of working.[4]

FINITE GAMES

The infinite game we're playing includes leading a new way of working (within the bigger infinite context of enduring value and relevance). New teams should be aware of this—this is the bigger, pioneering purpose they serve.

And yet, at the same time giving new teams a finite game to play is useful—that is, giving them a tighter focus that serves to capture and distribute new value to the enterprise. The tension between exploration and execution is something that new teams will need to dance within, because we do not want to become lost in either.

In *The Game Changer* I introduced a simple definition for games that can be applied here. All games are the interplay of goals, rules and feedback. A good game is a goal-driven, challenge-intense and feedback-rich experience geared towards progress. These three components correlate to modern elements of intrinsic motivation—the motivation inherent within the work itself (as distinct from extrinsic or internal drivers). These elements are purpose, mastery and autonomy.[5]

4| Of course, strategy can simply be prescribed to business units and existing teams. In this model, once a directive is declared and delegated, goals, targets, key performance indicators and other metrics can be set—allowing the unit to simply proceed to execute as per busyness as usual. This may be an approach that's apt for the established (old) mode of working, but it will not capitalise on the richness inherent within new ways of working.

5| Of course, motivation is much more complex than this. But these elements serve to cover the main fields of intrinsic motivation. To learn more, check out the fine work of Daniel Pink and his book *Drive: The surprising truth about what motivates us.*

Goals link to *purpose*, and serve as a focal point for our efforts. But, within this new way of working, our goals are lightly held. We don't anchor them down with specific incentives, and as such we can adapt them to serve the greater purpose as our learning grows.

Rules link to *mastery*. We need parameters in order to focus our efforts. By actively anticipating constraints, we enhance our creativity and ability to create more relevant and meaningful progress. The reason many people choose to play board games, sport games or video games is because of the inherent challenge within them. We could all be very efficient at the game of golf if we wanted to—we could simply walk up to the hole and drop the ball directly into it, thereby 'winning' without even taking a shot. But, of course, games don't work like this—they have rules to make them difficult. People don't play games to avoid work but to engage in *well-designed* work. With new ways of working, we have a chance to continually design and redesign the way we work, to ensure that the rules we play by are keeping us challenged and on track for meaningful progress.

Feedback links to *autonomy*. If the latency between our effort and meaningful feedback is minimal, we are more likely to continue to invest effort into things. What this means for our new ways of working is that we need to keep feedback loops tight. Experimentation ought to be progressed rapidly, with updates occurring regularly (see chapter 21). Whereas in traditional business units people may find a sense of progress by referring to default measures, in new ways of working the 'default' is always shifting. Our reference point comes from conversation and shared learning with the team, which works because of how tightly clustered and connected the team is (see chapter 17).

Essentially, by creating new ways of working, you're creating a new game. You're directly answering the question, 'If we were to start again from scratch today, what would we do differently?'

And you're doing it—initially, at a small and considered scale, and attached to a focused new stream of value for the enterprise. Why? Because, much like with the experimentation to establish the viability of different options, here you are establishing the viability of new ways of working.[6]

6| And, of course, if it doesn't work, the ramifications are minimal. This follows a very similar pathway to the experimental approach outlined in chapter 10 (see figure 10.1 on p. 133). In this instance, 'new ways of working' becomes the option we seek to validate.

PROTECT AGAINST INFECTION

These new ways of working will likely be an affront to other, more conservative elements and people within your enterprise—at least initially.

And, like the white blood cells in our immune system that protect us from infections and foreign invaders, elements within the larger enterprise system will seek to protect it from foreign (new) ways of working.

Well—two can play at that.

As a pioneering leader, one of the most important roles you will play is in the *defence* of new ways of working. The last thing you want to see happen is this new way of working becoming contaminated with old things like heavily weighted scorecards, ridiculously tokenistic compliance measures from HR, or anything that detracts the new team from their mission, meaningful progress and the bigger purpose they serve.

By reducing the cascade of rubbish defaults and the admin burden a new team might otherwise endure, you're ensuring they can better focus on new thinking and generating meaningful progress.

DIAL UP DIVERSITY

Given that you're looking to keep things small at first, the initial team needs to have a diverse enough set of multidisciplinary skills and talent density to proceed with autonomy.

But, inevitably, gaps in skills and capabilities will become apparent as time progresses. If you're distributing authority well, this new team will function much like an embedded startup. Therefore, if they need talent, they will have the authority to hire it (just like a startup would). In this instance, you'll have another opportunity to protect the team from unnecessary admin burden—preserving their ability to be self-sufficient.

MAKE PROGRESS VISIBLE

At this stage, other teams working in more traditional modes likely become jealous of this new team. Why do they get to have all the fun? What are these cowboys doing? It's not fair. How come they get to eat pizza in the office? They're a bunch of loose cannons, and a threat to the business. And so on.[7]

Stories can get out of hand, and our intention here is not to create an 'us and them' mentality[8] but, rather, to demonstrate the benefits of this new mode of working. This means that progress needs to be visible and shared frequently.

Depending upon the work this new team is undertaking, this sharing may be challenging—but some novel ways are available. In addition to standard communication pieces (like posting updates, articles and reports onto shared communication platforms) new teams can invite key stakeholders in to work with them. This honours the expertise and work of people from outside their team, and ensures that their efforts remain connected to the wider enterprise.

New teams can also host casual learning events—inviting folks from other teams along to participate in a shared update on work completed, and the new things learned (see chapter 21). This provides a chance for other teams to see the contribution this new team is making. As a result, everyone learns more, and new teams endear themselves further to the enterprise by demonstrating the value of their work.

7| What other teams may not see or hear about are the late hours this team pulls to progress an important project. Or how all team members self-regulate their hours of work—with many going above and beyond the call of duty to make a difference. From an outside perspective, people may see a lack of order and mess—but, from the inside, this team is clearly progressing breakthroughs in weeks, instead of the months a traditional team would take.

8| At least, not in a negative sense. It works to our favour, however, if more teams and leaders want to shift towards this new way of working—because this will only serve to speed up our progress towards a more responsive organisation.

SPREAD THE INFLUENCE

Much like our experimentations in part IV, the adoption of new ways of working is something that can scale. Rather than force other business units and teams to adopt these new ways, we simply demonstrate the value of them, and allow them to make the shift themselves. When more teams in the enterprise are comfortable with this new way of working, and when they see the results, appetite for this kind of pioneering progress and change may greatly increase. The learning from all the mistakes made with the first new team can also be incorporated—which should serve to smooth out some of the kinks in the process as other teams switch from the old mode to a new mode of working.

Don't force it, don't rush it. But by all means accelerate, catalyse and promote it. By starting with a bimodal approach—a new mode working alongside the old modes—we can begin to unlock meaningful progress relatively quickly and safely.

17. Meaningful Progress

The ultimate purpose of Quest-Augmented Strategy is to *enable* an enterprise to explore, find, validate, integrate and pursue viable strategic options that ensure its business model and identity remain viable into the future.

Meaningful progress is the antithesis of stagnation and decline.

Through meaningful progress, an enterprise maintains enduring value and relevance. And meaningful progress sees an enterprise outfox the Inevitable Kraken of Doom—by not only identifying new potential growth arcs, but also having the pioneering leadership and adaptive work culture to pursue them.

But this may still seem pretty vague and wordy. How do we really know what constitutes meaningful progress?

FINDING A SENSE OF PROGRESS

We can go about finding a sense of progress in at least two main ways.

We can easily measure progress quantitatively (with numbers). Using this approach, we declare our objectives, establish milestones and create a visible, clear and measurable sense of progress. We see what we are striving towards, and we reverse-engineer the steps to get there. And the clearer the goal, the easier it is for progress to be measured.

I occasionally use quantified measures to track progress in my health and fitness goals. This includes an app that clearly communicates how frequently, fast and far I've run within any given period of time. Right now — at the time of writing this book — it has come to my attention that I have developed a bit of a 'writer's physique'.[1] And so I'm now using quantitative measures to track my nutritional goals, too.

For teams working on a mission or a specific project, tapping into a quantified sense of progress can be incredibly motivating. Seeing that you're getting closer to your target allows you to benefit from 'the goal gradient effect' (a sensation in which our motivation and effort increases the closer we get to our goals).[2]

The trouble is, we can get carried away with this approach. It's just too easy. The numbers can provide a clear and immediate sense of progress. They make us feel productive. We have boxes to tick, and we don't have to think so hard.

As we explored in chapter 2, this can create an insidious Delusion of Progress — a scenario in which we avoid the more challenging and ambiguous yet meaningful work, by defaulting to easy/clear tasks that provide a rich and immediate sense of progress. The stronger the goals, measures and incentives, the more likely we are to see behavioural distortion away from the more ambiguous work that matters.

And so, quantifiable measures are not the only way to obtain a sense of progress. Nor are they the most appropriate for explorative work because of the potential incoherencies nested within the inherent complexity of uncertain future contexts.

We must also review progress qualitatively (with words). Here, we reconnect with our overarching strategic intent, and review our efforts in light of what's most important. We establish rituals and strategic rallying points, and gather together to assess what we have learned and how we are tracking. Through doing so, we learn, adapt and recalibrate to change as it emerges.

This sense of progress is grounded in shared conversations — something that should happen regularly. The only way to really 'see' a sense of

---

1 | I blame winter. And the peanut-butter cookies at my local cafe. They are the devil.

2 | The downside of this effect is that we can manufacture a perpetual false sense of urgency in order to benefit from this effect. It works — but it does make for perpetual franticness as we jump from one urgent deadline to another.

progress via qualitative inputs is to craft a time line of the evolving narrative. Short-term progress may be hard to see up close in this way—but if you zoom out to encompass a wider sense of time, great gains can be seen. 'Remember when, this time last year at the conference, we were talking about *x*? I can't believe how far we've come, and how much we've learnt since then!'

Naturally, we need to get a sense of progress from both quantitative and qualitative perspectives. If we are restricted to quantitative measures only, we may lose perspective on what really matters. But by only reviewing progress qualitatively, we may get caught in a spiral of introspection and reflection.

Both of these perspectives are brought to life through our rituals (see chapter 21), but two further perspectives are important in assessing meaningful progress: our areas of responsibility, and our most important projects (discussed in chapter 18).

AREAS OF RESPONSIBILITY

You can measure your progress by assessing how you're progressing in all areas of responsibility. Your responsibility can be infinite, and includes all of the *implicit* things associated with the various roles you play.

You may think this is fairly simple, but the more you move away from a clearly defined role and into the fuzzy territory of leadership, the broader your areas of responsibility become. And that's just one role.

When you also begin to integrate the responsibilities you have from all the other roles you play in your life—partner, parent, daughter or son, and friend to different people—things start to get mighty complex. And, again, thanks to the Delusion of Progress we can find ourselves progressing towards quantified goals while the fuzzier and more implicit elements of our roles suffer. We work really hard to hit targets and numbers...while missing out on family time, neglecting to take care of our health, and/or failing to support the growth and development of our team.

I can't offer a perfect solution to this. If you're striving to achieve balance across all of these areas, however, know that this is only possible over time. Balance does not occur within any given moment. The only thing we can do to ensure we are making meaningful progress across all our areas of responsibility is to create rituals that disrupt our normal pattern of behaviour. Things that pull us out of autopilot, and give us space to reflect and review our work from a space of dissociated metacognition.

(Ah, the joys of writing a linear book. I'd love to discuss rituals right now—but they're in the final chapter. I also fear that, with the number of times I've referenced them, I may have built them up so much that, by the time you do see them, you'll be all like, 'Meh'. And so let's preview one little thing, briefly.)

Daily journalling—especially when combined with a reflection on gratitudes—is an excellent way to safeguard against massive imbalances in your areas of responsibility. This can be as simple as investing ten minutes at the start of your day to reflect upon the day's priorities—the things that constitute meaningful progress—and how you are tracking across your areas of responsibility. By embracing a simple ritual like this, you create space for more thorough thinking, and give yourself a chance to engage in dissociated metacognition and evaluate what is most important.

PROJECTS

The alternative to areas of responsibility when assessing meaningful progress is looking at your most important projects, and the missions we choose to undertake in order to progress important work.

An area of responsibility may seem like an infinite marathon with no finish line, but a well-designed project will have a deliverable. Therefore, it is much more like a sprint. Or a long jog.[3] Or a marathon with a finish line.

Whereas areas of responsibility are implicit, and require an emphasis on qualitative reflection, projects are *explicit*, and benefit from clear quantitative measures. Projects, therefore, happen at many different levels and across many different time frames. Making lunch is a project. Reconciling the accounts for your taxes is a project. Recruiting a new executive is a project. Hosting a dinner party is a project. And so on.

In the next chapter, we explore these ideas in more detail, specifically honing in on our most important projects.

3| It was at this point I realised my metaphor wasn't working.

18. Mission Impossible

Y ou can think of missions as 'projects with imperative'.

In agile methodology, one might call missions *sprints*. In other contexts, one might call them (finite) *games*. Whatever you call them, a few key factors make missions most effective: they need to be compelling, focused and finite.

MISSIONS SERVE A MUST

All missions exist within a meaningful context—a greater imperative that provides a compelling sense of urgency. Missions aren't simply 'nice to haves' and nor are they 'should haves'—they are '*must* haves'.

A sense of purpose is a very powerful element of intrinsic motivation. Within a well-defined mission, almost no questioning occurs around how important it is. This may seem to go against the main philosophy of this book, but when it's time to declare a mission, there is no question—this is what we must do.

At its extreme, we see this spirit manifest during times of crisis. Some of my clients are brilliant in such times—they rally together with a shared sense of purpose and focus, taking on insurmountable challenges because, well, they have no other option.[1] It's just what you gotta do.

---

1 | Examples of this include folks who lead and staff call centres within insurance firms during extreme weather events and natural disasters, and developers and IT staff who rally together in response to a major security incident. Another example might be a team working to pull together a tender in time.

At times like these, people put in extraordinary levels of discretionary effort, because they know their work matters.

While reaching the same levels of commitment generated in a crisis during non-crisis times may be hard, any effort to impart the imperative of important projects will serve to enhance intrinsic motivation. The more people can see that their effort is contributing to something bigger than themselves—something meaningful—the more motivated they will be to contribute.

MISSIONS ARE FOCUSED

When someone is on a mission, they are set to achieve only one thing—their mission objectives. There's no messing around.

Again, this may seem in direct contrast to the main thesis of this book—and it is. Here, we are talking about a *narrowing* of focus, and a striving towards a very specific objective in the short to mid term. This is *totally* the opposite of leading a quest.

But sometimes we need periods of hyperfocus—that is, productivity blitzes to smash through important work. The framing of a mission, and the focus it brings, is particularly useful if the work is formulaic. If you have a precedent to follow, all the better. The mission-critical path can be mapped out and executed with excellence.

The infinite game of enduring relevance will consist of many such missions—finite games strung together with purpose.[2]

MISSIONS ARE FINITE

All missions have a clear start point, time frame and deliverable. Essentially, they are time-bracketed.

A good mission will start with a detailed briefing—something that instils the imperative and importance of the mission (context) while outlining

---

2| There are some caveats, of course. But we'll get to them in a bit.

any relevant parameters/constraints. The objectives will be clear and crisp. No doubt[3] will exist as to what needs to be achieved.

Missions *need* to have end points. They are a defined sprint—not an infinite marathon. End points also allow us to use Parkinson's Law to our advantage—the notion that work expands to fill the time available for its completion. By setting tight, focused missions (or sprints), we can potentially catalyse meaningful progress and growth.

If we don't have an end point, we risk forgetting what our context is—what the meaning of our work is, and the bigger purpose we serve. Without end points, we fixate upon the *what*, and forget the *why*.

A FEW CAVEATS

So: urgent, focused and finite missions. What could possibligh go wrong?[4]

I've made this point previously in *The Game Changer*, and better researchers than myself have compiled several reasons specific goals can be dangerous. To paraphrase the Harvard Business School paper 'Goals Gone Wild: The systematic side effects of over-prescribing goal setting', we need to be very careful with goals. Rather than consider them as harmless 'over-the-counter' treatments for motivation, we need to instead imagine goals as 'prescription-strength medication that requires careful dosing, consideration of harmful side effects, and close supervision.'

If you're going to use specific goals, at least be considered about it. At a self-assigned individual level over a short period of time, you probably have little to worry about. You can self-regulate. Likewise, if you're working in agile sprints with a small team, you'll have in-built rituals and moments to review the relevance of your mission.

But if you assign a new team a goal, you need to be very careful about how you frame it.[5] This is particularly important with a new team demonstrating a new mode of working.

3| No doubt?

4| To paraphrase *The Simpsons*, season six, episode four.

5| The *prescription* element is the key here. Technically, a mission is an important assignment given to a group of people. It's different from them choosing to explore the assignment themselves. By prescribing focus, you remove some autonomy from the individual or team. But, if you can make the why big enough, it may be framed as a choice. *Your mission, should you choose to accept...*

Ideally, we ought to treat goals with the same reverence as we would a mission—only using them if they're really important.

So, know when to declare a mission, and then keep it short, sharp and focused.

The best examples of these usually take the form of 'hackathons'—short but incredibly intense periods of focused work designed to solve a problem and/or develop an innovation. The imperative, focus and time frames[6] for such missions are clear. All barriers to collaboration are removed, and diversity is optimised.[7] Where people would normally be in different office locations, for a hackathon they're all in the same location.[8]

This intense focus can bring about great innovations. For example, Facebook's 'Like' button—what is now one of its most recognisable features and brand assets—was conceived as part of a hackathon.

Australian enterprise software developer Atlassian runs similar events called 'ShipIt' days.[9] Every quarter, teams have twenty-four hours to gather and work on whatever inspires them most—from destroying 'arch nemesis bugs' to projects that improve the workspace. In this instance, the time parameters and the imperative are there—and the focus of the mission emerges.

Now, you may think, *Oh, that's fine for them—they are mostly software companies. We are a bit more traditional.* To which I say, really? Screw that! That doesn't sound pioneering. And besides, if you look at what's happening today, companies are either choosing to act more like a software company—or they're being disrupted by one. So, get experimenting! Do your research, explore options and conduct some small, smart, cheap and safe experiments. You may be surprised by what you can cook up.

Missions can work very well when framed appropriately and used sparingly. The rest of the time? Continue to explore, share, learn and experiment. Embrace rituals that connect and continuously calibrate our efforts towards meaningful progress.

---

6 | Typically twenty-four to forty-eight hours, though some may last a week.

7 | This can be a great time to work with customers, or to combine clusters/hubs/nodes that might otherwise not get a chance to work together as closely.

8 | Or, they're very savvy and connected via live video uplink. But, in any event—they're tight.

9 | Atlassian is a highly connected and responsive organisation—search for a video of its ShipIt days and you'll see what I mean.

Summary

Part VI

◊ The more responsive and connected your enterprise becomes, the more the lines between elements of Quest-Augmented Strategy will blur. This is a good thing.

◊ A bimodal approach sees the facilitation of two distinct modes of work. The traditional (default) mode of work emphasises safety, accuracy and predictability. The other (new) mode emphasises speed, agility and efficacy.

◊ In order to execute pioneering growth for an enterprise, we need to form new modes. These modes can demonstrate and lead new ways of working.

◊ Start by choosing an appropriately pioneering small team. Give them more authority and autonomy, and a clear purpose to pursue—and then try not to intervene. Instead, protect this group from being infected by old ways of working, and support them in being self-sufficient.

◊ When this new team creates visibility of progress in an open and inclusive manner, other elements of the enterprise may wish to adopt this mode of working.

◊ And so we take a similar experimental approach as shared in part IV. By starting small and testing what works, we can begin to 'scale in' or transition more teams into this new mode of working.

◊   Meaningful progress is ultimately the main intention for this. We can measure progress quantitatively, and review it qualitatively. Quantitative measures tend to have more immediate power, but can lead to the Delusion of Progress. We need both.

◊   Areas of responsibility are the things required of us in each of the roles we play. In this context, meaningful progress is implicit and requires us to be able to reflect qualitatively. Daily journalling and regular team conversations help this.

◊   Projects and missions are much more explicit, and benefit greatly from quantitative measures of progress.

◊   Missions are projects with imperative. They are compelling, have a specific goal and are executed within a limited amount of time.

◊   Specific goals carry their dangers, but if we are sparing in our usage of them, the narrowed focus they generate can enable us to facilitate remarkable achievements. Hacakathons and similar intense collaborative efforts are examples of this in action.

———————————

Pioneering Culture

A guide to embedding Pioneering Leadership and
Quest-Augmented Strategy into workplace culture.

I t's so very easy to read a good book, frown sagely, stare upwards to the horizon, nod to yourself and affix a determined aspect... only to proceed to do nothing new or different. Or, to strike a heroic pose — arms akimbo — and proceed with the best intentions ... only to find yourself sucked back into the vortex of non-progressive busywork.

Let's not let this happen.

Regardless of what role you play, you have the ability to influence and shape the culture of your enterprise.[1]

In this book we have unpacked a refreshed approach to (Quest-Augmented) strategy and (pioneering) leadership. In this part, we focus on embedding these elements within leadership and workplace culture — the foundation of any enterprise.

If you recall our rainbow of growth and despair, you'll remember that the arrowhead to our growth curve is determined by three things: strategy, leadership and culture (see figure 4.1 on p. 46). It's the combination of

---

1 | Never underestimate this. All culture change begins with an individual — and you can start today.

these three factors that influence whether an organisation steers towards pioneering growth, new value and enduring relevance—or towards stagnation, decay and the Kraken of Doom.

In the final yet perhaps most fundamental element of *How to Lead a Quest*, we are going to cast our focus on the pivotal behaviours that serve to influence and shape your enterprise culture.

19. Lost in Translation

'Culture' can easily remain an ethereal and nebulous thing, and this is not helped by the way many corporate leaders talk about it. The usual cultural pillars are commonly plastered in corporate taglines and on the back of business cards—excellence, integrity, collaboration, innovation, safety, value, sustainability and so on—and then everyone calls it a day. But the real question is, what do these things *actually mean*, really?

This lack of clarity happens with disturbing frequency. A leader says to their team, 'Folks, we need to communicate with each other better.' Everyone nods—for who can argue with a statement like that?[1] But then, what proceeds may be very different from the intention the leader had in mind.

The leader may think that the team isn't sharing important updates—or that they are, but they're buried away in long email chains. She'd like her team to make more decisions together, in person, or at least through a medium other than email. But some of her team may believe 'communicating better' means, 'I need to send more emails' or 'I need to include more information about what I'm working on' or 'I need to talk with more people in the team before I make a decision.' And then, later, the leader finds herself frustrated as to why her team 'isn't listening' to her. She starts forwarding articles to the team about email

---

1 | It's akin to that person on a teleconference who suggests, 'We need to be strategic', or the CEO who kicks off a conference with, 'We need to be innovative; we need to think outside the box.' Great. So, what does this mean in terms of behaviour?

etiquette. Members of her team think, *Oh, what a good idea to share articles via email!* and then proceed to send even more emails with links to interesting articles. Then come the lol kittehs. And then the team's technology Luddite starts forwarding internet memes we all saw *years* ago. Brimstone, fire and chaos ensue.

FROM CONCEPTUAL TO CONCRETE

Culture becomes clarified when we shift our focus from conceptual notions to concrete examples.

One of the most useful definitions of 'culture' is that it is simply a set of behaviours replicated within a context.

Naturally, many behaviours occur within any given day or period of time — from checking emails to re-tucking your shirt into your pants to chatting with colleagues. But, out of the many things we repeatedly do, some are pivotal. These behaviours help to define a culture.[2]

Getting lost in pretty words is easy. I remember coming in to assist a client and their senior leadership team with the final stages of a new strategic vision. Because I was brought in late in the piece, a lot of groundwork had been completed — to which I could only respectfully nod and listen. But one of the key elements of their strategy 'going forward' was this line: 'We want all staff to feel empowered to improve the business without permission'. The team were quite proud of this.

And I said, 'Great! So, what does this mean?'

To which they replied, 'Well, it means that if our staff see an opportunity to improve the business, they don't need to wait for permission — they can make the changes and improve it!'

When people explain things with repeated phraseology, I know we are in trouble.[3] So I asked for an example of how this might play out. Their eyes darted to each other, some brows were furrowed, and one person

---

2| And they shift, relative to our context (see chapter 21).

3| I was once accosted at an airport by some folks who were trying to sell expensive bottles of special water that was supposedly engineered to help people feel better on long-haul flights. One of the ingredients was 'pine extract'. I asked about it, and they said that pine extract is essentially 'the extract from pine'. Suffice to say, they didn't win me over.

suggested an example. 'Say one of our frontline staff hears a complaint from a customer—maybe the customer didn't understand the application process for one of our products. Well, we'd want our staff to feel empowered to take action and improve it—they don't need to wait for our permission.' I could see other folks didn't quite agree with this example. Someone suggested that they already had a procedure for reviewing insight like this—the feedback gets passed on and reviewed. Another suggested the strategy was more about empowering staff to have ideas that could improve the business—not just reacting to complaints, but also coming up with ideas on how they can proactively improve the business. But when I probed them on this, I discovered the company had no structures or rituals to support this. The leaders had no congruent understanding about how their people could feel empowered in this context.

If left unchecked, this statement could have become another one of those cute lines developed at a leadership off-site event that translates into zero difference to workplace culture.

This is not an uncommon experience. Strategy is angsty work, and because of the Curse of Efficiency, our time is often tight. We can declare victory prematurely,[4] and feel as though we've 'nailed it' with an elegant set of words. But, as is often the case, the devil is in the detail.

What then followed in my discussions with this team was work in translating this strategic intent into the leadership behaviours that will make it happen. The first step in this process is *empathy*.

STORYBOARDING STRATEGY TO CULTURE

If we return to the previous example—the desire to have all staff 'feel empowered to improve the business without permission'—we find we need to ask ourselves a few questions.[5] To address an example like this, you can storyboard the intersection of new strategy and culture to clarify strategic intent and identify opportunities for leadership. The following sections outline how it works.

4| Partly to ease cognitive angst.

5| The same applies to any pivot in strategic intent, if you hope to translate it into a 'new normal' way of doing things.

Develop personas

Firstly, think about the key folks who will be affected by this change, or whose behaviours you want to shift. They might be the frontline staff of a particular business unit, your leaders' own direct reports, or folks from a range of different functions. Create three to five 'avatars' to represent these different personas (simple stick figures can do). Don't worry so much about their personalities, but instead emphasise the 'role' each of these personas undertakes. For example, you might have 'Jill, who works as team leader of our call centre', 'Mohammed, who oversees IT support', 'Moira, who is on the frontline' and so on (as appropriate). For each of these personas, ask: what are their priorities? What is the purpose of their role? What does progress look like in their world? What factors currently influence their behaviour?

Explore scenarios

Having identified relevant personas, the next step is to identify scenarios in which pioneering leadership is required. In the case of our current example, we could explore scenarios in which our various personas might have the opportunity to improve the business 'without permission'. And, having identified the opportunity, we then ask: what might trigger them to act to improve the business without permission? How would they know? What indicates that we value this behaviour, and what can serve to reinforce it?

Map pathways

We then explore the various pathways each of the personas might undertake to achieve the desired strategic intent. They have plenty of pathways to choose—for now, just focus on the obvious ones. Chances are, you'll come across *friction*.

Identify friction

Friction exists between our best intentions and the outcomes we desire. When exploring the pathways various personas may undertake to improve the business, we must be attuned to friction—the stuff that gets in the way, or makes it harder for folks to engage in business improvement. These points are where we have the greatest opportunity to demonstrate leadership and clarify strategic intent.

Find opportunities for leadership

One of the greatest things a leader can do is remove friction. Using our example, imagine a scenario where someone identifies a clear opportunity to improve the business. What pathway do they take? How do leaders ensure that they feel empowered to improve the business, without permission? What does leadership behaviour look like in each of these scenarios, with each persona and at each friction point?

What does it look like if frontline staff come to you with an idea? Do you deflect it to their manager? Or do you thank them and say you'll raise it at the next meeting? And do you? And, either way, how is the person kept updated? What's the feedback loop for them? Do they learn that such initiative is valued, or do they realise its encouragement is just empty corporate-speak? What other ways might your leadership team model the new strategic intent in their own behaviours?

Through this exploration of *how* new strategic intent manifests in everyday work culture, we start to make it real. Such conversations will likely trigger some debate among your leadership team — this is good, because the process will clarify understanding among your team, enhancing the likelihood that strategy will translate into workplace culture.[6]

Here be Dragons. Leaders must be very careful not to become too prescriptive in how they translate strategy. Yes! Another paradox. You see, if we become *too* prescriptive, people stop thinking for themselves. We end up with a new set of policies and procedures, and people simply follow the rules (which is ironic, given our example). We can't just leave the intersection between strategy and culture as a vague yet pithy statement. But we also can't afford to map out every single possible scenario and friction point in which our strategic intent will need to manifest.

Hence, we turn to keystone behaviours.

6| I know; tough, right? Much easier to default to what we always do. Faster, too.*
* But nay! For we are on a hero's journey here. Huzzah! *rattles sabre*

KEYSTONE BEHAVIOURS

Out of myriad possible behaviours you might demonstrate to shift and shape a culture, some are pivotal. We focus on these.

In masonry, a keystone is the stone placed at the summit of an arc, and it has the effect of locking everything in place. Keystone behaviours have a similar effect — they serve to lock everything in place. They are the clear manifestations of enterprise values and strategic intent.

I remember working with a large bank in Australia, and being surprised at how quickly they paid the confirmation invoice for an event that was more than nine months away. In my experience, the larger the organisation, the slower the payment (and the more hoops we need to jump through). I expressed this to one of the organisation's senior leaders, and they informed me that this is very deliberate. 'We value the role small business plays in Australia, and we know what other organisations are like. We make an effort to support small business wherever we can — this is just one example.'[7]

In another example, I remember chatting with the CFO of a large enterprise after running a workshop at their annual event. I had delivered a keynote to their staff the previous day, and had seen the CFO present in the morning. What surprised me was that he not only attended the workshop I facilitated (a mere 'breakout session'), but also actually sat up front, taking notes and asking very considered questions. He was displaying all of the behaviours associated with an avid learner. It's something I don't usually see.

I said as much to him after the workshop, and he explained this hadn't always been the case. His enterprise valued learning — they rightly knew it is what gives them a competitive edge, and the one thing that ensures they stay relevant. But the senior leadership team had noticed their own staff didn't seem to value learning. At similar workshops, staff would often simply check emails, or leave the room to take phone calls. When the CFO and his colleagues reflected on this, they realised that they were modelling the very same behaviour.

---

7 | Actually the conversation didn't happen as formally as this, but you get the gist.

And so, they decided, if learning was truly important to their enterprise — if it was something they valued, and a key element of their strategic intent — then they needed to model it. And so they did, focusing on key behaviours like sitting at the front, taking notes and asking questions at workshops like this. Similar keystone behaviours extended through the enterprise. Leaders would use internal social media platforms to share articles they found that challenged their thinking, or questions they found themselves pondering.

Through a combination of specific keystone behaviours demonstrated over time, they began to notice a discernible shift in how the rest of the enterprise approached learning. This is something you can affect too.

A good discussion for your leaders might lead with the following questions: how might our enterprise values and our strategic intent be represented in our behaviours? And what, specifically, are the keystone behaviours we can rally around?

In the next chapter, we'll explore three elements of culture: structures, artefacts and rituals.

20. Structures, Artefacts and Rituals

In addition to viewing culture as a set of behaviours within a given context (as discussed in chapter 19), it can also be useful to look at culture through an anthropological lens. Here, we identify three elements: structures, artefacts and rituals.

Throughout history, these three components have been present in every culture. And, once attuned, you'll begin to see these elements within any thriving enterprise culture. Let's start with structures.

STRUCTURES

The structures that shape culture can be thought of in two main ways: visible and invisible.

The visible structures within a workplace culture are the physical structures you see — the arrangement of workspaces, the art, the plants, and so on — and these play a key role in influencing a workplace culture.[1] Sometimes you walk into the head offices of an enterprise and immediately think, *Wow, this is different.* Intuitively, you know the space

---

1 | But only *a* key role. As my friend and cultural architect Mykel Dixon says, 'A ping pong table, a few scattered bean bags and a fridge full of craft beer does not a vibrant and engaged community make.'

is conducive to great work—the ceilings are high, the rooms are flooded with natural light and there are plants and art, and a range of different work zones have been created for different types of work.

Other times, you walk into an office and see a warren of monotonous cubicles. You feel as though you need to tiptoe past people, so as not to disturb them. No-one talks to each other—no wait; you can see some people talking over by the coffee machine. But they're speaking in hushed voices. Are they conspiring? Also, it looks like the coffee machine is *well* overdue for a service, and the kitchen is plastered with passive-aggressive reminders to clean up after yourself.

But most of the time you just see the default layout, with no surprises. And much like with default thinking, people begin to stop seeing the environment within which they work. Even simple things—such as what desks look like, and how they are arranged—can go by unquestioned for years.

But when leaders get deliberate about culture, they get deliberate about the physical structure of the work environment.

Valve Corporation, for example, is an enterprise that develops and distributes software. Like many enterprises in a similar game, collaboration is critical to the work they do, and a fundamental element of their culture. This is not just talk—they have designed the physical work environment to ensure that collaboration is as frictionless as possible. One such design feature? The desks have wheels.

In the Valve Employee Handbook (an artefact—we'll get to these in the next section), they suggest employees think of these wheels as a 'symbolic reminder that you should always be considering where you could move yourself to be more valuable. But also think of those wheels as literal wheels, because that's what they are, and you'll be able to actually move your desk with them.' And this is just one of many elements that make up the visible, physical structures that shape work culture.

So, when it comes to your enterprise culture, think about your strategic intent, and about the behaviours you'll need to see more of to drive it. Think of the things you say you value, and that you feel are important for the future of work. And then look at how the physical structure of work either enables or diminishes the things you want more of.

That's how you begin to shape work culture through visible structures.

There could be a whole book on this — in fact, there are. Several.[2] But I should probably move on to the more invisible structures that influence workplace culture.

These structures include policies, procedures, laws, systems, templates, organisational structure, hierarchies, role descriptions and frameworks (among other things).

Perhaps one of the biggest invisible drivers of culture is incentives and rewards. If these are left unchecked, all sorts of behavioural distortions can occur. This may be a career-limiting move on my behalf, but: show me a large multinational enterprise struggling to adapt to change and avoid decline, and I'll likely find senior executives heavily incentivised to hit annual (or quarterly) goals and targets.

Invisible structures also include the platforms we use to communicate and connect with each other. In some enterprises, these structures look like a default computer with default email software installed. Oh, and there's an intranet. Somewhere.

In more pioneering enterprises, the barriers between people are collapsing. If your enterprise values communication and the free sharing of ideas, learning and information — and it should — you ought to be investing in better communication platforms.

Internal and/or business social networks, collaboration and non-email communication tools — when implemented and led well — greatly *diminish* the noise that exists in large enterprises. This sounds counterintuitive, I know, but creating a third space for communications enhances a work culture's ability to make meaningful progress.[3]

Think about it. The two primary communication channels that exist in enterprises today are emails and meetings.

Emails, well. Where do we start? Emails are now a tragedy of the commons, and almost represent a global crisis. We're drowning in

---

2| But if you're interested in learning about the latest innovations and insights in this space, I recommend *Work Design Magazine* (workdesign.com). (I have no affiliation with them, btw.)

3| 'Slack' — a real-time messaging, archiving and search platform — has a simple tagline: 'Be less busy'.

email—and this is because the average time we take to respond to an email is greater, in aggregate, than the time the email took to create.[4] Using email as a platform to progress pioneering work and make meaningful progress—in among the Curse of Efficiency—is a horrendous idea. The channel is already saturated.

But we can't just arrange more meetings—either by phone, online or in-person. Meetings are disruptive. They exact a large toll in terms of people's collective attention, and should only occur as part of a purposeful ritual or learning experience, or because of a considered need to discuss an issue or arrive at a decision. But, even then, we can still leverage a third option.

And this third option looks like modern enterprise social networks, and collaboration and messaging platforms.[5] It's what all the cool kids are doing. As in, literally—look at any fast-growing or innovative company today, and you're almost guaranteed to find an alternative internal communications platform to email. A platform that allows for asynchronous communication and the free sharing of ideas, learning and insights. Something that enables the egalitarian formation of special interest groups that may pursue worthy hunches and contribute timely insight to our active quests.

Email will never go away, and we'll always need meetings. But these new communication structures will eclipse both emails and the number of meetings we need to hold internally, threading the way for more meaningful progress.

And so ends our short tour of the visible and invisible structures that influence culture. Next up: artefacts.

4| A global email charter, emailcharter.org, has been established in an attempt to reverse this (in fact, some of my clients have been inspired by this and created their own internal email charters).

5| I occasionally hear, 'We tried that—didn't work.' After a few questions, I discover none of the enterprise leaders embraced the system or modelled the behaviours they wanted to see. Instead of getting over the initial (and relatively small) learning curve, they defaulted to old habits—namely, emails and meetings—and this cascaded throughout the enterprise. But! If they had taken a more Quest-Augmented approach, things might have been different.

ARTEFACTS

An artefact is the physical manifestation of a culture.[6]

Take the Olympic Torch, for example. Here's a global cultural artefact that is drenched in meaning. At one level, it commemorates Prometheus's theft of fire from Zeus (both from Greek mythology—one the son of a Titan and the other the ruler of the Greek gods). But now it also represents the spirit of the Olympic Games, and great efforts are taken to parade this symbol through countries and keep the flame lit.

Other recognisable artefacts might include badges (as used in Scouts), certificates, trophies and the medals people receive in recognition of good service to a country. The value of these artefacts is not in the materials that make them, but in the meaning that they represent. They are the legacy of achievements deemed worthy within a cultural context.[7]

Staff uniforms are a very visible example of a cultural artefact. Some enterprise cultures favour conformity and a unified, professional look—particularly for frontline staff. *Enclothed cognition* is a term researchers use to describe the systematic influence clothes have on a wearer's psychological processes. An article published in the *Journal of Experimental Psychology*, for example, outlined that students who wore a lab coat performed tasks in the lab with more attention and care than those who didn't. If this lab coat was described as a 'doctor's coat' the effect was even more pronounced (especially when compared to it being described as a 'painter's coat'). In each instance, the same lab coat was used—but different meaning was attached to the artefact.

Therefore, if an enterprise wants to ensure that their (perhaps thousands of) frontline staff perform professionally and efficiently, a crisp, common uniform makes sense, and provides a 'tribe-like' element of commonality.

6| When archaeologists dig up the remains of ancient civilisations, the artefacts they find offer the greatest insight into the culture. Some cultural artefacts are, of course, intangible (like enduring stories or 'social artefacts'), but for the sake of simplicity we'll keep the focus on the more physical/visible kinds.

7| Do the virtual badges used in gamified applications count as worthy achievements? Well, like all things, this depends on the challenge within which a badge (or award) is bestowed. Rewards outside the context of meaningful challenge are meaningless.

But if the cultural context would benefit from greater diversity, authenticity and ingenuity, relaxing dress code standards might be appropriate.[8] What often makes a startup employee easily distinguishable to outsiders is a branded t-shirt or hoodie. While this is almost a cliché, first investor in Facebook and PayPal co-founder Peter Thiel argues that tech workers care about this very much. To them, everyone in the company needs to be 'different in the same way'—and so the result is a tribe of like-minded people equally devoted to the startup's mission.

I've had the 'pleasure of working alongside Elmwood—a global, award-winning brand design consultancy—as part of world-leading business and culture transformation work for McDonalds. If you visit the Elmwood office in Melbourne, you'll be treated to a very, very cool workspace. But what's most fascinating is that each of the Elmwood offices throughout the world share similar cultural artefacts. The foyer has a wall of Polaroid shots of staff from around the world (so that you can quickly put names to faces). They have an almost cafe-like hangout space where staff can meet, and even a funky green rhinoceros/hippopotamus thing in every office. The result is that any Elmwood employee can visit any Elmwood office in the world and immediately feel at home.

Some enterprises go a step further, and deliberately seek to capture their culture in the form of *books*.

In 2012, Valve Corporation—the same company that has desks on wheels—produced its Employee Handbook for new employees. It carried the tagline, 'A fearless adventure in knowing what to do when no-one's there telling you what to do' and contained stories, guidelines and examples to assist new staff assimilate into their culture. They even have a section dedicated to things they aren't good at—they openly accept, for example, that their relatively flat company structure has its downsides. If you haven't seen this yet, you can easily check it out by searching for Valve Employee Handbook online. Read it, and—like everything, including this book—take it with a pinch of salt and ask yourself: what

---

8| And remember: culture is a set of behaviours within a given context. That context can change, so it's possible to have different cultures within an enterprise—the professionally dressed frontline staff, for example, and the hoodie-wearing tech crew behind the scenes. What then becomes interesting in this context is when we ask: how do we unify different teams under the same enterprise context, without requiring the same uniform? After all, uniformity is an affront to diversity.

might *our* enterprise employee handbook look like if we were to have a pioneering future?

Similarly, Facebook has its 'little red book',[9] which explains the company's history, mission and culture to new employees. As the company grew, Facebook faced a lot of different challenges. The discussions and debates that were had during these times helped to shape their enterprise culture. The book contains these stories and the ideas that reflect the spirit of Facebook. 'Facebook was not originally created to be a company,' the book opens. 'It was built to accomplish a social mission — to make the world more open and connected.' The book also reminds employees that people don't use Facebook because they like Facebook — they use Facebook because they like their friends. The result is an artefact that describes and reflects the values and ideals of their culture.

And, of course, we cannot talk about culture without mentioning the work-culture poster child Zappos, an online clothing and shoe retailer. Zappos prides itself on world-leading customer service, and its CEO, Tony Hsieh, is a pioneer in new ways of working. Their culture book consists of a collage of unedited submissions from employees within the 'Zappos family'. These submissions include art, stories and photos, and they serve to reflect what the Zappos culture means to each employee. A new version of the culture book is created each year, so that it accurately reflects the true collective thoughts and feelings of employees. This culture book is available for the public to download.

So what might *your* enterprise culture book look like? Would it be courageous and bold, reflecting a compelling quest to make a difference? Would it have an edge? Would it take a stand for something? And would it reflect the real stories and values your enterprise culture embodies? Or... would it look like a standard enterprise brochure, with stock photography and a well-rounded, polished and politically correct mission statement that says nothing and does nothing different?

Artefacts are powerful objects that reflect meaning and represent culture. If you reckon your enterprise might struggle to craft a compelling culture book or artefact, you've got some work to do.

The best place to start? Rituals.

---

9 | The original 'little red book' was authored by Mao Tse-tung, the founder of the Chinese Communist Party, and contained his speeches, quotes, writings and other propaganda.

RITUALS

Let's come back to our primary definition of culture being *a set of behaviours replicated within any given context.* This given context might be at the organisational level, the society level or the team level. It can even be at the individual level. Within any given context we have observable, measurable behaviours. A company that genuinely values innovation, for example, will have clear behaviours that can be observed in this regard—that is, the things they do, and the way they work. Therefore, any conversation about culture becomes much less about the talk, and much more about the walk.

Aristotle once said, 'We are what we repeatedly do'. So the question we must ask is, what *are* the things we repeatedly do?

If you pause to think about it, most of the things we do will naturally be in service to the Curse of Efficiency and the Delusion of Progress. Which, of course, makes sense—everyone is busy, and we have a finite amount of time, energy and attention. Stuff needs to be done, and we have established ways of doing it. So let's get on with it and do it, right?

And so one of the first things many folks do when they arrive at work is check email—perhaps telling themselves they're 'getting a head start' on the day. Or they may do so automatically, without conscious thought—a default behaviour. Whatever the motivations, by doing this they instantly set up their day for reactive work. And, perpetually, we'll find that our days consist of putting out fires and responding to *other* people's urgencies. And because this is so frequently the norm, some people seek to distinguish themselves within this context by exacerbating the situation. They stay back late, host more meetings, use ASAP liberally, and ensure that everyone in the postcode is cc'd into every email. Meetings happen, nothing different gets done, everyone's busy, and the cycle continues.

Until we break it. Or carve out time for new rituals to disrupt default thinking.

Rituals are conscious routines we hold sacrosanct.

They're what keep individuals and cultures connected and congruent to their values, and on track to progress the things that matter.

In the next chapter, we'll explore a range of rituals that can liberate enterprise leaders from the perils of default thinking, the Curse of Efficiency and the Delusion of Progress.

21. Contextual Momentum

J ust pause reading this, and have a look at the date today.

...

I know, right? Can you believe how quickly the months have flown on by?

Most cannot. We find ourselves perpetually surprised by the passage of time. Months go by, and yet we still haven't progressed that important piece of pioneering work. We've been busy, and we keep saying we'll get around to it, but other urgent things always seem to crop up, and so we don't.

Part of this is due to the *default view* of most of our productivity tools (whether they be calendar apps, task managers, diaries or wall planners) confined to a day, a week or a month. And so our focus becomes contained within those parameters—we think in terms of daily, weekly or monthly priorities, and therefore struggle to progress our quests and the bigger projects that matter.

Rituals change this. They are the sacrosanct time we dedicate to ensuring meaningful progress. But how do we go about creating such rituals? When do these sacred routines occur, and what purpose do they serve?

MOMENTUM IN CONTEXT

If you get the big, compelling *why* behind leading a quest (outfoxing the Inevitable Kraken of Doom by unlocking new value, pioneering new growth arcs and securing enduring relevance—refer to figure 4.1 on p. 46), and the *what* (pioneering leadership and Quest-Augmented Strategy—refer to figure 5.1 on p. 60), then we may be ready to craft the *how*.

This takes the shape of a model I call 'contextual momentum'. I first introduced this framework within *The Game Changer*, and I've used this to help senior leadership teams establish new rituals for meaningful progress. Here, we focus on various time contexts to ensure we are engaging in the relevant pioneering thinking and doing at each level. It looks like this (see figure 21.1).

Figure 21.1: Contextual momentum

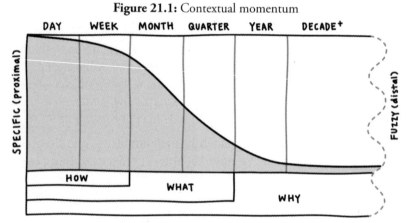

A few things are going on with this model. Let me explain its parameters, and then we'll get into the juicy bits relevant to leading a quest.

Firstly, you'll notice that the model represents a number of time contexts—from daily through to weekly, monthly, quarterly, yearly and decennially. Each of these contexts nests potential rituals of differing activity and focus (which we'll get to soon).

These time contexts are mapped across a spectrum—from specificity to fuzziness. This is almost like exploring Google Earth, where you can start in a detailed 'street view', and then zoom out to suburb view, city view, state view, country view and planet view. The more proximal the focus, the more specific and detailed we are. The more distal, the fuzzier things get.

Some enterprises get this important spectrum totally mixed up. Instead of embracing the sheer complexity of an uncertain future, they attempt to deny it by manufacturing specific distant goals. Some will go as far as putting specific numbers to it. Not only does this hobble the enterprise's ability to adapt along the way, but the emphasis on narrow, distant outcomes can also make how we can progress towards these goals unclear—particularly if progress requires us to challenge our own defaults. It's akin to a motivational speaker asking high school students to visualise exactly where they want to be in 10 years' time. 'What job will you have? What car will you drive?' I've heard a speaker ask. *Erm*, I think. *There are going to be entirely new industries in 10 years' time—the likes of which we can barely perceive right now.* Let's not rob ourselves of the ability to adapt.

Contextual momentum keeps our thinking and our activity in context. It serves meaningful progress, providing specific actions while preserving the ability to adapt.

You'll notice three lenses by which we view each time context. I suspect you are quite familiar with these by now:

◊ **The WHY lens** extends across all time contexts. This is where we connect our activities to purpose and meaning. When we stop and think, *Wait—why are we doing this?*, we are returning to the bigger why. This is powerful in any given moment or time interval.

◊ **The WHAT lens** is generally useful from the daily to quarterly level of focus. It's here that we determine our most important projects or experiments, and what our mission critical path may be. In some enterprises, extending this lens to a yearly level may be prudent—but in many cases *what* is important changes faster than we may think. A quarterly focus encourages us to maintain the pace, and balance thorough thinking with faster learning.

◊ **The HOW lens** is useful at the daily and weekly level, and frustrating or unnecessary at any other level. Have you ever been in an annual strategic summit where people find themselves debating tactical issues at the micro-level? It's just not really that helpful within that context. Likewise, if you're struggling to make meaningful progress at a daily

or weekly level, connecting with your bigger why may
help—but it may also be helpful to identify the friction
that's getting in the way, or to change your methodology.

Righto! Having now paced through our framework for contextual
momentum, let's drill down.

We're going to explore rituals that serve to integrate pioneering leadership
into enterprise culture, and assist you in progressing a quest. But! We're
not going to pace through this in a logical, sequential manner. If only
meaningful progress were that neat! First we'll start with *yearly* rituals you
can adopt and adapt to your context. Then, we'll explore *quarterly* rituals,
followed by *daily, weekly, monthly* and *decennially* anchored rituals.

YEARLY RITUALS

Here are some important rituals that should be performed at least
once per year. Such rituals are more concerned with bigger, contextual
questions and longer-term strategy and purpose. But don't be fooled by
their relative infrequency—this infrequency (when compared to other
rituals) doesn't mean they're less important. Quite the contrary: each
of these recommended rituals is so important that the time and effort
required to do them well precludes them from greater frequency.

Future mapping

At least once per year, you will want to get a large and diverse team[1]
immersed together in the imagination of a broad and diverse range of
possible future contexts (as outlined in part III). From this, we are able to
identify the common, overlapping incoherencies between possible future
contexts. From here, we can begin to harvest potential strategic options.

If this is the first time you are doing this, a good amount of time will
need to be dedicated to establishing relevant core 'themes' that seed and
initiate pioneering thinking and exploration. You will also need to have
an up-to-date representation of your business model and identity (as per
the strategic immersion ritual, covered next), your clearly articulated
current strategy, and someone to facilitate progress and hold the space
over two to four days.

1| For this team, thirty to fifty people is a good number to strive for if you run a large
enterprise.

The strategic immersion

At least once per year, you'll also want to get your smaller and more immediate team of leaders together for a strategic immersion. As outlined in part V, this will be for a minimum of two days, and is ideally held off-site.

Resist the temptation to bundle this ritual in with the future-mapping ritual to 'save time'. That's the Curse of Efficiency talking. These rituals serve two very different purposes — whereas future mapping is concerned with exploration and optionality, strategic immersion is focused on reviewing viable strategic options and making good decisions. Ideally, these rituals occur in tandem (six months apart) so as to allow for the development of a quiver of viable alternative options to default strategy.

The yearly conference

Conferences can be very effective ways to communicate strategic intent and connect your people with each other, and with the bigger purpose and evolving identity of your enterprise.[2] Also included will be operational updates, a review of achievements and setbacks, lessons learned and general progress made toward future coherence.

Conferences are also a great way to reduce the *path-length* between the clusters and silos within your enterprise, if your organisation isn't responsive or networked yet.

Your annual enterprise conference is primarily a *cultural* ritual, existing to serve the wider cultural norm you wish to cultivate. It's here that you may launch new 'culture books', highlight success stories, reward interesting failures,[3] and even have spontaneous jam sessions among staff.[4]

2| Presuming that you don't succumb to default thinking and design a conference program with a default agenda, default speakers sharing default messages in a default hotel venue with default hotel-branded notepads on default tables alongside default mints. This is made even worse when the Curse of Efficiency makes for an agenda built around five-minute increments. We can rethink this, and do much better.

3| You get what you focus on with failures. If you want more people exploring, experimenting, learning and sharing, you need to clearly indicate that this is of value. Even if it did not result in a 'success'.

4| Xero, a developer of cloud-based accounting software, uses an in-house band — made up of staff, accountants and bookkeepers — to provide entertainment at their annual events.

CHOOSE 'ONE WORD'

Each year, choose one word.

This began as a personal ritual—my attempt to counter the trend towards making New Year's resolutions specific and detailed. Every January my feeds would be flooded with folks talking about the importance of setting specific goals, and having a clear vision for your future.

And so, instead of having a specific goal and a detailed plan (and manufacturing the delusion of certainty such things bring), I began to simply choose one word to serve as a 'contextual beacon' for the year ahead. Over the years, I've shared this ritual with thousands of people, and it seems to resonate.

By choosing one word, you cast forth an *intention* for the year. And unlike a specific goal or resolution, one word gives you plenty of room to learn, grow and adapt.

A couple of years ago I chose the king archetype with the word *kingly*. For me, this choice was about stepping up, taking responsibility, staying true to my word, and serving the greater good (rather than trying to help anyone and everyone who asks). It was a powerful year, one that saw me publish my first book with Wiley and transition from motivation science into the space of frontier leadership and work culture.

The next year, I chose the word *prime* on account of how wonderful prime numbers are. These numbers appear seemingly random—but they're not. Nor are they predictable. This word called me to stay unique and not succumb to denominators. I also had elements around 'prime time' (given the PR I was then doing for *The Game Changer*) and being in the 'prime' of my life (I joined a CrossFit gym for a week).

As I write this book, my word for the year is *pirate*.[5] For me, 'kingly' brought with it a whole bunch of seriousness, whereas 'pirate' conjures the qualities of the opportunistic explorer. Commercially focused, unconventional and savvy, pirates are also jolly and buoyant. They drink rum and look after their mates.

5| Think of a clean version of JoÚny Depp's Captain Jack Sparrow (rather than a pirate with missing teeth and hook for a hand).

The point of these words is that they're distinct enough to serve as a beacon—a conceptual light to bring us back to our intention for the year, should we find ourselves wondering. But they're also fuzzy enough to allow us room to explore.

And this is something my clients have done with their teams. Not only is this a powerful ritual to encourage in people individually (and it's fascinating to hear what word each person chooses), but it can also be very useful for any team engaged in pioneering work. For example, one of the teams I work with chose *amplify* for the year. They were getting busier than ever, but did not want to simply expand to meet the volume of work. Amplifiers work best with a pure signal. And so, at each meeting, this word served to bring them back to this intent—what's the signal-to-noise ratio like? Is this activity of value, or are we just adding more noise?

I often integrate this 'one word' ritual into events I facilitate for clients. But this is something you can do yourself.

Imagine: if your life were an autobiography, what one word might describe the last 12 chapters (months)? And what one word might describe your intention for the *next* 12 months?

You can choose from three broad categories of words: abstract, active, and aspect/archetypal.

Abstract words

These include words like balance, lean, care, honour and mindful. They can also include emotive words like joy and courage. The key to abstract words is to really make them tangible and real—otherwise, they're just, well, abstract.

The way you make an abstract word real is to *package* it in a way people get. 'It's the year of style', for example, could be a phrase you use after anyone gives you a compliment (assuming that 'style' is the word for your year). If your word is 'art', you could start dropping 'such art' into the things you say and do.[6]

6| And yes, I'm referencing the Doge meme here. #suchwow

(continued)

CHOOSE 'ONE WORD' *(cont'd)*

Of all the categories of words, I find abstract words the most challenging to play with. If an abstract word resonates most with you, give thought to how you will manifest it in your every day.

Active words

These include words like unleash, create, ignite, build, consolidate, invigorate and make. They're verbs, and they're usually something we can easily gesticulate. Active words particularly come to life through our projects. If you choose the word 'create', for example, you can bet that people will want to know what you're creating.

I know someone who chose the word 'renovate'. He has house renovations he intends to do, yes. But, more importantly, he's identified a tendency to get distracted by shiny objects and new things. And so this year, he's bringing the focus back to the core elements of his business—renovating the core offerings in his business model. Digging a bit deeper into the etymology of the word, he also found that 'renovate' is closely related to words like restore, refresh and reinvigorate. And so, he's taking this approach to some of his relationships—more camping with family, more dinners with friends.

Aspect and archetype words

Aspect words are used when we want to take on the qualities of something. They include words like tiger, goddess, rockstar, explorer and samurai.

A friend of mine chose the word 'cat' for this year. Her intention was to bring more cat qualities into her world and work, à la Cat Woman. Think charming indifference, assumed authority, quiet arrogance, impeccable grooming—that kind of thing. This was a particularly wonderful challenge for someone cursed with generosity, considerateness and caring—for someone used to putting everyone else first, this makes for a powerful year.

Find qualities in something worth emulating. Summon your inner lion, alpaca or frog. Or make your year the year of tiger, and insist that people play 'Eye of the Tiger' before you walk into rooms.

Or perhaps an *archetype* word might fit you best for the year ahead? Maybe warrior, knight, queen, wizard, or rogue? These are words with which you take on the role of something and, in moments of uncertainty and doubt, ask yourself, 'What would a [*insert archetype*] do?' Or you ask yourself, 'Am I being [*insert archetype*]ly?'

This is a delightful ritual to have.

To help you on your way, here are three don'ts and three do's to be mindful of when it comes to your one word:

1. **Don't rush it.** There's art in the seeking. You don't need to land on your word immediately, nor do you need to find it in January — the Gregorian New Year is just a convenient time near a solstice when many people have a bit more time to reflect and reset. The new lunar year could work equally well. In any event: take your time.

2. **Don't anchor it to outcomes.** You're on a quest, not a mission. The very point of this activity is to leave you opportunity to grow and adapt. Choosing a word like 'success' or 'promoted' might detract from the journey, and set up an unhelpful pass/fail dichotomy. It's not black and white — most of your year will be grey, involving a series of mini-wins and minor setbacks. Keep your word big and fuzzy.

3. **Don't care too much about what other people think.** It's *your* word for the year. Choose what's right for you, not what you think you should choose in the eyes of others (including mine), and certainly not what others say you should choose (unless, of course, you are in full concordance). Be bold, risky and/or risqué.

But having said that...

1. **Do test it out.** Your word needs to survive social scrutiny — the last thing we want is a word that you're disinclined to share with others. Last year my friend Jen chose the word 'honour'. It had a lot of meaning for her, and fitted her well. But then the dangerlam[7] and

---

7 | That's Kim's professional name. I'm married to her.

(continued)

CHOOSE 'ONE WORD' *(cont'd)*

I killed it by promptly showing her a particularly dubious webcomic.[8]

2. **Do choose a word that makes you a bit uncomfortable.** While your word needs to be a good, intuitive fit for you, it shouldn't be easy. All progress and growth occurs just outside our comfort zone. And as such, your word should be something that's a little bit audacious, and a bit of a stretch. Last year my friend Alison chose the word 'unleash', and this year the dangerlam chose 'wild'. Make your word edgy. The edge is where we grow.

3. **Do make it fun for your friends and colleagues.** The people around you will play a huge part in how your year plays out. Your word is a social trigger. It's something people will ask you about as things progress. So, make it easy for them to hold you true to your meaningful intent. Phrase it into the things you do.

Earlier this year, I was having crepes with friends. We'd finished our main crepes, and then they ordered dessert crepes. 'I'll be good,' I said to myself, resisting the urge to order. But then the dessert crepes came out—burnt butter and caramel with double thickened cream. Damn, but I really wanted some crepe. I said as much, and they asked me, 'What would a pirate do?' (thinking that I'd decide to order myself a dessert crepe too). I did one better and seized my friend's crepe with my bare hands! Such pirate.[9]

Remember: it's a fuzzy beacon. It's not a goal, and it's not a plan. It's a light to pull you back on track, and to help you stay true to your intention should you waver.

Give this ritual a try.

8| The comic is available at oglaf.com/honor. Please don't look at the comic, though, because it contains penises and is entirely unprofessional, inappropriate and not safe for work. It's rather amusing, though. 'Show us your honour!' we'd say, and she'd just shake her head. Yeah, we ruined it for her.

9| It was actually much more polite than that. I tore off a 2 × 4 cm piece at the edge—the bit with no flavour. And then I promptly apologised, washed my hands and ordered a crepe of my own. But still!

QUARTERLY RITUALS

Your yearly rituals provide a meaningful context and purpose for your quarterly rituals. Of all the time signatures in our framework for contextual momentum (refer to figure 21.1 on p. 246), the quarterly rituals require the most deliberate attention.

Across all productivity and time management tools, you rarely have the option to view time from a quarterly perspective. And so days, weeks and months fly by — and, before you know it, another year has passed in which we haven't progressed any of the pioneering projects that matter.

Quarterly rituals keep us on track with the *what* in service to the *why*.

Reviewing options and experiments

After identifying common incoherencies across multiple possible future contexts (as part of the 'future mapping' ritual), it's important that the conversation and learning around potential options is kept current and fresh. This is helped by having a good internal communications platform and the continuous monitoring of diverse feeds. Of course, the existing experiments are also at play — some of which will be progressed with enhanced methodologies, and some of which will be encouraging us to rethink the hypothetical stance we take with an option.

By dedicating at least a day or two to reviewing our quiver of options and the drivers for change, we can have a better sense of what future contexts are more likely to manifest. This then enables us to determine which experiments we need to prioritise.

Reviewing strategy

Similar to our options review, you need to reconnect with your guiding strategy at least once a quarter. Not only does this keep strategy front of mind and integrated into the fabric of our work, but it also serves to mitigate the Delusion of Progress. Rather than chipping away at a project or program over a whole year, if a quarterly strategy review reveals that that stream of activity is no longer viable or relevant to the future, a whole heap of time, money and effort can be saved early. As a result, an enterprise can stay focused on progressing the projects that matter.

Here is also a time to review updates on options in development, and experiments in progress. Timely feedback may allow certain experiments to progress options toward a more viable status quicker than they would if strategic reviews happen less frequently.

Now is also a good time to determine which—out of all the things you could do—are the projects, missions or experiments that matter. I suggest you choose three projects to focus on each quarter.

If we choose just one, we'll procrastifectionate[10] over it, and it won't get done. If we choose two, we'll enter binary judgement mode and make one more important than the other.

No—three is the magic number. Because once we have three declared projects that matter, we can then seek to actively *fail* half of them.[11] Gosh, did I just use the F-word? I think I did.

Remember—the opposite of success is not failure. It's apathy. And a lot of conservative risk aversion is merely apathy in disguise. And, besides, in science there's no such thing as failure—there are only flawed methodologies and disproven hypotheses (as per figure 10.1 on p. 133). The only way we can disprove a hypothesis is by collecting evidence, which means we're actually *doing something.*

Attending an external event

Each quarter, attend at least one conference, meeting or event *outside* of your own enterprise. This can be done as a team—or folks (including yourself) can attend events or learning opportunities of their own choosing, reporting back and sharing their learning on the comms platform and as part of a monthly ritual.

The event you choose to attend could be anything from a guest presentation from a visiting scholar or an online webinar[12], to a startup pitch night, a local meetup, a breakfast networking event, or a cool

---

10| The powers of procrastination and perfectionism, combined!

11| Big thanks to Peter Cook for introducing this philosophy to me.

12| Okay this one's pretty lame, actually. But hey—it's better than nothing. Maybe.

conference. Ideally, the things you choose to attend will provide *new* learning.

Now, you might think, *Why do I need to attend an event? Can't I just download the executive summary?* You can, of course. And that would be very efficient. But you know what will likely happen—you'll proceed with the best of intentions, only to find yourself caught up in some busyness at some point.

Actual events disrupt this, and wake us up from our default thinking and efficiency. They offer us a chance to expose ourselves to new patterns and new ways of thinking. This serves to mitigate the threat of the filter bubble and insular thinking—the phenomenon in which we become ignorant of ideas outside our own experience.

Even if the event we attend turns out to be crap, we have an opportunity to be curious—why does this event suck? What can we learn here?

Hosting a low-key learning event

This is particularly important for teams progressing the exploration of options, and for any pioneering team working in a new mode. And the event doesn't have to be a lot of fuss—it could simply be 'a crash course' in understanding a new tecÚology or an emerging trend.

The benefits of this are twofold. Firstly, the event provides a visible progress to the rest of the enterprise about the value this team (and the mode in which they operate) generates.[13] Secondly, this ritual is good at focusing a new team. Knowing you have to teach/share/deliver new learning to others does wonders for enhancing your own capacity to learn.[14]

13| This is very important—stakeholder management is an infinite game.

14| I actually used this strategy to catalyse the early formation of this book. In conjunction with the University of Melbourne's Centre for Workplace Leadership, we hosted a series of free monthly 'think tanks'. You can find out more about our events at cleverhappenings.com

DAILY RITUALS

Yes, we're doing a jump here[15]—from yearly rituals, to quarterly rituals, to the routines you hold sacrosanct each and every day. Naturally, these will differ for everyone. Some folks I know, for example, go on a run or hit the gym every morning. If they miss out on this activity, they feel as though their day is missing something—they just don't feel as productive or motivated.

I wish I had that kind of chemical imbalance. For me, things like running and physical activity are very deliberate acts. It takes time to build it into a habit—a routine with a consistent rhythm.

But the same could be said about pioneering work, and the activities required to lead a quest and pursue meaningful progress. Unless we deliberately carve out time to devote to the things that matter, we'll always be swayed by the Delusion of Progress.

Whereas most other rituals are group activities, most of the daily rituals suggested here can be undertaken as a solo act.

3 × mission critical actions

Many folks—myself included—have started their days by checking email. At one point early in my adventures, I was 'so efficient' that I'd be checking and responding to emails within minutes of my alarm going off.[16] Such is not the way to live and work, though, because all this does is set up our day for reactive work. We find ourselves responding to other people's urgencies, instead of investing effort into the things that contribute to meaningful progress.[17]

But each morning presents an opportunity to disrupt that pattern. Instead of beginning your day with email, create a new hard edge: no email[18] until

---

15| From why, to what, to how.

16| We've since opted to charge our phones beyond arm's reach of the bed.

17| Oh, we intend to get around to doing those things—once we've dealt with these other things first. But, by the time we get around to the things that *would* contribute to meaningful progress, it's the end of the day, and we're spent. And, besides—these things are so vague. Where do we even begin?

18| It's not just emails, of course—include here anything that can distract you from thorough thinking and pioneering work. For me, this includes phone calls and meetings (we try to avoid scheduling anything before 11 am). But for less extroverted folks, phone calls and meetings might be energising—and catalysing to pioneering work. The key is to get curious about what works to facilitate meaningful progress in your world, and design your days to support it.

10 am.[19] With this new time you have carved out, you have one very important thing to do: identify the three things you can do today that will contribute to meaningful progress. These are your mission-critical actions.[20]

By mission critical, I mean all the things we discussed in chapter 18. The tight time frame mitigates the nasty side effects of specific goals. Instead, we are left with a focused imperative to achieve *before* we get absorbed back into our busy default work.

Monitoring feeds

In chapter 8 I introduced the importance of establishing diverse information feeds—sources of information that provide quality insight relevant to emerging hunches, trends, options and experiments. If you're looking to embed pioneering leadership into your culture, you'll want to be actively reviewing syndicated feeds and sharing relevant articles and insights with your team.[21]

Remember: we're all on an information diet, but most of what we consume is junk—unless we are mindful. Much like making yourself a good, healthy breakfast, each day offers you a chance to consciously choose what information you consume (and what you choose to share).

Journalling

I'd love to be able to recommend meditation as a daily ritual. It seems to be one of the most common rituals shared among effective leaders and extraordinary people. However, I'm yet to get into the rhythm of it. But, what *does* work very well for me (and for many) is journalling.

This is something I try to do at the start of every day. In fact, I bundle the three daily rituals I've shared so far into my morning. Whenever possible,

---

19 | This will differ for some—you might be able to stretch it until 11 am. Or you might be required to pull it back to 9.30 am. It's also influenced by how early you wake up, other areas of responsibility (like family) and the time and means of your daily commute. But, in any event, you can create a window *before* you open up your inbox.

20 | Not sure what these might be? Ah, well—review your projects and experiments that matter, your word for the year, and the current strategy you are running with. Something out of all that will emerge.

21 | This is also a chance to have a visible leadership presence on internal communications platforms.

I'll get up early, skate to a nearby cafe, order a magic[22], and begin to review relevant feeds. I'll then switch to a shlong[23] and begin journalling.

The first benefit of journalling is that it puts you into a dissociated metacognitive state. Whether you're reflecting or projecting, you can't help but liberate your perspective from busy default work—and this puts you in a great space to identify your mission critical actions for the day. But before I even begin to do this, I start with *gratitudes*.

One of the downsides to progress and constructive discontent is the 'discontent' bit. We are perpetually discontent, because more progress can *always* be achieved. We can always do more, and we always have things we can improve. Such a philosophy can be fatiguing—which is why gratitude is so important. Listing what we're grateful for gives us perspective, and reminds us that we are enough, and that everything is perfectly imperfect.

Digital sunsets

There is a certain irony as I write this (late into the night), but—it's important to switch off at the end of each day.

At its purest, a digital sunset is a ritual in which all digital devices are switched off at a certain point in the evening (ideally, before dinner). This may be very challenging for some, so the watered-down version simply means turning off all emails and notifications at a certain point in the evening.

As inefficient as this sounds, it creates a delightful paradox. By *not* working every minute of the day—and well into the night—we are *more* efficient and effective when we are working.

Just like we create a hard edge to the start of our day (in order to identify and progress our mission critical actions before we enter the land of distraction), creating a hard edge at the *end* of each day is equally important. This allows us to attend to some of our other areas of responsibility—like our relationships, sleep and health.[24]

22| This is Melbourne code for a double ristretto three-quarter flat white in a small cup.

23| I first learned of this one from a barista in Brisbane. It's code for a 'short long black'. This term that hasn't quite caught on anywhere else though. I can't imagine why.

24| Because, of course, if we don't look after these other areas of responsibility, they're going to suffer. This, in turn, will make us suffer. And if you're a leader, everyone suffers as a result.

WEEKLY RITUALS

Righto, now we are in the territory of things that would be wonderful to do daily—but just probably aren't feasible. We can't escape the fact that at least 80 per cent of our work must still be the default, business-as-usual things that must be done. But if you are able to embrace these small team rituals, your work will be much more pioneering, and much more conducive to meaningful progress.

Progress rallying

Once per week, rally your immediate reports together (ideally in the same physical space) for eleven to twelve minutes to review progress made.[25] Here is where you reconnect with any projects or experiments that matter, the strategy, and the bigger context in which you operate.

A visible progress map[26] is a good element to keep updated for these rally points, because it serves to provide a clear, quantitative sense as to what has been delivered and how we are progressing. The discussions that form around this serve to provide a qualitative sense of progress—if people are attuned to celebrating small but meaningful wins, this can create a momentum of good effort.[27]

This ritual also allows you to take more advantage of the Hawthorne Effect—the scenario in which our performance naturally elevates because we are observed. Each week, our actions are under the spotlight—not for critical review, but to reinforce the things that contribute to meaningful progress.

If you're pioneering, this is particularly important.[28] Rather than rely on implicit assumptions about what constitutes meaningful progress, a

---

25 | This time increment is deliberate—we want to keep the energy of these rallies high, and avoid having them turn into meetings. Keep the pace moving—if anything needs further discussion, the relevant people can continue the conversation *after* the progress rally wraps up.

26 | Like a high-level Gantt chart—a horizontal time line of the next three to twelve months of the strategy, along with any core deliverables required. Much like contextual momentum (see figure 21.1 on p. 246), proximal projects are more detailed.

27 | The opposite of this is people hiding behind default work and emails.

28 | Indeed, many software developers and anyone practising agile project methodologies will likely be doing this ritual daily. The high pace of learning and change requires that they do, so as to stay focused on meaningful progress and avoid duplicated or wasted effort.

shared discussion with the team will have everyone better understand the next steps needed.

Lunch and learn

This is another ritual that is intended to keep your team curious and connected. If you share a workspace, create a rotating roster. Once per week, someone nominates a relevant short video to share over lunch, along with a meaningful or relevant question for the team to discuss.

Plenty of timely, relevant and insightful videos are available online these days — though the key is not necessarily the video itself, but the conversations and thinking it may trigger.

Friction review

Friction is the enemy of efficiency and efficacy. It's what gets in the way of meaningful progress, and is usually the result of default thinking, and old policies, procedures and tecÚology that no longer serve our current context (let alone our emerging future context).

This ritual occurs on two levels. Individually, you should review and reflect on your week. What mission critical actions didn't you achieve? Was it an issue with your methodology?[29] Or did friction get in the way?

If the answer is your methodology, well, that's easy — *try a different approach.*

But if your answer was friction, this gets interesting.

The second level of this ritual is a *shared* review of friction — something you can do together at the end of the week.[30] If you've noticed a pattern of friction forming, and you suspect that others might experience similar friction, discuss it with your team. Perhaps you are in the midst of an incoherence right now. If that's the case, you know what to do. It's time to lead a quest, and find viable alternative options.

29| Usually we are too ambitious about what we can achieve in the short term. For mission critical actions (during days in which I have a heap of default work happening) I sometimes use an egg-timer set for 20 minutes. If I can't get it done within 20 minutes of focused work, I've probably made the action too big.

30| Possibly with Friday afternoon drinks.

MONTHLY RITUALS

Righto, now we are at the monthly interval. These things need to be scheduled in the calendar—they're too infrequent to be in the rhythm of, and not big enough to make a fuss of. But our monthly rituals are part of the *thread* that connects all of the things we do to meaningful progress.

Track alignment

Complexity and scope creep are very real. Part of the key to keeping this entropy at bay—and ensuring we don't burn out or succumb to efficient default (non) thinking—is to review where our efforts are going.

Each month, check in with your team and how you are tracking. What's working? Are any projects, experiments or activities no longer generating value? Do we have enough evidence to consider quitting them? What does the upcoming month look like? Are our activities aligned with the bigger strategy—or is it time to review and update the strategy?

This is a conversation that can easily occur over an hour or two. It's an important stop-check that may help to ensure our efforts don't go off track or significantly out of alignment to our overarching intention.

Book club

One of the most wonderful things to hear as an author[31] is how your book is being used. I can list at least half a dozen times[32] in which *The Game Changer* has been used as part of an enterprise team 'book club'.

Reading a book well requires time, and reflection. Whereas something shown at a weekly lunch and learn might expose people to new thinking and generate discussions in a short space of time, reading a book well requires thorough thinking and reflection.

This is not a passive activity. To read a book well, I suggest you use three different coloured highlighters.[33] The first coloured highlighter—let's make it yellow—is for those cool sentences, quotes and other stuff you'd be inclined to highlight anyway. Go for it.

---

31 | With the exception of nice online reviews.

32 | That's counting on *two* hands.

33 | Most eBook readers now also have the option to choose different coloured highlighters.

The second highlighter (let's make this blue or green) is for anything you read that makes you think, *Yeah, but...*[34] They're the things that cause you to question or disagree. A good book doesn't try to please everyone, and will contain things that you disagree with. The interesting thing is exploring why you disagree with certain points. What's informing this? What are the antecedents for this response? And what might others in your book club think?

By capturing these 'yeah-buts', your book club will benefit from richer conversations. Likewise, you will all also benefit from conversations orbiting around any 'yes-ands'. Use a pink highlighter for these. They are the statements within a book that make you think, *Oooh! We can do that! And if we combine X with Y, that'll work even better!*

By approaching a book like this,[35] and by having a monthly book club where you can discuss books, ideas and the inherent implications or imperatives for your enterprise, you foster more curiosity and thorough thinking. This, in turn, influences the ricÚess of options explored, and how deeply strategy might be augmented.

A long lunch

Each month, get out of the office and visit a good cafe or restaurant on a Friday afternoon for a late, long lunch. Mix up the seating and invite folks from other business units to join you. This is not a Fun Thing to force upon folks—rather, it's another circuit-breaker. Something designed to foster greater connection and deeper conversation across your team and the wider enterprise.

The *context* is what matters here. It's hard to rush conversations over a long lunch. Breaking bread with colleagues also eases tension, and allows ideas to be explored comfortably via different perspectives.

34| Chook mode.
35| *'Jason, you bastard. Why are you only telling us this now?'*

Some folks working at progressive enterprises might hear this suggestion and think, *Pfffft. Of course! We do this anyway. We don't even need to turn this into a formal ritual—it just happens.*

Others folks may think about how they could possibly justify the expense in their enterprise. Not in terms of money—people can pay for their own lunches—but in terms of time. *That's 90 minutes folks could be working…!* Such is the ridiculousness of the default norms that have emerged. In order to lead a quest, you need to look after your team, and invest in the activities that enrich thinking and form fellowship.

DECENNIAL RITUALS

And now we are well and truly back in the land of the fuzzy. If you don't know what the future holds, or what the meaning of life is—great! No clear answers are possible anyway—just keep searching.

I'm not sure that rituals can be sustained over decades, but one thing that is a useful concept to keep in mind is the sabbatical. At some point in your career—and I'm speaking to you, as an individual leader *outside* of the context of your enterprise—you'll want to embark upon a sabbatical. Take three to twelve months away from your normal work. During this time, your sole focus is to reflect, gain perspective and explore.

Of course, you can do this more frequently than once per decade. But, if it's been more than ten years since you last had a sustained period of time away from your usual work,[36] perhaps it's time to consider a mini-sabbatical. Yes, you have finances, handovers and other factors to keep in mind, and this may require some careful planning and

---

36| The key is not to stop working but, rather, to invest time immersed in a different context.

consideration. But, of the people I know who have done this, not a single one of them has regretted it.

And there we have it — a few rituals for you to play with. Of course, these are just ideas: suggestions to get you started. Refer back to figure 21.1 at the start of this chapter and ask yourself, 'What am I doing in each time frame to facilitate meaningful progress? What rituals do we have for pioneering leadership? How are we making clever happen?'

Summary

Part VII

◊   Culture is a set of behaviours replicated within any given context.

◊   It's easy for strategy intent to become lost in translation — particularly if it is discussed in conceptual terms, rather than concrete behaviours.

◊   In order to translate strategic intent into specific behaviours, we need to storyboard how strategy might play out within our culture. This is achieved by developing personas, exploring scenarios and mapping out the pathways each persona may take. For any area of potential friction — things that get in the way of desired behaviours — your leadership team can discuss how this can be mitigated.

◊   Part of this involves the identification of keystone behaviours. This is where your leadership team determines what specific behaviours are representative of enterprise values and your strategic intent, and models them.

◊   Structures and artefacts also influence work culture. Visible structures include all the physical things you see — for example, a workspace layout congruent to a culture of collaboration may have movable desks, or plenty of shared communal workstations or hot desks. Invisible structures include policies and procedures, and the systems we use to get work done. A key invisible structure is your internal communications platform — how people connect.

◊   Rituals are the conscious routines we hold sacrosanct. They
     are our deliberate efforts to engage in behaviours conducive
     to the cultural values of the enterprise. Such rituals can be
     mapped out over different time contexts, and engineered to
     serve ongoing momentum.

◊   You have plenty of ways to integrate pioneering leadership
     into workplace culture across different time frequencies and
     contexts. Rituals ensure that the right questions are being
     asked, and that meaningful progress is being achieved.

◊   A key thing that unites each of these rituals is that they are
     a disruption to default patterns of thinking and work. They
     encourage thorough thinking, curiosity and connection, and
     are essential for any enterprise looking to achieve enduring
     relevance.

Conclusion

T he two biggest threats to any enterprise are the infinite complexity of an uncertain future, and the fact that everyone is busy. And so darn efficient.

The default enterprise model has been built to instil order and resist change — but this is the very thing holding us back. As philosopher James Carse observes, 'Only that which can change can continue.'

In order to stay relevant, we must embrace a pioneering form of leadership. This means venturing beyond our default, efficient and established ways of working, and pursuing new pathways of growth.

We do this by embarking on quests into the uncertainty of possible future contexts, exploring scenarios in which our current business model may be rendered unviable or incoherent. Among common incoherencies, we explore potential strategic options that may enable our enterprise to mitigate risk and/or unlock new value. We continue to monitor the drivers of change. When a particular future context (and its associated incoherencies) seems likely to manifest, the alternative options identified can be explored. These pathways are tested rigorously. Through scientific experimentation, a set of viable alternative options are generated to enrich and augment strategic decision-making.

Alternative pathways allow enterprise leaders to pioneer beyond the default. All enterprises began this way but, at some point in the journey, efficiency eclipsed the need for exploration. Quests bring this back into balance, ensuring that you not only deliver excellence today, but also build for future relevance.

It's not an easy journey—it's a hero's journey.

And it starts with you.

———————

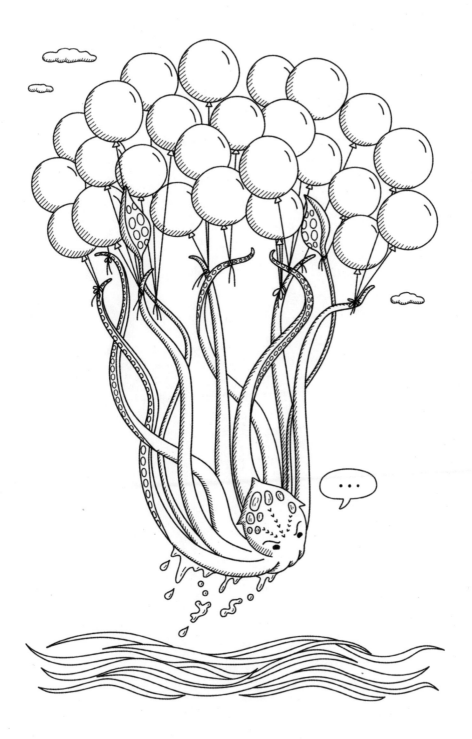

Index

Gartner 28, 100–102, 207–208
Gatti, Luca 94, 108
goals 219–221, 221–222, 224
Goethe, Johann Wolfgang von 50
Google, white space and 175
gratitude 152
growth arc, default 24–34
growth phase of default growth arc
  28–30

Hawthorne Effect 103, 261
hero's journey 43–45, 197
Hill, Alison 192
Hill, Darren 192
hunches 85–87

IBM 23–24
ideas, ranking 126–129, 163
identity of enterprises 88–89
ignorance, wilful 146–147
IKEA 88
Imber, Dr Amantha 108
imperfection 151–152
Implement 157
impostor syndrome 52–53
incentives 239
infinite games 41, 42, 62, 79
information feeds 102–104, 259
infrastructure in business models 90
intrapreneurs 55–57, 80
intuition *see* hunches
iPhone 47

Jobs, Steve 129
journalling 218, 259–260
judgements, resisting 100

Kahneman, Daniel 4, 179
Kodak 110–111
Kotter, John 192
Kraken of Doom, Inevitable 23, 24,
  32–34, 45–47
Kramer, Steven 16–17

Lafley, AG 41–42
latency in larger teams 77
leadership *see* pioneering leadership
Leslie, Mark 29

Making Ideas Happen 31,100
Martin, Roger 41–42
mastery, motivation and 210
maturity, plateau of in default growth
  arc 30–32
meaningful progress 19, 66, 70, 80,
  125, 170
  —measuring by projects 218
  —measuring qualitatively
    216–217, 224
  —measuring quantitatively
    215–216, 224
  —measuring through areas of
    responsibility 217–218, 224
  —rituals and 259
Milliner, Mark 86
missions 67, 224
  —focus and 220
  —necessity of context to 219
  —objectives and 221
  —timelines and 220–221
  —urgency and 219–220
Morrison, Lieutenant General David
  145
motivation 16–17, 209–210,
  219–220
Mount Everest 151

narrative, framing possible futures
  through 106–110, 120
Netflix 131
networked enterprise 193–197
newspaper template, framing
  possible futures through 108–109,
  120
Nokia 47–48
NOMOS Glashütte 95–96
norms 11–12

...and therein lies the rub.

Books end. They are finite.
No more pages. All done.

"Fin."

But *progress,* ah! Progress is infinite. And there are
always new and wonderful things to learn.

If you'd like to stay savvy with progress, you can join the
thousands of folk who subscribe to my museletter:

drjasonfox.com/ahoy
(a small surprise awaits you)

That's dangerlam,
meta-drawing.

Connect with WILEY ▶▶▶

WILEY
Browse and purchase the full range of Wiley publications on our official website.

www.wiley.com

Check out the Wiley blog for news, articles and information from Wiley and our authors.

www.wileybizaus.com

Join the conversation on Twitter and keep up to date on the latest news and events in business.

@WileyBizAus

Sign up for Wiley newsletters to learn about our latest publications, upcoming events and conferences, and discounts available to our customers.

www.wiley.com/email

Wiley titles are also produced in e-book formats. Available from all good retailers.

WILEY